New Casebo

SONS AND LOVERS

C000151234

New Casebooks

New Casebooks

SONS AND LOVERS

EDITED BY RICK RYLANCE

Introduction, selection and editorial matter
© Rick Rylance   1996

All rights reserved. No reproduction, copy or transmission of
this publication may be made without written permission.

No paragraph of this publication may be reproduced, copied or
transmitted save with written permission or in accordance with
the provisions of the Copyright, Designs and Patents Act 1988,
or under the terms of any licence permitting limited copying
issued by the Copyright Licensing Agency, 90 Tottenham Court
Road, London WIP 9HE.

Any person who does any unauthorised act in relation to this
publication may be liable to criminal prosecution and civil
claims for damages.

First published 1996 by
MACMILLAN PRESS LTD
Houndmills, Basingstoke, Hampshire RG21 6XS
and London
Companies and representatives
throughout the world

ISBN 0-333-54905-8 hardcover
ISBN 0-333-54906-6 paperback

A catalogue record for this book is available
from the British Library.

10 9   8   7   6   5   4   3   2   1
05 04 03 02 01 00 99 98 97 96

Printed in Malaysia

Contents

Acknowledgements

The editor and publishers wish to thank the following for permission to use copyright material:

Diane S. Bonds, for an extract from *Language and the Self in D. H. Lawrence* (1988), UMI Research Press, by permission of the author; Paul Delany, for 'Lawrence and the Decline of the Industrial Spirit' from *The Challenge of D. H. Lawrence*, ed. Michael Squires and Keith Cushman (1990), by permission of The University of Wisconsin Press; Terry Eagleton, for an extract from *Literary Theory: An Introduction* (1983), by permission of Blackwell Publishers; Sigmund Freud, for an extract from *Sexuality and the Psyche of Love*, ed. Philip Rieff (1963), trans. Joan Riviere, Collier Books, Macmillan Co., by permission of Sigmund Freud Copyrights; John Goode, for an extract from 'D. H. Lawrence', from *The Sphere History of English Literature: The Twentieth Century* (1970), Barrie & Jenkins, by permission of the author; Graham Holderness, for an extract from *D. H. Lawrence: History, Ideology and Fiction* (1982), by permission of Gill & Macmillan Publishers; Frank Kermode, for an extract from *Lawrence* (1973) Fontana, by permission of HarperCollins Publishers and Peters Fraser & Dunlop Group Ltd on behalf of the author; Louis Martz, for 'A Portrait of Miriam: A Study in the Design of *Sons and Lovers*' from *Imagined Worlds: Essays on Some English Novels and Novelists in Honour of John Butt*, ed. Maynard Mack and Ian Gregor (1968), Methuen & Co, by permission of Routledge; Kate Millet, for an extract from *Sexual Politics* (1977). Copyright © 1977 by Kate Millet, by permission of Georges Borchardt, Inc. on behalf of the author; Tony Pinkney, for an extract from *D. H Lawrence* (1990), Harvester, by permission of Harvester

Wheatsheaf; Scott R. Sanders, for extracts from *D. H. Lawrence: The World of His Novels* (1973), Vision Press, by permission of the author; Hilary Simpson, for an extract from *D. H. Lawrence and Feminism* (1982), Croom Helm, by permission of Routledge.

Every effort has been made to trace all the copyright holders but if any have been inadvertently overlooked the publishers will be pleased to make the necessary arrangement at the first opportunity.

General Editors' Preface

The purpose of this series of New Casebooks is to reveal some of the ways in which contemporary criticism has changed our understanding of commonly studied texts and writers and, indeed, of the nature of criticism itself. Central to the series is a concern with modern critical theory and its effect on current approaches to the study of literature. Each New Casebook editor has been asked to select a sequence of essays which will introduce the reader to the new critical approaches to the text or texts being discussed in the volume and also illuminate the rich interchange between critical theory and critical practice that characterises so much current writing about literature.

In this focus on modern critical thinking and practice New Casebooks aim not only to inform but also to stimulate, with volumes seeking to reflect both the controversy and the excitement of current criticism. Because much of this criticism is difficult and often employs an unfamiliar critical language, editors have been asked to give the reader as much help as they feel is appropriate, but without simplifying the essays or the issues they raise. Again, editors have been asked to supply a list of further reading which will enable readers to follow up issues raised by the essays in the volume.

The project of New Casebooks, then, is to bring together in an illuminating way those critics who best illustrate the ways in which contemporary criticism has established new methods of analysing texts and who have reinvigorated the important debate about how we 'read' literature. The hope is, of course, that New Casebooks will not only open up this debate to a wider audience, but will also encourage students to extend their own ideas, and think afresh about their responses to the texts they are studying.

John Peck and Martin Coyle
University of Wales, Cardiff

Introduction

RICK RYLANCE

The purpose of this collection is to provide ready access to a variety of modern approaches to *Sons and Lovers*. The selection is designed to illustrate recent trends in work on Lawrence and, more widely, to reflect developments in critical practice since the last Casebook volume on the novel was published in 1969.[1] The essays fall into three groups: those with an interest in the autobiographical and psychoanalytic dimensions of the novel (essays 1–3), those concerned primarily with the analysis of gender and sexual relations (essays 4–7), and those investigating the historical and social context (essays 8–12). But running through most is a particular interest in the novel's stylistic and narrative techniques, and readers will find many helpful points of development from piece to piece.

Critics have been interested in sexual, psychoanalytic, social and formal issues since *Sons and Lovers* was first published in 1913. But the methodological spirit in which these topics have been approached recently is very different. Most of the critics collected in the 1969 Casebook, for instance, following the critical principles of the day, searched the novel for evidence of coherence, growth and moral wisdom. *Sons and Lovers* was assumed to have a cohesive stylistic and formal organisation and demonstrate a view of life from which something could be learnt. Today, these things are no longer looked for. Feminist and socialist critics, to take the most obvious examples, are more interested in the novel's ideological limits and possibilities while, in the discussion of literary form, much recent criticism emphasises, not the integrity of the text, but ambiguities, eddies of meaning and disturbing subtexts. Some con-

temporary criticism asks increasingly abrasive questions of literature, but it would be wrong to assume that all of the critics collected here share this approach. Frank Kermode, Louis Martz and
Paul Delany, for instance, work from very different premises,
though with the same thought-provoking intelligence as their more
politically committed colleagues.

I   AUTOBIOGRAPHY AND PSYCHOANALYSIS

Modern criticism has been guarded about biographical interpretations of literary texts for the obvious reason that when writers use
material from their own lives they shape it for purposes other than
confession or personal record. Nonetheless much commentary on
Sons and Lovers has been dominated by this autobiographical issue
because the novel is so clearly based on Lawrence's own experience
and critics have been regularly forced into the awkward corner of
both accepting and denying the importance of the issue. Gāmini
Salgādo, for instance, in the first Casebook, rightly insisted that *Sons
and Lovers* should be read as a novel and not a personal apologia,
but over a third of his introduction is taken up with the problem.
Similarly, F. R. Leavis's pathbreaking *D. H. Lawrence/Novelist*
(1955), whose very title signals a wish to get away from the fascination of Lawrence's life, remains captured by it. 'The advance to *Sons
and Lovers*', Leavis wrote, 'is one to the direct and wholly convention-free treatment of the personal problem: the immense improvement, the success, is bound up with the strict concentration on the
autobiographical.'[2] So, for Leavis, *Sons and Lovers* cleared the air
for Lawrence's more mature and, he thought, impersonal work.
However, one major change in criticism since Leavis has been an
eagerness to see such issues in historical rather than individual or
moral contexts.

It is now difficult to accept Leavis's account for a number of
reasons. For one thing, the novel is not as convention-free as he
claims. Though Lawrence did write something refreshingly original
compared to his two earlier novels, *The White Peacock* (1911) and
The Trespasser (1912), *Sons and Lovers* clearly uses a number of
conventions of its period. The first of these is the *Bildungsroman*,
or novel of personal development, which had been a leading
nineteenth-century form used, for example, by Dickens in *David
Copperfield* and George Eliot in *The Mill on the Floss*. When *Sons*

and Lovers was written, the form was enjoying a resurgence as a new generation of writers experienced a period of change and transition. One particular version of this form, as Tony Pinkney makes clear in essay 11, was the *Künstlerroman*, a novel about the growth of an artist. Pinkney argues that *Sons and Lovers* was written as nineteenth-century fictional forms gave way to newer ones, and artistic development was therefore a matter of urgent, self-conscious concern. The issues raised by Lawrence's use of his own history are not, then, simply of a personal kind.

Lawrence was conscious of this. In the novel he writes of Paul's situation as a *representative* one: 'He was like so many men of his own age. Sex had become so complicated in him that he would have denied that he ever could want Clara or Miriam or any woman whom he *knew*. Sex desire was a detached sort of thing, that did not belong to a woman.'[3] Lawrence insisted on this point time and again. In a famous letter to his editor, Edward Garnett, he wrote that the novel described 'the tragedy of thousands of young men in England', and he changed the title from 'Paul Morel' to the more generalising *Sons and Lovers*.[4] Likewise, in his 'Autobiographical Sketch' of 1927, the impersonal is emphasised:

> the women freed herself at least mentally and spiritually from the husband's domination, and then she became that great institution, the character-forming power, the mother of my generation. I am sure the character of nine-tenths of the men of my generation was formed by the mother: the characters of the daughters too.[5]

The phrasing here (Lawrence speaks of 'the woman' and 'the husband' in a way that echoes one of the stylistic tricks of *Sons and Lovers* itself), and his characterisation of the 'mother of my generation', powerfully suggest issues of wide contemporary interest, most notably as associated with the founder of psychoanalysis, Sigmund Freud.

It is worth emphasising, however, that Freud and Lawrence were not singular in these interests. The dynamics of what Freud labelled the 'Oedipus Complex' (after the tragic Greek who unwittingly killed his father and married his mother) became a consistent theme in English writing in the early decades of the century. Plots exploring 'Oedipal' situations not unlike that in *Sons and Lovers* feature in works by several of Lawrence's contemporaries both male and female. May Sinclair's *The Combined Maze* (1913) and *Mary Olivier: A Life* (1919), J. D. Beresford's *An Imperfect Mother*

(1920) and Noel Coward's first stage success *The Vortex* (1924) are all examples. The theme appealed because of vivid personal experience, but also because it represented a point of conflict between generations in an era when young writers sought consciously to define their modernity. For some – like Nicky Lancaster in *The Vortex* – the situation is tragic, and the ending of *Sons and Lovers* has been read in this way, but more commonly these works end at a point of impasse. Where classic Victorian fiction closes with a marriage settlement, these new works end in uncertainty without any clear step towards either a new family or individual independence.

In the first essay in this collection, Frank Kermode sets *Sons and Lovers* in this context. However, for Kermode, it is the new style Lawrence developed in *Sons and Lovers* which is the most important achievement, for it enabled these volatile, highly-charged situations to be described in new ways and patterns. Thus, he argues, *Sons and Lovers* is shaped not so much by an unfolding narrative, but by a pattern of symbolic and structural variations from episode to episode (for example, Paul's relations with his mother are replicated in his relations with Miriam). He also notes that Lawrence's method of 'over-painting' is well adapted to a way of depicting reality which stresses uncertainty, flux, repetition and partiality, often at a psychological level below consciousness.

In terms of content, Kermode establishes the connection with Freud's almost exactly contemporary essay – reprinted as essay 2 in this volume – 'The Most Prevalent Form of Degradation in Erotic Life' (sometimes translated as 'On the Universal Tendency to Debasement in the Sphere of Love'). Just as Lawrence spoke of Paul Morel's tragedy as that of thousands, so Freud generalised from a phenomenon he increasingly observed among his patients in Vienna. Why, he asks, should so many young men suffer from 'psychical impotence' (that is, the inability to have sex with specific partners)? Kermode argues that, taken together, novel and essay define a distinctive cultural event, an 'epochal sickness with deep roots in the past', which is particular to this period.[6]

Freud's argument is complex, but a summary might go as follows. He maintains – conventionally enough – that to 'ensure a fully normal attitude in love' the 'affectionate' and the 'sensual' feelings need to be united. But difficulties arise because the male child's affectionate attachment to his mother gathers erotic elements as his sensual interests develop (this is Freud's Oedipal scenario). As a central part of early male development, therefore, the affectionate and sensual feelings are driven apart by the prohibition on incest, and so-called normal development depends upon the suppression of unacceptable but powerful feelings. This goal, though, is not always reached, and the sexual development of a boy whose relationship with his mother continues to carry an erotic charge is likely to be difficult. 'Psychical impotence' occurs when a sexual partner resembles the individual's mother and he is caught between opposed feelings of desire and prohibition. Freud, however, gives the argument a further twist. Part II of his essay suggests that what we conventionally call 'abnormal' development – the failure to come to terms with forbidden desires and integrate the affectionate and sensual feelings – may actually be the dominant trend, and that most men in fact do divorce sexual desire from affection. This is observable, Freud suggests, in the traditional distinction in male thinking between the idealised wife and the degraded mistress or prostitute.

It is easy to see the connection between Paul Morel's situation in *Sons and Lovers* and the condition Freud describes as 'universally prevalent in civilised countries and not a disease of particular individuals'.[7] Kermode notes how the stalling of Paul and Miriam's sexual relationship might follow the Freudian model, and other readers have observed that Paul's perception of Miriam and Clara corresponds to Freud's description of the conventional ways in which Edwardian men classified women: Miriam is spiritualised, while Clara becomes his sensual mistress of lower social status. It is also not difficult to see how Paul's relationship with Clara might represent a mild version of the compulsion towards the 'psychical debasement of the sexual object' Freud describes.[8] Some of their sexual experience takes place by a muddy river, for instance, and David Trotter notes that, in his descriptions of Clara, Lawrence follows, and then distances himself from the conventions used in Edwardian sex novels.[9] Finally, there is the vexed issue of Miriam's 'frigidity'.

Freud's thinking on women's sexuality has been attacked by feminists (though many also find his account of male behaviour illuminating) and Lawrence's portrait of Miriam has been controversial for similar reasons. In 'The Most Prevalent Form of Degradation', Freud argues that the female equivalent of 'psychical impotence' is 'frigidity', the inability to engage in sexual activity at all, and this – encouraged by certain of Paul's statements in the novel – has been a reproach commonly levelled at Miriam by male critics.[10] However, Freud's proposition is not simple, and he is careful to relate the condition to social circumstances and not to an inevitable, blamewor-thy, female disposition. 'Frigidity' is caused, he argues, by the 'long period of delay [for women] between sexual maturity and sexual activity which is demanded by education for social reasons',[11] and this postponement propels women's sexual careers into fantasy. In *Sons and Lovers*, of course, one consistent way of describing Miriam is as a dreamy romantic: 'The girl was romantic in her soul. Everywhere was a Walter Scott heroine being loved by men with helmets or with plumes in their caps. She herself was something of a princess turned swine-girl, in her own imagination' (Ch. 7, p. 191). But it is an open question whether such fantasies are pathological in the way Freud describes.

Freudian interpretations of *Sons and Lovers* remain controver-sial, and individual readers will need to test in detail the adequacy of Freud's account of both male and female development in relation to Lawrence's novel. But one or two general considerations are im-portant. Though Lawrence had some second-hand knowledge of Freud's ideas when writing the later drafts of the novel, the degree of influence Freud exerted remains a matter of speculation. What is certain is that, by 1920 at least, Lawrence had fiercely rejected Freud.[12] One reason for this was a fundamental disagreement about the nature of the unconscious which Lawrence came to regard as an essentially healthy, sensual alternative to the imprisoning rationality of modern culture. He associated the unconscious with sponta-neous, natural life whereas, for Freud, the unconscious is formed by the repressions essential to living in social groups and can be very destructive. This disagreement about the nature of the unconscious, and the implications drawn by Freud from his analysis of it ('The Most Prevalent Form of Degradation' is massively pessimistic at the close), raises important general issues. Among these is the question of the different kinds of language used by the two writers. Kermode describes Lawrence's new, dynamic style as one of tenderness and a certain beauty as well as impulsive emotion. Freud's essay, however, is very different in tone, vocabulary and structure of un-derstanding. His writing is unemotional; the vocabulary reaches for metaphors from zoology, economics and engineering; and this cool language – though it admits passing historical factors such as the influence of a girl's education – has the effect of freezing these human events into a grim, inevitable routine.

The question of whether Freud intended to describe such a psy-chological treadmill is a contentious area of psychoanalytic theory.

But the issue is important, not least because it opens questions about the extent to which literary texts like *Sons and Lovers* can be 'explained' by non-literary theories such as psychoanalysis without a distorting reduction. Much modern criticism is ambivalent in its response to this problem. On the one hand there is widespread interest in non-literary theory as a way of approaching literature but, on the other, many also argue that, because literature does not need systematic meanings, it is uniquely able to articulate diverse ideas and therefore unsettle all conclusions. In this sense, *Sons and Lovers* might be thought to put as many questions to Freud, as Freud's essay provides ways of 'explaining' the novel.

Modern developments in psychoanalytic criticism – represented here by Terry Eagleton in essay 3 – have had to deal with these problems. Eagleton uses work by the French psychoanalyst Jacques Lacan and the Marxist theorist Louis Althusser to examine the ways in which Paul's identity is created in particular social conditions. Eagleton explains Althusser's and Lacan's ideas with typical lucidity and is especially interested in what they can tell us about why people come to believe ideological ideas about themselves and their circumstances. His account of *Sons and Lovers* stresses the complex explicit and implicit ideological dynamics of the Morel household and examines the ways in which, encouraged by his socially-aspiring mother, Paul mis-recognises his situation in a particular, class-specific way. Eagleton, therefore, follows the more orthodox Freudian account but extends it in social detail and enlarges our sense of the forces, both social and psychological, at play in the formulation of an individual's development. Crucially, he also pays attention to the form of novel, an area which has not always been adequately dealt with by psychoanalytic criticism. He argues that, because the narrative point-of-view in the book is predominantly that of Paul, it must be read as coloured by his particular interests, defences and convictions. As a result, the story given in *Sons and Lovers* from Paul's perspective has important gaps and distortions, most obviously in the representation of Walter Morel, a portrait of his own father which Lawrence, in fact, came to regret.

This method of reading the novel is different from the classical psychoanalytic approach which treated Paul's story as a Freudian case history. Eagleton recommends paying attention as much to what the text avoids, as to what it says. He thereby introduces, in effect, a dimension to the novel which is not unlike a person's unconscious because it contains material which has been repressed or denied and which needs to be teased out, rather as an analyst explores a patient's dreams or free-associations. Psychoanalytic criticism is thus given a new impetus, and critics like Eagleton can look to a narrative's textual or political unconscious where the older approach considered only more personal characteristics and was reluctant to take the measure of the literary nature of the material it studied.

II *GENDER, NARRATIVE AND THE PLURAL TEXT*

Like Eagleton and Kermode's contributions, the fourth essay, Louis Martz's 'Portrait of Miriam', is concerned with style and narrative method. Indeed, Martz's classic account in many ways established the direction of much recent thinking in this area. But the essay is not solely concerned with formal matters. What interests Martz is the way in which Miriam emerges from a narrative told primarily from Paul's point-of-view and his essay pioneered a shift in commentary away from a somewhat exclusive emphasis on Paul's predicament. As we shall see, this change in direction was supported by developments in feminist criticism, and Martz's essay – published in 1968 – was in tune with a more general alteration in attitudes to gender questions, though in itself it has no explicit political edge.

Martz takes issue with interpretations which present Miriam as insipidly and destructively over-spiritual. Although this view is in the text, he argues that it is best understood as Paul's interpretation. What is 'puzzling and peculiar' for Martz about the narrative technique of Chapters 7–11 is that the ostensible neutrality of the earlier and later parts is replaced by a pained intensity in which 'we cannot wholly trust the narrator's remarks ... for his commentary represents mainly an extension of Paul's consciousness ... [and] the voice of the narrator tends to echo and magnify the confusions that are arising within Paul himself.' This insight, demonstrated in impressive detail, has been a cornerstone of much subsequent criticism because it provokes serious doubts about the book's realism: 'we can never tell, from the stream of consciousness alone, where the real truth lies', Martz remarks.[13]

Though at the end of his essay Martz limits the corrosive effect of his insight, by offering a more consoling interpretation of its conclusion than would be accepted by many recent commentators, the important point is that he has begun to unravel our confidence in the novel's apparent realist objectivity. Later critics, such as Diane Bonds, Graham Holderness and Tony Pinkney in this volume, develop the argument further. They are sceptical that there is any useful sense in which fictional works can be described as realistic if that implies a neutral accuracy of record. Rather, the modern argument is that so-called realistic work is in fact composed of a set of subtle conventions which create an illusion of objectivity. Like Eagleton's, this line of argument is concerned to explore the unacknowledged biases and repressions which shape the narrative, and which produce, as Martz puts it, 'the portrait of Miriam that lies beneath the over-painted commentary of the Paul-narrator'.[14] This search for concealed principles of organisation – for a text's blindspots, omissions and biases – is one of the main innovations of recent criticism.

Kate Millett's book *Sexual Politics*, from which essay 5 is extracted, illustrates another. This frankly political, eye-opening attack on patriarchal assumptions became an international bestseller in 1969, the year after Louis Martz's essay was published. Millett is concerned with the political aspects of sexuality, and especially the issue of power and violence as a systematic condition of patriarchal culture. Lawrence is attacked, alongside other male writers including Freud, for representing male domination as an inevitable and, indeed, desirable condition. Though Millett admires Lawrence's refreshingly original depiction of working-class life, and the undoubted passion and energy of his writing, she deplores the way *Sons and Lovers* is centred on Paul's needs around which the female characters gather as satellites with no social or psychological existence of their own. Mrs Morel, for example, 'is utterly deprived of any avenue of achievement' and lives only through her male children.[15]

Millett's point is well made in relation to the conditions of life for women in Mrs Morel's situation. However, the argument assumes that Lawrence endorses this state of affairs, and another interpretation might be that *Sons and Lovers* exposes the condition without ratifying the social arrangements which underpin it. But Millett closely identifies Paul with Lawrence, and the novel is thus interpreted as Lawrence's ideological fantasy in which, as a further twist to the Oedipal conundrum, the mother's loss is compensated by a literary vision in which the women 'exist in Paul's orbit and to cater to his needs: Clara awakens him sexually, Miriam to worship his talent ... and Mrs Morel to provide always that enormous and expansive support, that dynamic motivation which can inspire the son of a coal miner to rise above the circumstances of his birth and become a great artist.'[16]

Millett interprets *Sons and Lovers* not as realism but as a 'heroic [male] romance'.[17] However, it is debatable whether she accurately reflects the mood and shape of the novel, and Millet has been criticised – not least by other feminists – for misrepresenting texts by selective quotation or summary. Judicious caution, though, is not what is interesting about *Sexual Politics*. Millett's strengths lie in her polemic, which stirs up issues and provokes questions rather than balances a judgement, and her exposure of the ways in which power functions in the novel in an interpersonal way. Although she unproblematically identifies Paul with Lawrence her account of this disturbing area of manipulation in the book is both revealing and important.

Later feminist critics, like Diane Bonds in essay 6, extend these insights. Like Martz, Bonds is interested in how the language of the novel reveals more than it states, and she, too, focuses on Paul's manipulation of Miriam. She observes that Miriam is often described in ways which reveal a more robust personality than is allowed by the usual account of her as a dreamy, unsexual fantasist. Bonds thus follows Martz in identifying the unstable interplay of narrative voice and imagery and recognising how Paul's desires colour the narrative voice. But she is harder in her judgements: 'one might call ... [the narrative commentary] the view of a self-deceived neurotic couched in the language of an objective, authoritative onlooker who has access to all the facts.'[18] This change in evaluation reflects feminist recognition of the political aspect of intersubjective role-play, manipulation and deception.

One of Bonds' most valuable ideas concerns the way Paul leads the gauche Miriam into judgements about herself by his orchestration of her language. Throughout, Bonds argues, Paul directs a severely judgemental, but equally evasive, discourse in which Miriam remains his puppet. But Bonds rejects Martz's isolation of the central third of the novel as the solely problematic area in this respect and is unhappy with his reading of the ending as an orthodox *Bildungsroman* in which the hero gains mature self-understanding. For Bonds this neat, wholesome resolution of what she calls 'the narrator's shiftiness' is questionable because issues of sexual power are avoided, and because contemporary conceptions of literary language oppose such deceptive tidiness. Indeed, much recent thinking in this area is interested, not in the equanimity of a text's resolutions, but in the disturbing subtexts revealed through metaphors, imagery, contradictions and evasions.

Bonds' essay draws on a body of ideas often loosely grouped as 'poststructuralism', a demanding but influential body of enquiry originating in France in the late 1960s. Poststructuralist thought stresses the precariousness of all truth claims and emphasises the instability of the language in which they are expressed. Truth claims, it is said, are powerful acts of assertion, efforts to master a problem (or, indeed, other people) rather than cool statements of fact or analysis. They impose an interpretation, rather than discover truth. In *Sons and Lovers*, for example, Paul does not reveal 'the truth' about Miriam. He imposes on her, and perhaps the reader too, by an act of powerful conscious or unconscious will. However, careful attention to the detail of such acts reveals contradictions. Bonds' particular example is the way Paul's convictions about painting – he believes in a spontaneous, free kind of art which catches the immediate, lively presence of a subject – are contradicted by his imposition of stereotyped images onto Miriam.

What happens in personal terms, poststructuralists argue, also happens in more abstract forms of discourse like literary criticism. For example, when older critics stressed the coherence of *Sons and Lovers*, poststructuralists contend that this is a limiting interpretation similar to Paul's 'interpretation' of Miriam. In making it, features of the text are suppressed by a governing, but often silent, set of interests. For literary critics, especially in America, the most influential thinker in this area has been the philosopher Jacques Derrida. Derrida's 'deconstruction' is concerned to destabilise accepted ideas and investigate concealed or repressed meanings. One concept used by Derrida, and by Bonds in her account of Paul's painting, is the philosophical idea of 'presence'. Deep or spontaneous convictions of all kinds fall into this category. They are the permanent 'presences' which hold our world-view together, and deconstructionists are expert at teasing out the contradictions, slippages in argument and unexamined assumptions embedded in the expression of them. This exploration of what is sometimes called the text's 'plurality' has been an increasingly vigorous feature of recent criticism.[19]

It will be clear by now that feminist approaches to literature are neither simple nor unified, and Hilary Simpson, in essay 7, represents another strand. Her analysis is more historically grounded than that of either Millett or Bonds and is based on her study of feminist activism in Lawrence's own day, some sense of which is present in *Sons and Lovers*. Taking issue with Millett's 'savage account' of Paul's treatment of Clara, Simpson uses her historical material to contextualise it. Though she carefully establishes Lawrence's ambivalent attitudes to Clara's feminism, Simpson makes an interesting defence of the controversial way in which she eventually returns to her violent husband. The parallel she makes with what happens to Miriam is also illuminating, as is the careful account of Paul's stereotypical male response to an assertive, independent-minded woman.

Simpson's essay raises two important general issues. The first of these is the difficulty of judging complex texts by 'politically correct', modern-day criteria. For example, can we say that *Sons and Lovers* indulges what many see as Paul's stereotyped and manipulative conduct, or does the novel help us understand it through a more ample analysis? This issue runs into a larger one. As Simpson says, Lawrence's ambivalence towards feminism was an aspect of his general uncertainty about political issues. Though at times he held strong convictions, his enduring attitude towards politics was one of severe mistrust of social generalisations and a feeling that his real interests were with individuals. As a result, Lawrence often depicts negatively political campaigners of all kinds, and tends to dismiss whole communities as narrow and inhibiting from the point of view of his isolated central characters.[20] One version of this can be seen in Paul Morel's uneasy relations with his father and the mining town of Bestwood. Indeed, it might be said that what unites Paul, Miriam, Clara and Mrs Morel, despite their antagonisms, is the painful fact that none of them is comfortable in their immediate social environments. This is a leading issue in the concluding group of essays.

III *SONS AND LOVERS* IN SOCIAL CONTEXT

Lawrence is often rightly admired for the inward way in which he writes about Nottingham and the mining country and issues of social class. His originality in this respect struck his first readers immediately and the next four essays – by Goode, Holderness, Sanders and Pinkney – examine this aspect of *Sons and Lovers*. They centre on three related issues: the quality of the novel's depiction of a working-class, industrial environment, the depiction of Paul's increasing isolation and alienation, and the vexed question of the novel's realism. The last of these is, once again, particularly important. For these critics, the instability of the text – its disturbed narrative voice, its complex, 'over-painted' style, its rickety sense of formal propriety – says something not just about the development of fictional forms in Britain in this crucial period, but also about the relationship between literary forms and the particular social and class experience *Sons and Lovers* records. In this, each critic owes much, in different ways, to the great British socialist critic Raymond Williams who pioneered this kind of analysis. Williams's brief account of *Sons and Lovers* in his book *The English Novel from Dickens to Lawrence* (1970) interprets the novel as a work of transition. Paul's story is understood as one of translation from a community with ambiguously valued but settled social and human relations, to a different and more solitary social world. At the same time, the new language Lawrence found for this experience remade the conventions of nineteenth-century fiction into a form which is still used in Britain as a way of interpreting working-class lives.[21]

John Goode's piece is an extract from one of the best modern essays offering an overall account of Lawrence's career in these terms. He begins with the problem of form and, like many of his contemporaries, finds it unsettled. For him *Sons and Lovers* has no stable generic shape and coggles between *Bildungsroman*, urban realism, country pastoral and a more heavily symbolic kind of writing. Goode relates this instability to the series of dislocations in social status and cultural expectation experienced by the Morel family. So *Sons and Lovers* reflects Lawrence's efforts to represent new kinds of class experience and social process by adapting and challenging some of the realist conventions of novels written largely for middle-class readers.

In both formal and thematic terms, the novel represents the passage from an older community to a more lonely, individual voice. This is a process of both loss and gain, and Goode finds it at each point of personal conflict in the novel. The Oedipal intimacies of the book are not, for him, matters of individual psychology. They are entangled in the social aspirations which underpin the narrative, unsettle the family and end for Paul in painful isolation as he forms his identity by rejection rather than positive choice. At the close, Paul becomes for Goode 'a kind of Robinson Crusoe figure, stripped of everything but the shut fist and clenched mouth'.[22] As such he represents his age: the working-class boy settling to a middle-class career, the man from a small community moving to the city, the child of industrialism ambiguously becoming an artist, the friend, son and lover ending in modern isolation.

Most critics interested in the social context of *Sons and Lovers* follow this argument and read the book as a narrative of individuation and estrangement. Graham Holderness, in essay 9, also relates the originality of composition in *Sons and Lovers* to Lawrence's origins. Holderness, though, is keen that responses to the novel should not slip into easy generalisation. The Morels, he points out, are not a typical working-class family. Indeed, it is their very difference from their neighbours which is the source of many of the tensions with which the family is riven, and neither he nor Goode idealises a community in which, among other things, such bitter domestic conflict is ingrained. However, if the book portrays the limitations of this community, then by the close the snares surrounding Paul's freedom from it are also glaringly apparent and the last chapter is significantly entitled 'Derelict'. For Holderness, the novel is a searching examination of the powerful Edwardian ideologies of self-improvement and social mobility. Individuality, and freedom of a kind, are discovered; but so, too, are loneliness and alienation.

Scott Sanders in essay 10 approaches these questions from a different perspective again. He also is interested in themes of restricted individual development, but he argues that this choice of theme in a sense limits the book's account of Bestwood. The novel, as it were, has to be written from a distance, from the point of view of an individual (both Lawrence and Paul Morel) who has separated himself from the environment described. This, in fact, is a persisting structural difficulty in writing about working-class experience, but in *Sons and Lovers* Sanders feels that it has three specific consequences. First, attention to issues of class difference is displaced onto issues of psychological and gender difference (though John Goode's argument that social issues are nonetheless always present in the description of personal and psychological conflict might be borne in mind). Second, Sanders makes the excellent point, demonstrated in careful detail, that the language of Paul's childhood is the language of his socially aspiring mother, and that Paul's consciousness is formed in and by this language. This in itself takes him some distance from his neighbours. The third point concerns Walter Morel, and Sanders is one of the few critics to give much sustained attention to him. He understands Morel (Lawrence often calls him merely 'the miner') as caught between two inhospitable ideologies related to the work ethic: the world of the mining company outside the household, and the world of social aspiration within it. As a result Walter's story is also one of isolation. No one else in the novel talks as he does at any length, and he almost literally disappears from the text. In a world of increasing individuation – Sanders, like Goode, draws a parallel with Robinson Crusoe – Walter is left lonely and abandoned by an aspiring family which excludes him. Throughout the novel, Sanders concludes, the characters are driven by forces which are portrayed as impersonally beyond them. Even sexual experience is often described in terms which are abstract, detached or anonymous. For him, this is a rendition of a world which has lost human bearings, community and mutuality.

Tony Pinkney in essay 11 is a somewhat different kind of socialist critic. Influenced by the work of Terry Eagleton, and the theoretical analysis associated with the journal *New Left Review*, Pinkney also describes *Sons and Lovers* as a novel whose form is determined by larger forces. Devised as nineteenth-century realism, he argues that the novel was then disturbed by forces which unsettle its classic realist ambitions and accommodations. Most arrestingly, Pinkney identifies Miriam with the pre-realist, more subversive Gothic, a fictional form associated with the liminal areas of dream, repressed desire and sexuality rather than the mundane social worlds of Edwardian realism. Pinkney's identification of this aspect of the novel mirrors a significant return of interest in the Gothic recently amongst modern feminist critics and novelists who are interested in it as a means for exploring the hinterland of distinctively female desires. But Pinkney identifies other unstable components in the style of *Sons and Lovers*. These include an oscillation between the two poetic schools of Imagism and Georgianism with both of which Lawrence was connected. This divided style, Pinkney argues, reflects, in a representatively 'modernist' way, the rootlessness and transition which is the novel's theme.

Approaches to *Sons and Lovers* concerned with the novel's social aspect produce both variety and consensus. There is agreement that the novel deals with the phenomenon of late nineteenth-century individualism, and all accounts agree that the novel's realism is complex and problematic. Tony Pinkney offers the most audacious account of this, seeing in the text a play of incongruous stylistic forces reflecting the cultural history in which the novel is interested. But the other essays also struggle with these complexities. Indeed, there has been a particularly full debate about literary realism in recent years as established definitions have crumbled. Because fictional realism cannot be established by some simple check against a putative real-life event, there are enormous areas of dispute about what is meant by such a term. Among socialist critics, for example, there has been a shift from a sometimes crude valorisation of 'social-realism' to an appreciation that the way texts make readers conscious of reality is more complex than passive transcription. At the same time, as we have seen, modern thinking about literary language stresses not its representational qualities, but the plurality of the meanings it makes available, and most critics now agree that there is good reason to recognise strong, alternative currents of meaning below the ostensibly mimetic surface of *Sons and Lovers*.

In the four essays by Goode, Holderness, Sanders and Pinkney, one touchstone in the effort to define the novel's realism is the work of the Hungarian critic Georg Lukács, a Marxist of considerable influence in the post-war period. Lukács valued the nineteenth-century realist novel especially. For him it was the literary form which was uniquely able to balance attention to the personal and the social and understand the two together. By portraying typical individuals, Lukács argued, the great nineteenth-century European novelists like Balzac, Dickens and Tolstoy were able to grasp the essentials of the historical process in ways that more 'modernist' work – with its fragmented techniques and emphasis on alienation and psychological collapse – was unable to do.[23] Despite reservations, this kind of argument is used by Goode, Holderness and Sanders to interpret *Sons and Lovers* as having an understanding of the changing society it describes. For them Paul Morel represents his age. But, as Tony Pinkney points out, there are difficulties in Lukács' assumption that fiction can reflect society in this way, and he instead describes a text riven by social change without establishing any coherent grip upon it. Pinkney's account of the novel as a volatile, splintered work, offering a crackerjack variety of styles and aspects, is of a piece with the contemporary, 'post-modern' critical outlook which downplays representationalism and emphasises writing which is both disturbing and disturbed.

The final essay in this collection, by Paul Delany, also deals with questions of historical change, but in a very different way. In a wide-ranging discussion of Lawrence's attitudes to industrialisation,

Delany engages an aspect of *Sons and Lovers* which is significant because Lawrence himself held such strong anti-industrial views. The essay places Lawrence in a wider tradition of radical, anti-industrial social criticism and asks us to consider the depiction of Bestwood in *Sons and Lovers* in this light. Delany's attention to the evolution in these arguments, many of which were shared by enthusiastic early commentators on Lawrence, is a reminder that, in the last decade of the twentieth century, it is more than eighty years since *Sons and Lovers* was published. Perhaps the importance of the novel is that it still engages such a range of responses, through a changing history, and speaks critically and questioningly to readers at the other end of a turbulent century.

NOTES

1. Gāmini Salgādo (ed.), *D. H. Lawrence: Sons and Lovers: A Casebook* (London, 1969).

2. F. R. Leavis, *D. H. Lawrence/Novelist* (1955: Harmondsworth, 1964), p. 19.

3. D. H. Lawrence, *Sons and Lovers*, Penguin edition, ed. Keith Sagar (Harmondsworth, 1981), ch. 10, p. 335. Subsequent reference will be to this edition and will follow quotations.

4. *The Letters of D. H. Lawrence*, vol. 1, ed. James T. Boulton (Cambridge, 1979), p. 477. Compare the closing paragraph of Lawrence's unpublished 'Foreword' to *Sons and Lovers*: 'The old son-lover was Oedipus. The name of the new one is legion.' D. H. Lawrence, *Sons and Lovers*, ed. Helen Baron and Karl Baron (Cambridge, 1992), p. 473.

5. D. H. Lawrence, '[Autobiographical Fragment]', *Phoenix: The Posthumous Papers of D. H. Lawrence*, ed. Edward D. MacDonald (London, 1936), p. 818.

6. See below p. 26.

7. See below p. 32.

8. See below pp. 32, 33–4.

9. David Trotter, *The English Novel in History 1895–1920* (London, 1993), ch. 13. For an interesting, opposite evaluation of the sex scenes by the river, however, see Paul Delany's article '*Sons and Lovers*: The Morel Marriage as a War of Position', *D. H. Lawrence Review*, 21 (1989), 162.

10. See, for example, Keith Sagar, *The Art of D. H. Lawrence* (Cambridge, 1966), pp. 25–32 (reprinted in the earlier Casebook on the novel, edited by Gāmini Salgādo, pp. 208–15), and Peter Balbert, *D. H. Lawrence and the Phallic Imagination: Essays on Sexual Identity and Feminist Misreading* (London, 1989). For an overview, see Adrienne E. Gavin, 'Miriam's Mirror: Reflections on the Labelling of Miriam Leivers', *D. H. Lawrence Review*, 24 (1992), 27–42.

11. See below p. 35.

12. See D. H. Lawrence, *Fantasia of the Unconscious and Psychoanalysis and the Unconscious* (Harmondsworth, 1971). These essays were written in 1921 and 1920 respectively.

13. See below pp. 56–7.

14. See below p. 57.

15. See below p. 76.

16. See below p. 75.

17. See below p. 79.

18. See below p. 105.

19. For general comment on Lawrence and deconstruction see Gerald Doherty, 'White Mythologies: D. H. Lawrence and the Deconstructive Turn', *Criticism*, 29 (1987), 477–96.

20. For further discussion see Rick Rylance, 'Lawrence's Politics' in *Rethinking Lawrence*, ed. Keith Brown (Milton Keynes, 1990), pp. 163–80.

21. Raymond Williams, *The English Novel From Dickens to Lawrence* (London, 1970).

22. See below p. 131.

23. Georg Lukács, *Studies in European Realism: A Sociological Survey of the Writings of Balzac, Stendhal, Tolstoy, Gorki and Others*, trans. Edith Bone (London, 1950).

A Note on the Text of *Sons and Lovers*

Two different versions of *Sons and Lovers* can now be bought. The more commonly available one, used in most paperback editions, reprints the text of the 1913 English first edition. This version of the novel was significantly changed from Lawrence's original manuscript by his editor Edward Garnett who altered it because he considered it too long and because he feared a scandal like those which later dogged Lawrence's career. (For example, his next novel *The Rainbow* was prosecuted under the Obscene Publications Act and withdrawn from sale.) Garnett edited the manuscript of *Sons and Lovers* skilfully but firmly. He eliminated a number of passages of sensual or erotic description which he guessed might be thought offensive, and some other material, including several descriptions of William's early life, as he strove to balance commercial, aesthetic and ideological pressures and bring the book to a manageable size for the publishers. In total, 85 passages of between 2 and 185 lines were deleted. These 'lost' passages, however, have been restored in the recent edition of the novel edited by Helen and Carl Baron for the prestigious new Cambridge Edition of Lawrence's works.

It is an open question which version of the novel is preferable. But, whatever the arguments (and it is worth bearing in mind that Lawrence agreed to Garnett's changes and, indeed, dedicated the novel to him), practical considerations dictate that this Casebook should use the 'older' text based on the first edition as a point of reference. This is for two reasons. First, it was the text used by all of the critics collected here, and, second, it continues to be the text most likely to be used by readers today. However, a problem remains because there are many different editions of it and these paginate the novel very differently. Indeed, the critics collected in this volume referenced their comments to three different editions, creating major inconsistencies in page numbering which would inevitably have caused confusion.

I have therefore standardised all page references to the Penguin edition of *Sons and Lovers* edited by Keith Sagar in 1981. I think this is probably the one most widely in circulation, and it is the edition used by several of the more recent contributors here. But details of two other excellent editions – including the Cambridge volume, whose expensive hardback version has a massive array of superb editorial notes – are to be found in the Further Reading.

1

The Writing of *Sons and Lovers*

FRANK KERMODE

Sons and Lovers, the masterpiece of Lawrence's first phase, was begun in October 1910. In November he ended his engagement to Jessie Chambers, and on 3 December began one with Louie Burrows. His mother died on 10 December. He restarted the novel, then called *Paul Morel*, early in 1911, but set it aside to write *The Trespasser*. Resuming the *Bildungsroman*, he finished it in May 1912, and rewrote it that autumn. Much of importance occurred between these versions. In January 1912 illness forced him to give up teaching; he returned to the Nottingham area and met Frieda Weekley, the German wife of a professor at Nottingham University College. The composition of his autobiographical novel therefore coincided with a period of multiple crises in his life. It was begun before the death of his mother, which is its climax; it was rewritten at the behest of an early lover, Miriam, and then again under the eye of Frieda after their elopement. It would be difficult to think of any other writer who wrote his life into successive texts of his fiction as Lawrence did; he habitually confronted his tale with new experience, and new interpretations of the past. There is in consequence an abundance, even a confusion, of life; one cannot feel that the published version is the last possible rehandling of the tale; and this openness is not the consequence of inefficiency. Flexibility, the power of a story to challenge a reader (including himself) is one of the marks of the novel as Lawrence wanted it to be, liberated from the burden of finality and completeness placed on it by his enemies, the novelists who, in his opinion, mistook structure for life, and novelistic custom for natural law.

Sons and Lovers is probably still the best known of the novels, and it would be wrong to cavil at this, for it is certainly a great achievement. In the first part the brief inset of the courtship of Paul's parents, the father's gaiety, his 'sensuous flame of life' melting the mother's puritanism, has that singleminded veracity of impression which was consistent, in Lawrence, with more abstract intentions. Morel in his caressing dialect speaks, as Dorothy Van Ghent notes, Lawrence's language of physical tenderness (she adds that the name of Mellors, the gamekeeper of *Lady Chatterley's Lover* who speaks that language also is a virtual anagram of Morel).[1] This is the dark dancing miner whom marriage will reduce, both physically and morally; whose son will be lost to a mother who makes refinement the instrument of her conquest. The placing of the parents and children, as of the ravaged landscape and its colliers, is done with extraordinary narrative tact and energy. Morel, obscurely fighting for a manhood sapped at the root by the absorbing care of the mother, cuts off the one-year-old William's curls and causes his wife the most intense suffering of her life (Lawrence remembered this and used the same narrative theme to a different but related purpose in *St Mawr*, when Mrs Witt cuts the hair of the groom Lewis). Mrs Morel is locked out by an angry husband; under a great moon she buries her face in a lily, and returns to the house smeared with pollen. This scene is so intensely realised – night scents and sounds, grey-white light, fear and cold – that the mind is satisfied without further interpretation, though interpretation, if offered, will be absorbed. Does the lily, a flower which Lawrence admired for its sexual blossoms and mired roots, daub Mrs Morel satirically, or is there sympathy between them? Miriam is later taken to task for trying to identify with or possess the flowers she is admiring. But Mrs Morel is for once identified with the night; when her normal prudence returns she makes her husband let her in, and his punishment for the misdeed is to be further reduced. There are other scenes in which narrative is transcended, caught up into some symbolic mode, without damage to the relation of acts and persons; for example, the moment when the blood of the mother, struck by the husband, drops into the baby Paul's hair. This boy sleeps with his mother, and lovingly cleans the mire off her fine shoes; episodes of everyday life will tell their own story better when the entire narrative context is capable of assuming, at any moment, large symbolic meanings; an understanding of how this worked is what chiefly distinguishes Lawrence as a critic of fiction, especially in his studies of American literature. Thus it is not enough to say that the perversely close relation of Paul with his mother precludes the possibility, at least during her life, of his satisfactorily choosing a sexual partner; Miriam is not merely a rival but also, in some ways a double; the rejection of her for the mother is also a rejection of the mother.

So too with Morel, the detested father; his defeat is not simply Oedipal; it is also the defeat of the dark virility of the pit, of unashamed and easy male grace and strength, beauty with its roots in muck. And all these meanings are in the complexity of the text, its power to suggest meanings other than that vouched for by a narrator apparently half-committed to Paul's own preference for the mother.

It has been argued that the narrative method alters in Part II; that objective omniscience gives way to a subtler mode, in which we can no longer trust the narrator: 'the point of view adopted is that of Paul; but since confusion, self-deception, and desperate self-justification are essential to that point of view, we can never tell ... where the real truth lies' except 'by seeking out the portrait of Miriam that lies beneath the over-painted commentary of the Paul-narrator.'[2] This nonce-technique Louis L. Martz regards as having served on one occasion only; but Lawrence is the great over-painter, his habitual method is to confront the text again and again, to re-handle it in precisely this style. The product grows progressively more complex in relation to the intention; that is why he insists that we do not isolate an intention and trust it. Trust the tale. If there is more than one Miriam under its surface paint, then so be it. In fact any novel, by virtue of its length, the intermittency of such controls as 'point of view', and the indeterminate nature of narrative, permits a great many such doublings, and consequently an indefinite range of interpretation. And Lawrence, with his fierce confidence in the novel as the *best* way of understanding reality, is not merely permissive; at his best he encourages the fiction to take away the power of meaning from its author. Rewriting, or 'overpainting', was his usual way of achieving this. So there is nothing unusual about his employment of the method in *Sons and Lovers*, though Martz is right to find it there, and his demonstration of its effect on the representation of Miriam is finely achieved.

Jessie Chambers did not like the Miriam she saw – unwilling to let go, subtly wrong in her attitude to the non-human or the animal, too much, in the end, the woman who buttons up or reduces men. She saw how much the confusions of Paul had coloured her image, how unfair his condemnation and rejection of her for a failure in which he shared at least equally. Yet all this is in the book; it is he who, possessed, resents her possessiveness, he whose 'sex desire was a sort of detached thing that did not belong to a woman' (p. 335). The only woman who might really please him would be one he did not know (compare the story 'Love Among the Haystacks', probably written in 1911). And it is he who forces the girl to accept him sexually: 'He said that possession was a great moment in life' (p. 345). This is what Lawrence later came to call sex in the head. When Miriam makes her sacrifice he identifies the initiatory experience with death. Miriam has two faces, the vital and sensitive, often snubbed by Paul, and the timid, restrained and possessive, both of which somewhat resemble Mrs Morel. Both are visible, simultaneously.

So with Clara: the success with which Lawrence renders the pleasures of this sexual relationship is not always recognised. It is true that she is a licensed mother-substitute; the first thing Paul does after making love to her is to clean her boots. But the very completeness of his sexual satisfaction sets it apart from life; she is for night, not day. Dawes, so often called a reflection of Morel, is Clara's true husband; Paul ritually fights him and comes to terms with the married couple, as he might with his reconciled parents, but the death that inhabits his sex manifests itself in the same chapter as the fight, when his mother confesses her cancer.

Such are the complexities which life, and reflection upon it, brought into the over-painting of *Sons and Lovers*. The cutting of all the knots is the death of the mother, in the chapter called 'Release'. Paul says goodbye to her, and to Clara; he oscillates between death and a mechanical kind of life, swings back briefly and for the last time to Miriam, and then departs for the future, 'a nothingness and yet not nothing' (p.492), walking towards light not darkness. The novel originates in an intense and prolonged personal crisis; it is remarkable that it should be so unselfish, so unsentimental. One could hardly ask for further proof of the seriousness with which Lawrence believed that 'the novel, properly handled, can reveal the most secret places of life',[3] as no other discourse can, and do so beyond the intention, and despite the defences, of its author.

Much has been said of the relation of *Sons and Lovers* to Freud; its theme is Oedipal, and in the later stages of composition

Lawrence had learned something about Freud from Frieda – his first contact with a thinker he was repeatedly to attack. The degree to which the personal relationships in the novel comply with Freud's account of mother-fixation is surely a tribute to the accuracy of Freud's generalisation rather than a proof of Lawrence's indebtedness. Freud observed and generalised, Lawrence observed, but believed that the text of a novel was more than an occasion for drawing abstract conclusions. Freud was, as it happens, the kind of scientist Lawrence believed to be incapacitated, by the very nature of his interests and methods, from giving a truthful version of reality. It is nevertheless true, as Simon O. Lesser has remarked,[4] that there are interesting common elements in *Sons and Lovers* and Freud's important, and almost contemporaneous paper, 'The Most Prevalent Form of Degradation in Erotic Life' (1912). This is the disorder Freud calls 'psychical impotence' – impotence which has no physical cause, and is manifested only in relation to some women. There is a conflict between affection and sex, traceable to an incestuous fixation on mother or sister. It may not take the extreme form of impotence, and indeed in most people it does not; but Freud is clear that 'very few people of culture' can achieve an ideal fusion of tenderness and sensuality, and this manifests itself in a lack of sexual desire for women who inspire affection, and is remedied 'in the presence of a lower type of sexual object'. The consequence is an inability to get on with one's well-brought-up wife. And he believes that 'whoever is to be free and happy in love must overcome his deference for women and come to terms with the idea of incest with mother or sister'. Honest men admit the sex act to be degrading; honest women are obliged by the culture to make it secret, and of course the trouble of the men rubs off on them also. The sexual difficulties of the age, Freud was sure, stemmed from the basic Oedipal situation, assisted by another unchangeable condition, the proximity of the genital and excrementatory organs in an animal which, since it learnt to walk upright, has tried culturally to sever the associations between them. It cannot be done; the genitals remain animal, and so does love, which perhaps will never 'be reconciled with the demands of culture'.

This diagnosis is certainly directed towards a situation of which Lawrence was aware, though for him 'the demands of culture' originated in and were insisted upon by woman. Paul is almost aware – as is Morel – that his relationship with his mother is not entirely a matter of sexless 'affection' – he is at times a phantom husband. And he knows, however obscurely, that one reason why Miriam will not do is that he attributes to her a denial of animal nature which he associates with superior women – with Clara he has much better sex because she is, in a measure, inferior. The story makes it plain enough that an explanation similar to Freud's is also lurking in it.

Lawrence's own reaction to the sex-culture dilemma proposed by Freud would certainly have been, 'To hell with culture'. And this meant, partly, to hell with women, its agents. Later he was explicitly to reject the Oedipal hypothesis, though he defended with increasing ferocity the position that women inhibited the full expression of a man's inmost self, defiled his angel. His reflections on the genital-excrementatory syndrome persisted through many years, and in practice his answer was to teach the woman better by enforcing it on her in its animal reality. Yet it is clear enough that Freud and Lawrence, however different their instruments and diagnoses, were in a sense talking about the same thing, an epochal sickness with deep roots in the past, and, as to its symptoms as well as its causes, a malfunction of sexual relationships within the culture. Philip Rieff calls them both 'honest heresiarchs', who tried to show us that we were sick from our ideals, and succeeded anyway in demonstrating that we were sick of them.[5] Their intellectual traditions were very different, and Lawrence's opinions, mystical and rational, have their origin in English radical thought, not in the clinics of Vienna; but their concurrence, as far as it goes, is testimony that, as Europe moved into the Great War, to speak well of the obvious ills of civilisation one had to reflect deeply on sons and what they love.

Lawrence was soon to feel a need to give systematic form to such reflections; the war developed them and made them urgent, but they are implicit in *Sons and Lovers* and in the poems of *Look! We Have Come Through!* which celebrate recovery and marriage. *Sons and Lovers* is the only major work of Lawrence which had no doctrinal double, in which there is no possible dissension between life and what he called 'metaphysic'. Henceforth all is different.

From Frank Kermode, *Lawrence* (London, 1973), pp. 16–23.

NOTES

[Sir Frank Kermode is one of Britain's most distinguished contemporary critics. During a long career, his interests have ranged widely in Renaissance and twentieth-century writing, and he has had a particular interest in the theory of narrative which emerges here in his brief but illuminating remarks on the style of *Sons and Lovers*. His book on Lawrence, from which this extract is taken, was published in 1973 in the influential 'Modern Masters' series of which Kermode was General Editor. The book gives an accessible account of Lawrence's career and stresses the 'prophetic' side of his writing. This, Kermode contends, dominated Lawrence's later career but can also be glimpsed in the more symbolic parts of *Sons and Lovers*. What is original about Kermode's treatment of this theme, however, is his emphasis on the immediate historical context of Lawrence's interest in psychological and prophetic issues, and he illuminatingly relates Lawrence's work to that of significant contemporaries such as, in this extract, Freud. Page references to *Sons and Lovers* are incorporated into the text and are to the Penguin edition edited by Keith Sagar (1981). Ed.]

1. Dorothy Van Ghent, *The English Novel: Form and Function* (New York, 1953), pp. 245–61; reprinted, with other excellent critical material on this novel, in *D. H. Lawrence, Sons and Lovers: Text, Background, and Criticism*, ed. Julian Moynahan (Harmondsworth, 1968), pp. 527–46.

2. Louis L. Martz, 'Portrait of Miriam', in *Imagined Worlds*, ed. M. Mack and I. Gregor (London, 1968). [Reprinted in this volume, p. 57. Ed.]

3. D. H. Lawrence, *Lady Chatterley's Lover*, ch. VIII.

4. Simon O. Lesser, *Fiction and the Unconscious* (London, 1957), pp. 175–8.

5. Philip Rieff, 'Two Honest Men', *The Listener*, LXIII (5 May 1960), reprinted in Moynahan (ed.), *Sons and Lovers: Text, Background, and Criticism*, pp. 518–26.

2

The Most Prevalent Form of Degradation in Erotic Life

SIGMUND FREUD

I

If a practising psychoanalyst asks himself what disorder he is most often called upon to remedy, he is obliged to reply – apart from anxiety in all its many forms – psychical impotence. This strange disorder affects men of a strongly libidinous nature, and is manifested by a refusal on the part of the sexual organs to execute the sexual act, although both before and after the attempt they can show themselves intact and competent to do so, and although a strong mental inclination to carry out the act is present. The man gets his first inkling in the direction of understanding his condition by discovering that he fails in this way only with certain women, whereas it never happens with others. He knows then that the inhibition of his masculine potency is due to some quality in the sexual object, and sometimes he describes having had a sensation of holding back, of having perceived some check within him which interfered successfully with his conscious intention. What this inner opposition is, however, he cannot guess, or what quality in the sexual object makes it active. If the failure has been repeated several times he probably concludes, by the familiar erroneous line of argument, that a recollection of the first occasion acted as a disturbance by causing anxiety and brought about the subsequent failures; the first occasion itself he refers to some 'accidental' occurrence.

Psychoanalytic studies of psychical impotence have already been carried out and published by various writers.[1] Every analyst can, from his own experience, confirm the explanations adduced in them. The disorder is in fact due to the inhibiting influence of certain complexes in the mind that are withdrawn from the knowledge of the person in question. As the most universal feature of this pathogenic material an incestuous fixation on mother and sister which has not been surmounted stands out. In addition to this, the influence of accidental impressions of a painful kind connected with infantile sexuality comes into consideration, together with those factors which in general reduce the amount of libido available for the female sexual object.[2]

When cases of severe psychical impotence are subjected to exhaustive study by means of psychoanalysis, the following psycho-sexual processes are found to be operative. Here again – as very probably in all neurotic disorders – the root of the trouble lies in an arrest occurring during the course of development of the libido to that ultimate form which may be called normal. To ensure a fully normal attitude in love, two currents of feeling have to unite – we may describe them as the tender, affectionate feelings and the sensual feelings – and this confluence of the two currents has in these cases not been achieved.

Of these two currents affection is the older. It springs from the very earliest years of childhood, and was formed on the foundation provided by the interests of the self-preservative instinct; it is directed towards the members of the family and those who have care of the child. From the very beginning elements from the sexual instincts are taken up into it – component-parts of the erotic interest – which are more or less clearly visible in childhood and are invariably discovered in the neurotic by psychoanalysis in later years. This tender feeling represents the earliest childish choice of object. From this we see that the sexual instincts find their first *objects* along the paths laid down by the ego-instincts and in accordance with the value set by the latter on their objects, in just the same way that the first sexual *satisfactions* are experienced, i.e. in connection with the bodily functions necessary for self-preservation. The 'affection' shown to the child by its parents and attendants which seldom fails to betray its erotic character ('a child is an erotic plaything') does a great deal to increase the erotic contributions to the cathexes that are put forth by the ego-instincts in the child, and to raise them to a level which is bound to leave its mark on future development, especially when certain other circumstances leading to the same result are present.

These fixations of the child's feelings of affection are maintained through childhood, continually absorbing erotic elements, which are thus deflected from their sexual aims. Then, when the age of puberty is reached, there supervenes upon this state of things a powerful current of 'sensual' feeling the aims of which can no longer be disguised. It never fails, apparently, to pursue the earlier paths and to invest the objects of the primary infantile choice with currents of libido that are now far stronger. But in relation to these objects it is confronted by the obstacle of the incest-barrier that has in the meanwhile been erected; consequently it seeks as soon as possible to pass on from these objects unsuited for real satisfaction to others in the world outside, with whom a real sexual life may be carried on. These new objects are still chosen after the pattern (imago) of the infantile ones; in time, however, they attract to themselves the tender feeling that had been anchored to those others. A man shall leave father and mother – according to the Biblical precept – and cleave to his wife; then are tenderness and sensuality united. The greatest intensity of sensual passion will bring with it the highest mental estimation of the object (the normal overestimation of the sexual object characteristic of men).

Two factors will determine whether this advance in the development of the libido is accomplished successfully or otherwise. First, there is the degree of frustration in reality which is opposed to the new object-choice and reduces its value for the person concerned. For there is no sense in entering upon a choice of object if one is not to be allowed to choose at all or has no prospect of being able to choose one fit for the part. The second factor is the degree of attraction that may be exercised by the infantile objects which should be relinquished, and this is proportionate to the erotic cathexis already attaching to them in childhood. If these two factors are sufficiently powerful, the general mechanism leading to the formation of neurosis will come into operation. The libido turns away from reality, and is absorbed into the creation of phantasy (introversion), strengthens the images of the first sexual objects, and becomes fixated to them. The incest-barrier, however, necessarily has the effect that the libido attaching to these objects should remain in the unconscious. The sensual current of feeling is now attached to unconscious ideas of objects, and discharge of it in onanistic acts contributes to a strengthening of this fixation. It constitutes no change in this state of affairs if the step forward to extraneous objects which miscarried in reality is now made in phantasy, if in the phantasied situations leading up to onanistic gratification the extraneous objects are but replacements of the original ones. The phantasies become capable of entering consciousness by this replacement, but in the direction of applying the libido externally in the real world no advance has been made.

In this way it may happen that the whole current of sensual feeling in a young man may remain attached in the unconscious to incestuous objects, or, to put it in another way, may be fixated to incestuous phantasies. The result of this is then total impotence, which is perhaps even reinforced by an actual weakening, developing concurrently, of the organs destined to execute the sexual act.

Less severe conditions will suffice to bring about what is usually called psychical impotence. It is not necessary that the whole amount of sensual feeling should be fated to conceal itself behind the tender feelings; it may remain sufficiently strong and unchecked to secure some outlet for itself in reality. The sexual activity of such people shows unmistakable signs, however, that it has not behind it the whole mental energy belonging to the instinct. It is capricious, easily upset, often clumsily carried out, and not very pleasurable. Above all, however, it avoids all association with feelings of tenderness. A restriction has thus been laid upon the object-choice. The sensual feeling that has remained active seeks only objects evoking no reminder of the incestuous persons forbidden to it; the impression made by someone who seems deserving of high estimation leads, not to a sensual excitation, but to feelings of tenderness which remain erotically ineffectual. The erotic life of such people remains dissociated, divided between two channels, the same two that are personified in art as heavenly and earthly (or animal) love. Where such men love they have no desire and where they desire they cannot love. In order to keep their sensuality out of contact with the objects they love, they seek out objects whom they need not love; and, in accordance with the laws of the 'sensitivity of complexes' and the 'return of the repressed', the strange refusal implied in psychical impotence is made whenever the objects selected in order to avoid incest possess some trait, often quite inconspicuous, reminiscent of the objects that must be avoided.

The principal means of protection used by men against this complaint consists in *lowering* the sexual object in their own estimation, while reserving for the incestuous object and for those who represent it the overestimation normally felt for the sexual object. As soon as the sexual object fulfils the condition of being degraded, sensual feeling can have free play, considerable sexual capacity and a high degree of pleasure can be developed. Another factor also contributes to this result. There is usually little refinement in the ways of obtaining erotic pleasure habitual to people in whom the tender and the sensual currents of feeling are not properly merged; they have remained addicted to perverse sexual aims which they feel it a considerable deprivation not to gratify, yet to such men this seems possible only with a sexual object who in their estimate is degraded and worth little.

The motives behind the phantasies mentioned in the preceding paper,[3] by which boys degrade the mother to the level of a prostitute, now become intelligible. They represent efforts to bridge the gulf between the two currents of erotic feelings, at least in phantasy: by degrading her, to win the mother as an object for sensual desires.

II

So far we have pursued our inquiry into psychical impotence from a medico-psychological angle which is not justified by the title of this paper. It will prove however, that this introduction was necessary in order to provide an approach to our actual theme.

We have reduced psychical impotence to a disunion between the tender and sensual currents of erotic feeling, and have explained this inhibition in development itself as an effect of strong fixations in childhood and of frustration in reality later, after the incest-barrier has intervened. There is one principal objection to raise against this doctrine: it does too much, it explains why certain persons suffer from psychical impotence, but it makes it seem puzzling that others can escape the affliction. Since all the factors that appear to be involved, the strong fixation in childhood, the incest-barrier, and the frustration in the years of development after puberty, are demonstrably present in practically all civilised persons, one would be justified in expecting that psychical impotence was universally prevalent in civilised countries and not a disease of particular individuals.

It would not be difficult to escape from this conclusion by pointing to the quantitative element in the causation of disease, that greater or lesser amount of each single factor which determines whether or not recognisable disease results. But although this argument is in my opinion sound, I do not myself intend to employ it in refuting the objection advanced above. I shall, on the contrary, put forward the proposition that psychical impotence is far more widespread than is generally supposed, and that some degree of this condition does in fact characterise the erotic life of civilised peoples.

If one enlarges the meaning of the term psychical impotence, and ceases to limit it to failure to perform the act of coitus, although an intention to derive pleasure from it is present and the genital apparatus is intact, it would comprise, to begin with, all those men who are described as psycho-anaesthetic, i.e. who never fail in the act but who perform it without special pleasure – a state of things which is commoner than one might think. Psychoanalytic study of such cases has discovered the same aetiological factors in them as those found in psychical impotence, when employed in the narrower sense, without at first discovering any explanation of the symptomatic difference between the two. By an analogy which is easy to justify, one is led on from these anaesthetic men to consider the enormous number of frigid women, whose attitude to love can in fact not be described or understood better than by equating it with psychical impotence in men, although the latter is more conspicuous.[4]

If, however, instead of attributing a wide significance to the term psychical impotence, we look about for instances of its peculiar symptomatology in less marked forms, we shall not be able to deny that the behaviour in love of the men of present-day civilisation bears in general the character of the psychically impotent type. In only very few people of culture are the two strains of tenderness and sensuality duly fused into one; the man almost always feels his sexual activity hampered by his respect for the woman and only develops full sexual potency when he finds himself in the presence of a lower type of sexual object; and this again is partly conditioned by the circumstance that his sexual aims include those of perverse sexual components, which he does not like to gratify with a woman he respects. Full sexual satisfaction only comes when he can give himself up wholeheartedly to enjoyment, which with his well-brought-up wife, for instance, he does not venture to do. Hence comes his need for a less exalted sexual object, a woman ethically inferior, to whom he need ascribe no aesthetic misgivings, and who does not know the rest of his life and cannot criticise him. It is to such a woman that he prefers to devote his sexual potency, even when all the tenderness in him belongs to one of a higher type. It is possible, too, that the tendency so often observed in men of the highest rank in society to take a woman of a low class as a permanent mistress, or even as a wife, is nothing but a consequence of the need for a lower type of sexual object on which, psychologically, the possibility of complete gratification depends.

I do not hesitate to lay the responsibility also for this very common condition in the erotic life of civilised men on the two factors operative in absolute psychical impotence, namely, the very strong incestuous fixation of childhood and the frustration by reality suffered during adolescence. It has an ugly sound and a paradoxical as well, but nevertheless it must be said that whoever is to be really free and happy in love must have overcome his deference for women and come to terms with the idea of incest with mother or sister. Anyone who in the face of this test subjects himself to serious self-examination will indubitably find that at the bottom of his heart he too regards the sexual act as something degrading, which soils and contaminates not only the body. And he will only be able to look for the origin of this attitude, which he will certainly not willingly acknowledge, in that period of his youth in which his sexual passions were already strongly developed but in which gratification of them with an object outside the family was almost as completely prohibited as with an incestuous one.

The women of our civilised world are similarly affected by their up-bringing and further, too, by the reaction upon them of this attitude in men. Naturally the effect upon a woman is just as unfavourable if the man comes to her without his full potency as if, after overestimating her in the early stages of falling in love, he then, having successfully possessed himself of her, sets her at naught. Women show little need to degrade the sexual object; no doubt this has some connection with the circumstance that as a rule they develop little of the sexual overestimation natural to men. The long abstinence from sexuality to which they are forced and the lingering of their sensuality in phantasy have in them, however, another important consequence. It is often not possible for them later on to undo the connection thus formed in their minds between sensual activities and something forbidden, and they turn out to be psychically impotent, i.e. frigid, when at last such activities do become permissible. This is the source of the desire in so many women to keep even legitimate relations secret for a time; and of the appearance of the capacity for normal sensation in others as soon as the condition of prohibition is restored by a secret intrigue – untrue to the husband, they can keep a second order of faith with the lover.

In my opinion the necessary condition of forbiddenness in the erotic life of women holds the same place as the man's need to lower his sexual object. Both are the consequence of the long period of delay between sexual maturity and sexual activity which is demanded by education for social reasons. The aim of both is to overcome the psychical impotence resulting from the lack of union between tenderness and sensuality. That the effect of the same causes differs so greatly in men and in women is perhaps due to another difference in the behaviour of the two sexes. Women belonging to the higher levels of civilisation do not usually transgress the prohibition against sexual activities during the period of waiting, and thus they acquire this close association between the forbidden and the sexual. Men usually overstep the prohibition under the condition of lowering the standard of object they require, and so carry this condition on into their subsequent erotic life.

In view of the strenuous efforts being made in the civilised world at the present day to reform sexual life, it is not superfluous to remind the reader that psychoanalytic investigations have no more bias in any direction than has any other scientific research. In tracing back to its concealed sources what is manifest, psychoanalysis has no aim but that of disclosing connections. It can but be satisfied if what it has brought to light is of use in effecting reforms by substituting more advantageous for injurious conditions. It cannot, however, predict whether other, perhaps even greater, sacrifices may not result from other institutions.

III

The fact that the restrictions imposed by cultural education upon erotic life involve a general lowering of the sexual object may prompt us to turn our eyes from the object to the instincts themselves. The injurious results of the deprivation of sexual enjoyment at the beginning manifest themselves in lack of full satisfaction when sexual desire is later given free rein in marriage. But, on the other hand, unrestrained sexual liberty from the beginning leads to no better result. It is easy to show that the value the mind sets on erotic needs instantly sinks as soon as satisfaction becomes readily obtainable. Some obstacle is necessary to swell the tide of the libido to its height; and at all periods of history, wherever natural barriers in the way of satisfaction have not sufficed, mankind has erected conventional ones in order to be able to enjoy love. This is true both of individuals and of nations. In times during which no obstacles to sexual satisfaction existed, such as, may be, during the decline of the civilisations of antiquity, love became worthless, life became empty, and strong reaction-formations were necessary before the indispensable emotional value of love could be recovered. In this context it may be stated that the ascetic tendency of Christianity had the effect of raising the psychical value of love in a way that heathen antiquity could never achieve; it developed greatest significance in the lives of the ascetic monks, which were almost entirely occupied with struggles against libidinous temptation.

One's first inclination undoubtedly is to see in this difficulty a universal characteristic of our organic instincts. It is certainly true in a general way that the importance of an instinctual desire is mentally increased by frustration of it. Suppose one made the experiment of exposing a number of utterly different human beings to hunger under the same conditions. As the imperative need for food rose in them all their individual differences would be effaced and instead the uniform manifestations of one unsatisfied instinct would appear. But is it also true, conversely, that the mental value of an instinct invariably sinks with gratification of it? One thinks, for instance, of the relation of the wine-drinker to wine. Is it not a fact that wine always affords the drinker the same toxic satisfaction – one that in poetry has so often been likened to the erotic and that science as well may regard as comparable? Has one ever heard of a drinker being forced constantly to change his wine because he soon gets tired of always drinking the same? On the contrary, habit binds a man more and more to the particular kind of wine he drinks. Do we ever find a drinker impelled to go to another country where the wine is dearer or where alcohol is prohibited, in order to stimulate his dwindling pleasure in it by these obstacles? Nothing of the sort. If we listen to what our great lovers of alcohol say about their attitude to wine, for instance, B. Böcklin,[5] it sounds like the most perfect harmony, a model of a happy marriage. Why is the relation of the lover to his sexual object so very different?

However strange it may sound, I think the possibility must be considered that something in the nature of the sexual instinct itself is unfavourable to the achievement of absolute gratification. When we think of the long and difficult evolution the instinct goes through, two factors to which this difficulty might be ascribed at once emerge. First, in consequence of the two 'thrusts' of sexual development impelling towards choice of an object, together with the intervention of the incest-barrier between the two, the ultimate object selected is never the original one but only a surrogate for it. Psychoanalysis has shown us, however, that when the original object of an instinctual desire becomes lost in consequence of repression, it is often replaced by an endless series of substitute-objects, none of which ever give full satisfaction. This may explain the lack of stability in object-choice, the 'craving for stimulus', which is so often a feature of the love of adults.

Secondly, we know that at its beginning the sexual instinct is divided into a large number of components – or, rather, it develops from them – not all of which can be carried on into its final form; some have to be suppressed or turned to other uses before the final form results. Above all, the coprophilic elements in the instinct have proved incompatible with our aesthetic ideas, probably since the time when man developed an upright posture and so removed his organ of smell from the ground; further, a considerable proportion of the sadistic elements belonging to the erotic instinct have to be abandoned. All such developmental processes, however, relate only to the upper layers of the complicated structure. The fundamental processes which promote erotic excitation remain always the same. Excremental things are all too intimately and inseparably bound up with sexual things; the position of the genital organs – *inter urinas et faeces* – remains the decisive and unchangeable factor. One might say, modifying a well-known saying of the great Napoleon's, 'Anatomy is destiny'. The genitals themselves have not undergone the development of the rest of the human form in the direction of beauty; they have retained their animal cast; and so even today love, too, is in essence as animal as it ever was. The erotic instincts are hard to mould; training of them achieves now too much, now too little. What culture tries to make out of them seems attainable only at the cost of a sensible loss of pleasure; the persistence of the impulses that are not enrolled in adult sexual activity makes itself felt in an absence of satisfaction.

So perhaps we must make up our minds to the idea that altogether it is not possible for the claims of the sexual instinct to be reconciled with the demands of culture, that in consequence of his cultural development renunciation and suffering, as well as the danger of his extinction at some far future time, are not to be eluded by the race of man. This gloomy prognosis rests, it is true, on the single conjecture that the lack of satisfaction accompanying culture is the necessary consequence of certain peculiarities developed by the sexual instinct under the pressure of culture. This very incapacity in the sexual instinct to yield full satisfaction as soon as it submits to the first demands of culture becomes the source, however, of the grandest cultural achievements, which are brought to birth by ever greater sublimation of the components of the sexual instinct. For what motive would induce man to put his sexual energy to other uses if by any disposal of it he could obtain fully satisfying pleasure? He would never let go of this pleasure and would make no further progress. It seems, therefore, that the irreconcilable antagonism between the demands of the two instincts – the sexual and the egoistic – have made man capable of ever greater achievements, though, it is true, under the continual menace of danger, such as that of the neuroses to which at the present time the weaker are succumbing.

The purpose of science is neither to alarm nor to reassure. But I myself freely admit that such far-reaching conclusions as those drawn here should be built up on a broader foundation, and that perhaps developments in other directions will enable mankind to remedy the effects of these, which we have here been considering in isolation.

From Sigmund Freud, *Sexuality and the Psychology of Love*, ed. Philip Rieff (New York, 1963), pp. 58–70. First published 1912; translated by Joan Riviere.

NOTES

[Sigmund Freud was, of course, one of the intellectual giants of the twentieth century whose work has shaped ideas in most areas of the humanities and social and psychological sciences. Though not a piece of literary criticism, 'The Most Prevalent Form of Degradation in Erotic Life' is reprinted because there are such clear connections between it and *Sons and Lovers*. The two were published within a year of each other and commentators immediately made connections between psychoanalytic theory and Lawrence's novel. Reprinting Freud's essay means that readers are able to get first-hand experience of a stimulating text which is often reduced in commentary and test for themselves the advantages and limitations of Freud's account of male and female psychological development along the lines indicated in the general Introduction. It also means that there is material to develop Frank Kermode's point that, read together, *Sons and Lovers* and Freud's essay give the reader a historical sense of the debate about sexual and psychological issues at the turn of the century.

'The Most Prevalent Form of Degradation' (sometimes translated as 'On the Universal Tendency to Debasement in the Sphere of Love') is one of three essays Freud published between 1910 and 1918 under the overall title 'Contributions to the Psychology of Love'. The others are 'A Special Type of Object Choice Made By Men' (1910) and 'The Taboo of Virginity' (1918). They are examples of Freud's fast-developing work on the sexual dynamics of the family in the light of his unearthing of the 'Oedipus Complex', a term he introduced in 1910 though the basic theory had been around somewhat longer. The argument of Freud's essay is summarised in the Introduction, but readers might pay particular attention to how it is structured, especially the way Freud seems at first to accept conventional ideas about love and sexuality before undermining these as the essay progresses. Though Freud's and Lawrence's views differed in important ways, one thing they have in common is that they both challenge prevailing conceptions of so-called 'normal' behaviour. Ed.]

1. M. Steiner, *Die funkionelle Impotenz des Mannes und ihre Behandlung;* W. Stekel, in *Nervöse Angstzustande und ihre Behandlung;* Ferenczi, 'Analytic Interpretation and Treatment of Psychosexual Impotence'.

2. W. Stekel, *Nervöse Angstzustande,* p. 191 *et seq.*

3. [In an earlier paper in his series 'Contributions to the Psychology of Love' Freud argued that, in the confused period before full sexual knowledge, the growing boy first establishes the distinction between the pure mother and the sexually available, degraded prostitute, and then seeks 'cynically' to blur the distinction as his feelings towards his mother are more and more eroticised. Thus is established the well-known polarity of madonna and whore which, Freud believed, begins in infantile sexual fantasy. See 'A Special Type of Object Choice Made by Men' (1910). Ed.]

4. At the same time I willingly admit that the frigidity of women is a complicated subject which can be approached from another angle.

5. G. Floerke, *Zehn Jahr mit Böcklin,* 2 Aufl. 1902, p. 16.

3

Psychoanalysis and Society in *Sons and Lovers*

TERRY EAGLETON

In order to pursue further the implications of Lacan's thought for the human subject, we shall have to take a brief detour though a famous essay written under Lacan's influence by the French Marxist philosopher Louis Althusser. In 'Ideology and Ideological State Apparatuses', contained in his book *Lenin and Philosophy* (1971), Althusser tries to illuminate, with the implicit aid of Lacanian psychoanalytic theory, the working of ideology in society. How is it, the essay asks, that human subjects very often come to submit themselves to the dominant ideologies of their societies – ideologies which Althusser sees as vital to maintaining the power of a ruling class? By what mechanisms does this come about? Althusser has sometimes been seen as a 'structuralist' Marxist, in that for him human individuals are the product of many different social determinants, and thus have no essential unity. As far as a science of human societies goes, such individuals can be studied simply as the functions, or effects, of this or that social structure – as occupying a place in a mode of production, as a member of a specific social class, and so on. But this of course is not at all the way we actually experience ourselves. We tend to see ourselves rather as free, unified autonomous, self-generating individuals; and unless we did so we would be incapable of playing our parts in social life. For Althusser, what allows us to experience ourselves in this way is ideology. How is this to be understood?

As far as society is concerned, I as an individual am utterly dispensable. No doubt someone has to fulfil the functions I carry out (writing, teaching, lecturing and so on), since education has a crucial role to play in the reproduction of this kind of social system, but there is no particular reason why this individual should be myself. One reason why this thought does not lead me to join a circus or take an overdose is that this is not usually the way that I experience my own identity, nor the way I actually 'live out' my life. I do not *feel* myself to be a mere function of a social structure which could get along without me, true though this appears when I *analyse* the situation, but as somebody with a significant *relation* to society and the world at large, a relation which gives me enough sense of meaning and value to enable me to act purposefully. It is as though society were not just an impersonal structure to me, but a 'subject' which 'addresses' me personally – which recognises me, tells me that I am valued, and so makes me by that very act of recognition into a free, autonomous subject. I come to feel, not exactly as though the world exists for me alone, but as though it is significantly 'centred' on me, and I in turn am significantly 'centred' on it. Ideology, for Althusser, is the set of beliefs and practices which does this centring. It is far more subtle, pervasive and unconscious than a set of explicit doctrines: it is the very medium in which I 'live out' my relation to society, the realm of signs and social practices which binds me to the social structure and lends me a sense of coherent purpose and identity. Ideology in this sense may include the act of going to church, of casting a vote, of letting women pass first through doors; it may encompass not only such conscious predilections as my deep devotion to the monarchy but the way I dress and the kind of car I drive, my deeply unconscious images of others and of myself.

What Althusser does, in other words, is to rethink the concept of ideology in terms of Lacan's 'imaginary'. For the relation of an individual subject to society as a whole in Althusser's theory is rather like the relation of the small child to his or her mirror-image in Lacan's. In both cases, the human subject is supplied with a satisfyingly unified image of selfhood by identifying with an object which reflects this image back to it in a closed, narcissistic circle. In both cases, too, this image involves a *mis*recognition, since it idealises the subject's real situation. The child is not actually as integrated as its image in the mirror suggests; I am not actually the coherent, autonomous, self-generating subject I know myself to be in the ideological sphere, but the 'decentred' function of several social determinants. Duly enthralled by the image of myself I receive, I subject myself to it; and it is through this 'subjection' that I become a subject.

Most commentators would now agree that Althusser's suggestive essay is seriously flawed. It seems to assume, for example, that ideology is little more than an oppressive force which subjugates us, without allowing sufficient space for the realities of ideological *struggle*; and it involves some rather serious misinterpretations of Lacan. Nevertheless, it is one attempt to show the relevance of Lacanian theory to issues beyond the consulting room; it sees, rightly, that such a body of work has deep-seated implications for several fields beyond psychoanalysis itself. Indeed, by reinterpreting Freudianism in terms of language, a pre-eminently social activity, Lacan permits us to explore the relations between the unconscious and human society. One way of describing his work is to say that he makes us recognise that the unconscious is not some kind of seething, tumultuous, private region 'inside' us, but an effect of our relations with one another. The unconscious is, so to speak, 'outside' rather than 'within' us – or rather it exists 'between' us, as our relationships do. It is elusive not so much because it is buried deep within our minds, but because it is a kind of vast, tangled network which surrounds us and weaves itself through us, and which can therefore never be pinned down. The best image for such a network, which is both beyond us and yet is the very stuff of which we are made, is language itself; and indeed for Lacan the unconscious is a particular effect of language, a process of desire set in motion by difference. When we enter the symbolic order, we enter into language itself; yet this language, for Lacan as for the structuralists, is never something entirely within our individual control. On the contrary, as we have seen, language is what internally *divides* us, rather than an instrument we are confidently able to manipulate. Language always pre-exists us: it is always already 'in place', waiting to assign us our places within it. It is ready and waiting for us rather as our parents are; and we shall never wholly dominate it or subdue it to our own ends, just as we shall never be able entirely to shake off the dominant role which our parents play in our constitution. Language, the unconscious, the parents, the symbolic order: these terms in Lacan are not exactly synonymous, but they are intimately allied. They are sometimes spoken of by him as the 'Other' – as that which like language is always anterior to us and will always escape us, that which brought us into being as subjects in the first place but which always outruns our grasp. We have seen that for Lacan our unconscious desire is directed towards this Other, in the shape of some ultimately gratifying reality which we can never have; but it is also true for Lacan that our desire is in some way always *received* from the Other too. We desire what others – our parents, for instance – unconsciously desire for us; and desire can only happen because we are caught up in linguistic, sexual and social relations – the whole field of the 'Other' – which generate it.

Lacan himself is not much interested in the social relevance of his theories, and he certainly does not 'solve' the problem of the relation between society and the unconscious. Freudianism as a whole, however, does enable us to pose this question; and I want now to examine it in terms of a concrete literary example, D. H. Lawrence's novel *Sons and Lovers*. Even conservative critics, who suspect such phrases as the 'Oedipus complex' as alien jargon, sometimes admit that there is something at work in this text which looks remarkably like Freud's famous drama. (It is interesting, incidentally, how conventionally-minded critics seem quite content to employ such jargon as 'symbol', 'dramatic irony' and 'densely textured', while remaining oddly resistant to terms such as 'signifier' and 'decentring'.) At the time of writing *Sons and Lovers*, Lawrence, as far as we know, knew something of Freud's work at second hand from his German wife Frieda; but there seems no evidence that he had any direct or detailed acquaintance with it, a fact which might be taken as striking independent confirmation of Freud's doctrine. For it is surely the case that *Sons and Lovers*, without appearing to be at all aware of it, is a profoundly Oedipal novel: the young Paul Morel who sleeps in the same bed as his mother, treats her with the tenderness of a lover and feels strong animosity towards his father, grows up to be the man Morel, unable to sustain a fulfilling relationship with a woman, and in the end achieving possible release from this condition by killing his mother in an ambiguous act of love, revenge and self-liberation. Mrs Morel, for her part, is jealous of Paul's relationship with Miriam, behaving like a rival mistress. Paul rejects Miriam for his mother; but in rejecting Miriam he is also unconsciously rejecting his mother *in* her, in what he feels to be Miriam's stifling spiritual possessiveness.

Paul's psychological development, however, does not take place in a social void. His father, Walter Morel, is a miner, while his mother is of a slightly higher social class. Mrs Morel is concerned that Paul should not follow his father into the pit, and wants him to take a clerical job instead. She herself remains at home as a house-wife: the family set-up of the Morels is part of what is known as the 'sexual division of labour', which in capitalist society takes the form of the male parent being used as labour-power in the productive process while the female parent is left to provide the material and emotional 'maintenance' of him and the labour force of the future (the children). Mr Morel's estrangement from the intense emotional life of the home is due in part to this social division – one which alienates him from his own children, and brings them emotionally closer to the mother. If, as with Walter Morel, the father's work is especially exhausting and oppressive, his role in the family is likely to be further diminished: Morel is reduced to establishing human contact with his children through his practical skills about the house. His lack of education, moreover, makes it difficult for him to articulate his feelings, a fact which further increases the distance between himself and his family. The fatiguing, harshly disciplined nature of the work process helps to create in him a domestic irri-tability and violence which drives the children deeper into their mother's arms, and which spurs on her jealous possessiveness of them. To compensate for his inferior status at work, the father struggles to assert a traditional male authority at home, thus es-tranging his children from him still further.

In the case of the Morels, these social factors are further compli-cated by the class-distinction between them. Morel has what the novel takes to be a characteristically proletarian inarticulateness, physicality and passivity: *Sons and Lovers* portrays the miners as creatures of the underworld who live the life of the body rather than the mind. This is a curious portraiture, since in 1912, the year in which Lawrence finished the book, the miners launched the biggest strike which Britain had ever seen. One year later, the year of the novel's publication, the worst mining disaster for a century resulted in a paltry fine for a seriously negligent management, and class-warfare was everywhere in the air throughout the British coalfields. These developments, with all their acute political awareness and complex organisation, were not the actions of mindless hulks. Mrs Morel (it is perhaps significant that we do not feel inclined to use her first name) is of lower-middle-class origin, reasonably well-educated, articulate and determined. She therefore symbolises what the young, sensitive and artistic Paul may hope to achieve: his emotional turning to her from the father is, inseparably, a turning from the impoverished, exploitative world of the colliery towards the life of emancipated consciousness. The potentially tragic tension in which Paul then finds himself trapped, and almost destroyed, springs from the fact that his mother – the very source of the energy which pushes him ambitiously beyond home and pit – is at the same time the powerful emotional force which draws him back.

A psychoanalytical reading of the novel, then, need not be an alternative to a social interpretation of it. We are speaking rather of two sides or aspects of a single human situation. We can discuss Paul's 'weak' image of his father and 'strong' image of his mother in both Oedipal and class terms; we can see how the human relationship between an absent, violent father, an ambitious, emotionally demanding mother and a sensitive child are understandable both in terms of unconscious processes and in terms of certain social forces and relations. (Some critics, of course, would find neither kind of approach acceptable, and opt for a 'human' reading of the novel instead. It is not easy to know what this 'human' is, which excludes the characters' concrete life-situations, their jobs and histories, the deeper significance of their personal relationships and identities, their sexuality and so on.) All of this, however, is still confined to what may be called 'content analysis', looking at what is said rather than how it is said, at 'theme' rather than 'forms'. But we can carry these considerations into 'form' itself – into such matters as how the novel delivers and structures its narrative, how it delineates character, what narrative point of view it adopts. It seems evident, for example, that the text itself largely, though by no means entirely, identifies with and endorses Paul's own viewpoint: since the narrative is seen chiefly through his eyes, we have no real source of testimony other than him. As Paul moves into the foreground of the story, his father recedes into the background. The novel is also in general more 'inward' in its treatment of Mrs Morel than it is of her husband; indeed we might argue that it is organised in a way which tends to highlight her and obscure him, a formal device which reinforces the protagonist's own attitudes. The very way in which the narrative is structured, in other words, to some extent conspires with Paul's own unconscious: it is not clear to us, for example, that Miriam as she is presented in the text, very much from Paul's own viewpoint, actually merits the irritable impatience which she evokes in him, and many readers have had the uneasy sense that the novel is in some way 'unjust' to her. (The real-life Miriam, Jessie Chambers, hotly shared this opinion, but this for our present purposes is neither here nor there.) But how are we to validate this sense of injustice, when Paul's own viewpoint is consistently 'foregrounded' as our source of supposedly reliable evidence?

On the other hand, there are aspects of the novel which would seem to run counter to this 'angled' presentation. As H. M. Daleski has perceptively put it: 'The weight of hostile comment which Lawrence directs against Morel is balanced by the unconscious sympathy with which he is presented dramatically, while the overt celebration of Mrs Morel is challenged by the harshness of her character in action.'[1] In the terms we have used about Lacan, the novel does not exactly say what it means or mean what it says. This itself can partly be accounted for in psychoanalytical terms: the boy's Oedipal relation to his father is an ambiguous one, for the father is loved as well as unconsciously hated as a rival, and the child will seek to protect the father from his own unconscious aggression towards him. Another reason for this ambiguity, however, is that on one level the novel sees very well that though Paul must reject the narrowed, violent world of the miners for his venture into middle-class consciousness, such consciousness is by no means wholly to be admired. There is much that is dominative and life-denying as well as valuable in it, as we can see in the character of Mrs Morel. It is Walter Morel, so the text tells us, who has 'denied the god in him': but it is hard to feel that this heavy authorial interpolation, solemn and obtrusive as it is, really earns its keep. For the very novel which *tells* us this also *shows* us the opposite. It shows us the ways in which Morel is indeed still alive; it cannot stop us from seeing how the diminishing of him has much to do with its own narrative organisation, turning as it does from him to his son; and it also shows us, intentionally or not, that even if Morel *has* 'denied the god in him' then the blame is ultimately to be laid not on him but on the predatory capitalism which can find no better use for him than as a cog in the wheel of production. Paul himself, intent as he is on extricating himself from the father's world, cannot afford to confront these truths, and neither, explicitly, does the novel: in writing *Sons and Lovers* Lawrence was not just writing about the working class but writing his way out of it. But in such telling incidents as the final reunion of Baxter Dawes (in some ways a parallel figure to Morel) with his estranged wife Clara, the novel 'unconsciously' makes reparation for its upgrading of Paul (whom this incident shows in a much more negative light) at the expense of his father. Lawrence's final reparation for Morel will be Mellors, the 'feminine' yet powerful male protagonist of *Lady Chatterley's Lover*. Paul is never allowed by the novel to voice the kind of full, bitter criticism of his mother's possessiveness which some of the 'objective' evidence would seem to warrant; yet the way in which the relationship between mother and son is actually dramatised allows us to see why this should be so.

In reading *Sons and Lovers* with an eye to these aspects of the novel, we are constructing what may be called a 'sub-text' for the work – a text which runs within it, visible at certain 'symptomatic' points of ambiguity, evasion or overemphasis, and which we as readers are able to 'write' even if the novel itself does not. All literary works contain one or more such sub-texts, and there is a sense in which they may be spoken of as the 'unconscious' of the work itself. The work's insights, as with all writing, are deeply related to its blindnesses; what it does not say, and *how* it does not say it, may be as important as what it articulates; what seems absent, marginal or ambivalent about it may provide a central clue to its meanings. We are not simply rejecting or inverting 'what the novel says', arguing, for example, that Morel is the real hero and his wife the villain. Paul's viewpoint is not simply invalid: his mother is indeed an incomparably richer source of sympathy than his father. We are looking rather at what such statements must inevitably silence or suppress, examining the ways in which the novel is not quite identical with itself. Psychoanalytical criticism, in other words, can do more than hunt for phallic symbols: it can tell us something about how literary texts are actually formed, and reveal something of the meaning of that formation.

From Terry Eagleton, *Literary Theory: An Introduction* (Oxford, 1983), pp. 173–9.

NOTES

[Terry Eagleton is one of the most gifted of contemporary British literary critics. Working from the Marxist tradition, and with clear political commitments which direct his work, he commands an impressive range of intellectual reference as well as a gift for the vivid explanation of demanding and complex ideas. This extract is taken from his sophisticated and lively account of the main developments in twentieth-century criticism in which the chapter on psychoanalysis explores a range of ideas from Freud to the present day. His reading of *Sons and Lovers* makes use of theory pioneered by French thinkers associated with structuralism and poststructuralism in the 1960s and 1970s. Eagleton's lucid account of this material needs no additional comment, but readers might look to the way he connects psychoanalytic theories of individual development to social questions of an ideological kind. How, he asks, does Paul Morel's identity develop in his specific social and family circumstances, and how does this effect a story which is told primarily from his perspective? This attention to the narrative method in *Sons and Lovers* is particularly welcome as psychoanalytic criticism has often avoided questions touching on aspects of literary form. Eagleton's description of the literary text as being in some respects like a person's unconscious is part of a recently influential way of thinking about literary language and the way it is structured. Related ideas are explored by Diane Bonds (essay 6) and Tony Pinkney (essay 11). They are discussed in the Introduction and the headnote to essay 11. Ed.]

1. H. M. Daleski, *The Forked Flame: A Study of D. H. Lawrence* (London, 1968), p. 43.

4

A Portrait of Miriam:
A Study in the Design of
Sons and Lovers

LOUIS L. MARTZ

I

The girl was romantic in her soul.

And she was cut off from ordinary life by her religious intensity which made the world for her either a nunnery garden or a paradise, where sin and knowledge were not, or else an ugly, cruel thing.

And in sacrifice she was proud, in renunciation she was strong, for she did not trust herself to support everyday life.

'You don't want to love – your eternal and abnormal craving is to be loved. You aren't positive, you're negative. You absorb, absorb, as if you must fill yourself up with love, because you've got a shortage somewhere.' (pp. 191, 198, 271, 274)

With very few exceptions, the commentators on Lawrence's *Sons and Lovers* have tended to accept the view of Miriam's character as thus described by the narrator and by Paul Morel. Mark Spilka, for example, in his stimulating book, bases his interpretation of the novel on the assumption that Miriam has 'an unhealthy spirituality', is truly 'negative', that she really 'wheedles the soul out of things', as Paul Morel says, and that 'because of the stifling nature of Miriam's love, Paul refuses to marry her' – justifiably, since 'Miriam's frigidity is rooted in her own nature'.[1] But I believe that the portrait of Miriam is far more complex than either Paul or the narrator will allow, and that a study of her part in the book will cast some light upon the puzzling and peculiar technique of narration that Lawrence adopts when he comes to the central section of his novel, the five tormented chapters (7–11) running from 'Lad-and-Girl Love' through 'The Test on Miriam'.

As everyone has noticed, Part I of the novel (the first third of the book, concluding with the death of William) is written in the manner of Victorian realism: the omniscient narrator, working with firm control, sets forth the facts objectively. The countryside, the mining village, the family conflicts, the daily life of the household – all is given in clear, precise, convincing detail. The use of local dialect, the echoes of biblical style, the short, concise sentences combine to create in us a confidence in the narrator's command of his materials. His fairness to everyone is evident. If the father is predominantly shown as brutal and drunken, in those savage quarrels with the mother, he is also shown in his younger glory as a man who might have flourished with a different wife: 'Gertrude Coppard watched the young miner as he danced, a certain subtle exultation like glamour in his movement, and his face the flower of his body, ruddy, with tumbled black hair, and laughing alike whatever partner he bowed above' (p. 44). Even when the wife has turned away from him she can enjoy his music:

> Quite early, before six o'clock, she heard him whistling away to himself downstairs. He had a pleasant way of whistling, lively and musical. He nearly always whistled hymns. He had been a choir-boy with a beautiful voice, and had taken solos in Southwell cathedral. His morning whistling alone betrayed it.
>
> His wife lay listening to him tinkering away in the garden, his whistling ringing out as he sawed and hammered away. It always gave her a sense of warmth and peace to hear him thus as she lay in bed, the children not yet awake, in the bright early morning, happy in his man's fashion.   (pp. 53–4)

We watch Morel's relish in getting his breakfast and his joy in walking across the fields to his work in the early morning; we learn of those happy times when Morel is cobbling the family's boots, or mending kettles, or making fuses; we recognise his faithful labour at his gruelling job; and particulary we notice the love for him felt by the youngest child Arthur: 'Mrs Morel was glad this child loved the father' (p. 86). All these things give a sense of balance and proportion to Part I, making it clear that Paul's view is partial, unfair to the father, ignoring his basic humanity.

Paul's blindness towards his father's very existence as a human being is cruelly shown in the scene where Morel emerges from the pit to hear of William's death:

> 'And William is dead, and my mother's in London, and what will she be doing?' the boy asked himself, as if it were a conundrum.
>
> He watched chair after chair come up, and still no father. At last, standing beside a waggon, a man's form! The chair sank on its rests, Morel stepped off. He was slightly lame from an accident.
>
> 'Is it thee, Paul? Is 'e worse?'
>
> 'You've got to go to London.'
>
> The two walked off the pit-bank, where men were watching curiously. As they came out and went along the railway, with the sunny autumn field on one side and a wall of trucks on the other, Morel said in a frightened voice:
>
> "E's niver gone, child?'
>
> 'Yes.'
>
> 'When wor't?'
>
> The miner's voice was terrified.[2]
>
> 'Last night. We had a telegram from my mother.'
>
> Morel walked on a few strides, then leaned up against a truck side, his hand over his eyes. He was not crying. Paul stood looking round, waiting. On the weighing-machine a truck trundled slowly. Paul saw everything, except his father leaning against the truck as if he were tired.   (p. 182)

'Paul saw everything, except his father.' Only the omniscient narrator reveals the man Morel, battered from his work, frightened for his son's life, sunk in dumb agony at the news, while his intimate dialect plays off pitifully against the formal language of Paul, to stress the total division between the two.

Part I, then, is a triumph of narration in the old Victorian style. It is a long prologue, in which the issues are clearly defined, and in which, above all, the mother's overpowering influence is shown in the death of one son, while she turns toward Paul as her only remaining hope: '"I should have watched the living, not the dead", she told herself' (p. 186).

Meanwhile, as William is engaged in his fatal courtship, the figure of Miriam has been quietly introduced, in the natural, harmonious setting of the farm: 'Mother and son went into the small railed garden, where was a scent of red gillivers. By the open door were some floury loaves, put out to cool. A hen was just coming to peck them. Then, in the doorway suddenly appeared a girl in a dirty apron. She was about fourteen years old, had a rosy dark face, a bunch of short black curls, very fine and free, and dark eyes; shy, questioning, a little resentful of the strangers, she disappeared' (p. 169). Shortly after this follows the vivid incident in which the brothers jeer at Miriam for being afraid to let the hen peck the corn out of her hand:

> 'Now, Miriam', said Maurice, 'you come an' 'ave a go.'
> 'No', she cried, shrinking back.
> 'Ha! baby. The mardy-kid!' said her brothers.
> 'It doesn't hurt a bit', said Paul. 'It only just nips rather nicely.'
> 'No', she still cried, shaking her black curls and shrinking.
> 'She dursn't', said Geoffrey. 'She niver durst do anything except recite poitry.'
> 'Dursn't jump off a gate, dursn't tweedle, dursn't go on a slide, dursn't stop a girl hittin' her. She can do nowt but go about thinkin' herself somebody. "The Lady of the Lake." Yah!' cried Maurice.
>   (p. 171)

We are bound to align this with the later incident of the swing, both of which might be taken 'as revelations of Miriam's diminished vitality, her tendency to shrink back from life, whether she is making love, feeding chickens, trying to cope with Mrs Morel's dislike of her, or merely looking at flowers'.[3] But we should note that immediately after the passage just quoted Paul witnesses another aspect of Miriam:

> As he went round the back, he saw Miriam kneeling in front of the hen-coop, some maize in her hand, biting her lip, and crouching in an intense attitude. The hen was eyeing her wickedly. Very gingerly she put forward her hand. The hen bobbed for her. She drew back quickly with a cry, half of fear, half of chagrin.
> 'It won't hurt you', said Paul.
> She flushed crimson and started up.
> 'I only wanted to try', she said in a low voice.
> 'See, it doesn't hurt', he said, and, putting only two corns in his palm, he let the hen peck, peck, peck at his bare hand. 'It only makes you laugh', he said.
> She put her hand forward, and dragged it away, tried again, and started back with a cry. He frowned.
> 'Why, I'd let her take corn from my face', said Paul, 'only she bumps a bit. She's ever so neat. If she wasn't, look how much ground she'd peck up every day.'

He waited grimly, and watched. At last Miriam let the bird peck
from her hand. She gave a little cry – fear, and pain because of fear –
rather pathetic. But she had done it, and she did it again.

'There, you see', said the boy. 'It doesn't hurt, does it?'

She looked at him with dilated dark eyes.

'No', she laughed, trembling.   (p. 172)

The scene shows more than timidity; it shows, also, her extreme
sensitivity, along with her shy desire for new experience: she wants
to try, she wants to learn; if rightly encouraged she will and can
learn, and then she can respond with laughter and trembling excitement. This first view of Miriam, seen through the eyes of the objective narrator, is astir with life: for all her shyness and shrinking she
is nevertheless capable of a strong response. The whole initial
sketch is suffused with her 'beautiful warm colouring' and accompanied by her 'musical, quiet voice'. She is a girl of rich potential.

II

As Part II opens we become at once aware of a drastic shift in
method. The first two pages are given over to an elaborate interpretation of Miriam's character before she again appears, 'nearly sixteen,
very beautiful, with her warm colouring, her gravity, her eyes dilating
suddenly like an ecstasy' (p. 193). No such extended analysis of
anyone has appeared in Part I; there the characters have been allowed
to act out their parts before us, with only brief guiding touches by the
objective narrator. But here we sense a peculiar intensity in the analysis: the narrator seems to be preparing the way for some new and
difficult problem, and in so doing he seems to be dropping his manner
of impartiality. He is determined to set our minds in a certain direction, and this aim is reflected in the drifting length and involution of
the sentences. The style of writing here seems designed to reflect the
'mistiness' of the character he is describing, her remoteness from life:

> Her great companion was her mother. They were both brown-
> eyed, and inclined to be mystical, such women as treasure religion
> inside them, breathe it in their nostrils, and see the whole of life in a
> mist thereof. So to Miriam, Christ and God made one great figure,
> which she loved tremblingly and passionately when a tremendous
> sunset burned out the western sky, and Ediths, and Lucys, and
> Rowenas, Brian de Bois Guilberts, Rob Roys, and Guy Mannerings,
> rustled the sunny leaves in the morning, or sat in her bedroom aloft,
> alone, when it snowed. That was life to her. For the rest, she drudged

in the house, which work she would not have minded had not her clean red floor been mucked up immediately by the trampling farm-boots of her brothers. She madly wanted her little brother of four to let her swathe him and stifle him in her love; she went to church rev-erently, with bowed head, and quivered in anguish from the vulgarity of the other choir-girls and from the common-sounding voice of the curate; she fought with her brothers, whom she considered brutal louts; and she held not her father in too high esteem because he did not carry any mystical ideals cherished in his heart, but only wanted to have as easy a time as he could, and his meals when he was ready for them. (pp. 191–2)

She is also a girl who is 'mad to have learning whereon to pride herself'; and for all these causes she neglects and ignores her physi-cal being: 'Her beauty – that of a shy, wild, quiveringly sensitive thing – seemed nothing to her. Even her soul, so strong for rhap-sody, was not enough. She must have something to reinforce her pride, because she felt different from other people.' At the same time, her misty emotions lead her towards a desire to dominate Paul: 'Then he was so ill, and she felt he would be weak. Then she would be stronger than he. Then she could love him. If she could be mistress of him in his weakness, take care of him, if he could depend on her, if she could, as it were, have him in her arms, how she would love him!' (p. 192).

In all this the narrator is anticipating the views of Miriam fre-quently expressed by Paul himself: that she is too spiritual, too ab-stract, that she shrinks away from physical reality, and that she has a stifling desire to absorb and possess his soul. The incident of the swing that follows shortly after (pp. 199–201) would seem to bear out some of this: she is afraid to let Paul swing her high, and Lawrence phrases her fear in language that has unmistakable sexual overtones: 'She felt the accuracy with which he caught her, exactly at the right moment, and the exactly proportionate strength of his thrust, and she was afraid. Down to her bowels went the hot wave of fear. She was in his hands. Again, firm and inevitable came the thrust at the right moment. She gripped the rope, almost swooning' (p. 200). Yet she has led Paul to the swing, and she is fascinated by his free swinging: 'It roused a warmth in her. It were almost as if he were a flame that had lit a warmth in her whilst he swung in the middle air.' Who can say that Miriam is unable to learn this too, as she has learned with the hen, and as she is later shown to overcome her fear of crossing fences?

Occasionally she ran with Paul down the fields. Then her eyes blazed naked in a kind of ecstasy that frightened him. But she was physically afraid. If she were getting over a stile, she gripped his hands in a little hard anguish, and began to lose her presence of mind. And he could not persuade her to jump from even a small height. Her eyes dilated, became exposed and palpitating.

'No!' she cried, half laughing in terror – 'no!'

'You shall!' he cried once, and, jerking her forward, he brought her falling from the fence. But her wild 'Ah!' of pain, as if she were losing consciousness, cut him. She landed on her feet safely, and afterwards had courage in this respect.   (pp. 203–4)

Certainly she wants to learn; only a few lines after the swing episode we find this all-important passage:

But the girl gradually sought him out. If he brought up his sketchbook, it was she who pondered longest over the last picture. Then she would look up at him. Suddenly, her dark eyes alight like water that shakes with a stream of gold in the dark, she would ask:

'Why do I like this so?'

Always something in his breast shrank from these close, intimate, dazzled looks of hers.

'Why *do* you?' he asked.

'I don't know. It seems so true.'

'It's because – it's because there is scarcely any shadow in it; it's more shimmery, as if I'd painted the shimmering protoplasm in the leaves and everywhere, and not the stiffness of the shape. That seems dead to me. Only this shimmeriness is the real living. The shape is a dead crust. The shimmer is inside really.'

And she, with her little finger in her mouth, would ponder these sayings. They gave her a feeling of life again, and vivified things which had meant nothing to her. She managed to find some meaning in his struggling, abstract speeches. And they were the medium through which she came distinctly at her beloved objects.

(pp. 201–2)

It seems as though she is learning to reach out towards the 'shimmeriness' that is the 'real living'; with his help she is coming out of her 'mist' towards a distinct sight of 'her beloved objects'. *She* is learning, while *he* shrinks away from her intimate, shimmering eyes ('like water that shakes with a stream of gold in the dark'). She senses the meaning of his 'abstract speeches', she gets 'so near him', she creates in him 'a strange, roused sensation' (p. 202) – and as a result she enrages him for reasons that he cannot grasp. Is it because he is refusing to face the shimmer that is really inside Miriam?

So, when he sees her embracing her youngest brother 'almost as if she were in a trance, and swaying also as if she were swooned in an ecstasy of love', he bursts out with his irritation:

> 'What do you make such a *fuss* for?' cried Paul, all in suffering because of her extreme emotion. 'Why can't you be ordinary with him?'
> She let the child go, and rose, and said nothing. Her intensity, which would leave no emotion on a normal plane, irritated the youth into a frenzy. And this fearful, naked contact of her on small occasions shocked him. He was used to his mother's reserve. And on such occasions he was thankful in his heart and soul that he had his mother, so sane and wholesome. (p. 203)

One senses, as Miriam does at a later point, an alien influence here, twisting the mind of Paul and the narrator away from Miriam. Two pages later we see a dramatic juxtaposition of two warring actualities:

> He used to tell his mother all these things.
> 'I'm going to teach Miriam algebra', he said.
> 'Well', replied Mrs Morel, 'I hope she'll get fat on it.'
> When he went up to the farm on the Monday evening, it was drawing twilight. Miriam was just sweeping up the kitchen, and was kneeling at the hearth when he entered. Everyone was out but her. She looked round at him, flushed, her dark eyes shining, her fine hair falling about her face.
> 'Hello!' she said, soft and musical. 'I knew it was you.'
> 'How?'
> 'I knew your step. Nobody treads so quick and firm.'
> He sat down, sighing.
> 'Ready to do some algebra?' he asked, drawing a little book from his pocket. (p. 205)

Who is sane and wholesome, we may well ask? And whose thoughts are abstracted from life? We are beginning to learn that we cannot wholly trust the narrator's remarks in this central portion of the book, for his commentary represents mainly an extension of Paul's consciousness; everywhere, in his portion of the book, the voice of the narrator tends to echo and magnify the confusions that are arising within Paul himself. These are the contradictions in which some readers have seen a failure or a faltering in the novel, because 'the point of view is never adequately objectified and sustained to tell us which is true'.[4] But I feel rather that Lawrence has invented a successful technique by which he can manage the deep autobiographical problems that underlie the book. We are watching the strong graft of a stream of consciousness growing out of the live trunk of that Victorian prologue, and intertwining with the objectively presented action. The point of view adopted is that of Paul; but since confusion, self-deception, and desperate self-justification are essential to that point of view, we can never tell, from that stream of consciousness alone, where the real truth lies. But we can tell it from the action; we can tell it by seeking out the portrait of Miriam that lies beneath the overpainted commentary of the Paul-narrator. This technique of painting and overpainting produces a strange and unique tension in this part of the novel. The image of Miriam appears and then is clouded over; it is as though we were looking at her through a clouded window that is constantly being cleared, and fogged, and cleared again. It is an unprecedented and inimitable technique, discovered for this one necessary occasion. But it works.

How it works, we may see by looking once again at the frequently quoted passage where Miriam leads Paul, despite his reluctance ('They grumble so if I'm late') into the woods at dusk to find the 'wild-rose bush she had discovered'.

> The tree was tall and straggling. It had thrown its briers over a hawthorn-bush, and its long streamers trailed thick, right down to the grass, splashing the darkness everywhere with great split stars, pure white. In bosses of ivory and in large splashed stars the roses gleamed on the darkness of foliage and stems and grass. Paul and Miriam stood close together, silent, and watched. Point after point the steady roses shone out to them, seeming to kindle something in their souls. The dusk came like smoke around, and still did not put out the roses.
>
> Paul looked into Miriam's eyes. She was pale and expectant with wonder, her lips were parted, and her dark eyes lay open to him. His look seemed to travel down into her. Her soul quivered. It was the communion she wanted. He turned aside, as if pained. He turned to the bush.
>
> 'They seem as if they walk like butterflies, and shake themselves', he said.
>
> She looked at her roses. They were white, some incurved and holy, others expanded in an ecstasy. The tree was dark as a shadow. She lifted her hand impulsively to the flowers; she went forward and touched them in worship.
>
> 'Let us go', he said.

> There was a cool scent of ivory roses – a white, virgin scent.
> Something made him feel anxious and imprisoned. The two walked
> in silence. (p. 210)

What is this 'something' that makes him 'feel anxious and impris-
oned'? Is he like the hawthorn-bush, caught in the trailing streamers
of the rose-bush? Is it because she has insisted on a moment of soul-
communion which represents her tendency towards 'a blasphemous
possessorship'?[5] The narrator seems to be urging us in this direction. Yet in itself the scene may be taken to represent, amid this
wild profusion of natural growth, a moment of natural communion
in the human relationship, a potential marriage of senses and the
soul. This is, for Miriam, an 'ecstasy' in which nature is not abstracted, but realised in all its wild perfection. Paul breaks the mood
and runs away towards home. And when he reaches home we may
grasp the true manner of his imprisonment:

> Always when he went with Miriam, and it grew rather late, he
> knew his mother was fretting and getting angry about him – why, he
> could not understand. As he went into the house, flinging down his
> cap, his mother looked up at the clock. She had been sitting thinking
> because a chill to her eyes prevented her reading. She could feel Paul
> being drawn away by this girl. And she did not care for Miriam. 'She
> is one of those who will want to suck a man's soul out till he has
> none of his own left', she said to herself; 'and he is just such a gaby
> as to let himself be absorbed. She will never let him become a man;
> she never will.' So, while he was away with Miriam, Mrs Morel grew
> more and more worked up.
> She glanced at the clock and said, coldly and rather tired:
> 'You have been far enough to-night.'
> His soul, warm and exposed from contact with the girl, shrank.
> (pp. 210–11)

Miriam offers him the freedom of natural growth within a mature
relation, though Paul soon adopts the mother's view of Miriam's
'possessive' nature. He cannot help himself, but there is no reason
why readers of the book should accept the mother's view of
Miriam, which is everywhere shown to be motivated by the
mother's own possessiveness. The mother has described only herself
in the above quotation; she has not described Miriam, who is quite
a different being and has quite a different effect on Paul. The fact is
that Paul needs both his mother and Miriam for his true development, as he seems to realise quite early in the conflict: 'A sketch

finished, he always wanted to take it to Miriam. Then he was stimulated into knowledge of the work he had produced unconsciously.
In contact with Miriam he gained insight; his vision went deeper.
From his mother he drew the life-warmth, the strength to produce;
Miriam urged this warmth into intensity like a white light'
(p. 208). Or earlier we hear that Miriam's family 'kindled him and
made him glow to his work, whereas his mother's influence was to
make him quietly determined, patient, dogged, unwearied' (p. 198).

But the mother cannot bear to release him. Miriam must be met
by her with cold, unfriendly curtness, while the married woman,
Clara, may receive a friendly welcome from the mother. Clara
offers no threat: 'Mrs Morel measured herself against the younger
woman, and found herself easily stronger' (p. 386).

'Yes, I liked her', she says in answer to Paul's inquiry. 'But you'll
tire of her, my son; you know you will' (p. 394). And so she encourages the affair with Clara: the adulterous relation will serve the
son's physical needs, while the mother can retain the son's deeper
love and loyalty. Mrs Morel senses what she is doing, but evades
the facts:

> Mrs Morel considered. She would have been glad now for her son to
> fall in love with some woman who would – she did not know what.
> But he fretted so, got so furious suddenly, and again was melan-
> cholic. She wished he knew some nice woman – She did not know
> what she wished, but left it vague. At any rate she was not hostile to
> the idea of Clara.   (p. 300)

The mother's devices are pitiful, and at the same time contemptible,
as we have already seen from the painful episode in which she over-
whelms her son with raw and naked emotion:

> He had taken off his collar and tie, and rose, bare-throated, to go
> to bed. As he stooped to kiss his mother, she threw her arms round
> his neck, hid her face on his shoulder, and cried, in a whimpering
> voice, so unlike her own that he writhed in agony:
> 'I can't bear it. I could let another woman – but not her. She'd
> leave me no room, not a bit of room –'
> And immediately he hated Miriam bitterly.
> 'And I've never – you know, Paul – I've never had a husband – not
> really –'
> He stroked his mother's hair, and his mouth was on her throat.
> 'And she exults so in taking you from me – she's not like ordinary
> girls.'

> 'Well, I don't love her, mother,' he murmured, bowing his head
> and hiding his eyes on her shoulder in misery. His mother kissed him
> a long, fervent kiss.
> 'My boy!' she said, in a voice trembling with passionate love.
>
> (pp. 267–8)

'At your mischief again?' says the father, 'venomously', as he interrupts this scene of illicitly possessive passion. Mischief it is, corrosive and destructive to the marriage that Paul needs, the full relationship that Miriam offers, with her intimate love for nature.

It will be evident that I do not agree with the view that Spilka and others have taken of that flower-picking episode with Miriam and Clara, the view that takes the scene as a revelation of a basic flaw in Miriam: 'she kills life and has no right to it'.[6]

> 'Ah!' cried Miriam, and she looked at Paul, her dark eyes dilating.
> He smiled. Together they enjoyed the field of flowers. Clara, a little
> way off, was looking at the cowslips disconsolately. Paul and Miriam
> stayed close together, talking in subdued tones. He kneeled on one
> knee, quickly gathering the best blossoms, moving from tuft to tuft
> restlessly, talking softly all the time. Miriam plucked the flowers lov
> ingly, lingering over them. He always seemed to her too quick and
> almost scientific. Yet his bunches had a natural beauty more than
> hers. He loved them, but as if they were his and he had a right to
> them. She had more reverence for them: they held something she had
> not.   (p. 294)

The last clause has a wonderful ambiguity. If we take Paul's point of view, we will say that she is 'negative', that she lacks true life. If we ponder the whole action of the book, we will say that what she lacks is the full organic life of the flower, sexually complete within itself. She cannot grow into her full life without the principle that Paul, with his masculine creativity, here displays. The passage shows a man and a woman who are true counterparts, in mind and body. When, a little later, Paul sprinkles the flowers over Clara, he is performing an exclusively sensuous ritual that threatens more than a pagan love-death:

> Her breasts swung slightly in her blouse. The arching curve of her
> back was beautiful and strong; she wore no stays. Suddenly, without
> knowing, he was scattering a handful of cowslips over her hair and
> neck, saying:
>
> > 'Ashes to ashes, and dust to dust,
> > If the Lord won't have you the devil must.'

> The chill flowers fell on her neck. She looked up at him, with almost pitiful, scared grey eyes, wondering what he was doing. Flowers fell on her face, and she shut her eyes.
>
> Suddenly, standing there above her, he felt awkward.
>
> 'I thought you wanted a funeral', he said, ill at ease.
>
> (pp. 295–6)

It is Paul, under his mother's domination, who kills life, by refusing to move in organic relation with Miriam:

> He would not have it that they were lovers. The intimacy between them had been kept so abstract, such a matter of the soul, all thought and weary struggle into consciousness, that he saw it only as a platonic friendship. He stoutly denied there was anything else between them. Miriam was silent, or else she very quietly agreed. He was a fool who did not know what was happening to himself. By tacit agreement they ignored the remarks and insinuations of their acquaintances.
>
> 'We aren't lovers, we are friends', he said to her. '*We* know it. Let them talk. What does it matter what they say.'
>
> Sometimes, as they were walking together, she slipped her arm timidly into his. But he always resented it, and she knew it. It caused a violent conflict in him. With Miriam he was always on the high plane of abstraction, when his natural fire of love was transmitted into the fine steam[7] of thought. She would have it so.   (p. 224)

The last sentence is a fine example of the way in which the commentary of the Paul-narrator can contradict the tenor of the action: 'she slipped her arm timidly into his'. Clara knows better and tells Paul the truth in that revealing conversation just before 'the test on Miriam'. Paul has been describing how Miriam 'wants the soul out of my body': 'I know she wants a sort of soul union'.

> 'But how do you know what she wants?'
>
> 'I've been with her for seven years.'
>
> 'And you haven't found out the very first thing about her.'
>
> 'What's that?'
>
> 'That she doesn't want any of your soul communion. That's your own imagination. She wants you.'
>
> He pondered over this. Perhaps he was wrong.
>
> 'But she seems –' he began.
>
> 'You've never tried,' she answered.   (pp. 337–8)

This is not to deny that Miriam is shy, intense, spiritual, and, as a result of her upbringing, fearful and evasive of sexual facts. All these qualities belong to her character, for she is young, sensitive, and modest. My point is that her portrait does not consist simply of a static presentation of these aspects: her portrait is being enriched dynamically and progressively before our eyes, over a long period of years, from her early adolescence, through an awakening and potential fulfilment, to the utter extinction of her inner life and hope.

The truth of Clara's view has been borne out long before, as far back as that scene where Paul accuses Miriam of never laughing real laughter:

> 'But' – and she looked up at him with eyes frightened and struggling 'I do laugh at you – I do.'
> 'Never! There's always a kind of intensity. When you laugh I could always cry; it seems as if it shows up your suffering. Oh, you make me knit the brows of my very soul and cogitate.'
> Slowly she shook her head despairingly.
> 'I'm sure I don't want to', she said.
> 'I'm so damned spiritual with *you* always!' he cried.
> She remained silent, thinking, 'Then why don't you be otherwise'. But he saw her crouching, brooding figure, and it seemed to tear him in two. (p. 241)

And then, on the next page, as Paul repairs the bicycle tyre, we have an unmistakable glimpse of the vital image of Miriam, her strong physical feeling for him, and her true laughter:

> 'Fetch me a drop of water in a bowl', he said to her. 'I shall be late, and then I s'll catch it.'
> He lighted the hurricane lamp, took off his coat, turned up the bicycle, and set speedily to work. Miriam came with the bowl of water and stood close to him, watching. She loved to see his hands doing things. He was slim and vigorous, with a kind of easiness even in his most hasty movements. And busy at his work, he seemed to forget her. She loved him absorbedly. She wanted to run her hands down his sides. She always wanted to embrace him, so long as he did not want her.
> 'There!' he said, rising suddenly. 'Now, could you have done it quicker?'
> 'No!' she laughed.
> He straightened himself. His back was towards her. She put her two hands on his sides, and ran them quickly down.
> 'You are so *fine!*' she said.
> He laughed, hating her voice, but his blood roused to a wave of flame by her hands. She did not seem to realise *him* in all this. He might have been an object. She never realised the male he was. (p. 242)

Those last three sentences, the outgrowth of his torment, and the earlier remark, 'so long as he did not want her', provide clear examples of the way in which the overpainted commentary tends to obscure the basic portrait of Miriam. It is the same in the episode at Nethermere: 'He could not bear to look at Miriam. She seemed to want him, and he resisted. He resisted all the time. He wanted now to give her passion and tenderness, and he could not. He felt that she wanted the soul out of his body, and not him.'

> He went on, in his dead fashion:
> 'If only you could want *me*, and not want what I can reel off for you!'
> 'I!' she cried bitterly – 'I! Why, when would you let me take you?'
>   (p. 247)

His bursts of anger and 'hate', his feeling that Miriam is pulling the soul out of his body, are only his own tormented reactions to the agony he feels in being pulled so strongly away from his mother, as Daniel Weiss has said: 'It is that for the first time in his life he is facing a mature relationship between himself and another woman, *not* his mother, and that a different mode of love is being demanded from him. It is Miriam's refusal to allow him to regress to the Nirvana, the paradisal state of the infant, her insistence that he recognise her, that fills him with anguish.'[8]

As though to warn us against accepting Paul's responses and interpretations, Lawrence inserts in the middle of the crucial chapter, 'Strife in Love', a long, vigorous, attractive, and surprising scene where the father is shown totally in command of the household, on a Friday evening, when the miners make their reckoning in Morel's house. Complaining with warm, vigorous dialect about the cold room, as he emerges from his bath, Morel draws even his wife into laughter and reminiscent admiration:

> Morel looked down ruefully at his sides.
> 'Me!' he exclaimed. 'I'm nowt b'r a skinned rabbit. My bones fair juts out on me.'
> 'I should like to know where', retorted his wife.
> 'Iv'ry-wheer! I'm nobbut a sack o' faggots.'
> Mrs Morel laughed. He had still a wonderfully young body, muscular, without any fat. His skin was smooth and clear. It might have been the body of a man of twenty-eight, except that there were, perhaps, too many blue scars, like tattoo-marks, where the coal-dust remained under the skin, and that his chest was too hairy. But he

put his hand on his sides ruefully. It was his fixed belief that, because he did not get fat, he was as thin as a starved rat.

Paul looked at his father's thick, brownish hands all scarred, with broken nails, rubbing the fine smoothness of his sides, and the incongruity struck him. It seemed strange they were the same flesh.

'I suppose', he said to his father, 'you had a good figure once.'

'Eh!' exclaimed the miner, glancing round, startled and timid, like a child.

'He had', exclaimed Mrs Morel, 'if he didn't hurtle himself up as if he was trying to get in the smallest space he could.'

'Me!' exclaimed Morel – 'me a good figure! I wor niver much more n'r a skeleton.'

'Man!' cried his wife, 'don't be such a pulamiter!'

'Strewth!' he said. 'Tha's niver knowed me but what I looked as if I wor goin' off in a rapid decline.'

She sat and laughed.

'You've had a constitution like iron,' she said; 'and never a man had a better start, if it was body that counted. You should have seen him as a young man', she cried suddenly to Paul, drawing herself up to imitate her husband's once handsome bearing.

Morel watched her shyly. He saw again the passion she had had for him. It blazed upon her for a moment. He was shy, rather scared, and humble. Yet again he felt his old glow. And then immediately he felt the ruin he had made during these years. He wanted to bustle about, to run away from it.   (pp. 250-1)

Paul is the 'outsider' here, the one who does not enter into the family warmth, as we have seen a few lines earlier from his cold comment on his father's vigorous exclamations ('Why is a doorknob deader than anything else?'), and as we see a little later from the way in which he turns 'impatiently' from his books and pencil, after his father has asked him 'humbly' to count up the money. And at the close of the episode he dismisses his father viciously: 'It won't be long', he says to his mother. 'You can have my money. Let him go to hell' (p. 255). Morel does not deserve this, we feel, after all the warmth and vigour of his action here. Paul is cruel to anyone who threatens his mother's dominion, however briefly.

This Miriam feels instinctively, a few minutes later, when she looks at the stencilled design that Paul has made for his mother:

'Ah, how beautiful!' she cried.

The spread cloth, with its wonderful reddish roses and dark green stems, all so simple, and somehow so wicked-looking, lay at her feet. She went on her knees before it, her dark curls dropping. He saw her crouched voluptuously before his work, and his heart beat quickly. Suddenly she looked up at him.

'Why does it seem cruel?' she asked.

'What?'

'There seems a feeling of cruelty about it', she said.

'It's jolly good, whether or not', he replied, folding up his work with a lover's hands.   (pp. 255–6)

He has also made a 'smaller piece' for Miriam; but when he sees her fingering the work 'with trembling hands' he can only turn with embarrassment to tend the bread in the oven, and when she looks up at him 'with her dark eyes one flame of love' he can only laugh 'uncomfortably' and begin to talk 'about the design'. 'All his passion, all his wild blood, went into this intercourse with her, when he talked and conceived his work. She brought forth to him his imaginations. She did not understand, any more than a woman understands when she conceives a child in her womb. But this was life for her and for him' (p. 256). But, as the imagery of conception ironically implies, such talk is not all of life for either of them.

Immediately after this, the physical scuffle and flirtation with Beatrice shows another need, which Miriam recognises and would like to satisfy: 'His thick hair was tumbled over his forehead. Why might she not push it back for him, and remove the marks of Beatrice's comb? Why might she not press his body with her two hands? It looked so firm, and every whit living. And he would let other girls, why not her?' (p. 261) A moment later, as usual, Paul tries to 'abstract' their relationship into a French lesson, only to find that her French diary is 'mostly a love-letter' to him:

'Look,' he said quietly, 'the past participle conjugated with *avoir* agrees with the direct object when it precedes.'

She bent forward, trying to see and to understand. Her free, fine curls tickled his face. He started as if they had been red hot, shuddering. He saw her peering forward at the page, her red lips parted piteously, the black hair springing in fine strands across her tawny, ruddy cheek. She was coloured like a pomegranate for richness. His breath came short as he watched her. Suddenly she looked up at him. Her dark eyes were naked with their love, afraid, and yearning. His eyes, too, were dark, and they hurt her. They seemed to master her. She lost all her self-control, was exposed in fear. And he knew, before he could kiss her, he must drive something out of himself. And a touch of hate for her crept back again into his heart. He returned to her exercise.   (p. 262)

Miriam does not bear the slightest blame for the failure of this relationship: she is 'like a pomegranate for richness', like the bride in the Song of Solomon; she combines a pure beauty of sensuous appeal with all the soul that Paul the artist needs for his further development. And like that bride she is not passive, she tries to draw Paul out of his imprisonment, tries to draw his attention towards the wild beauty of 'the yellow, bursten flowers'. His response is to level at her the most cruel of all his desperate charges:

> 'Aren't they magnificent?' she murmured.
> 'Magnificent! it's a bit thick – they're pretty!'
> She bowed again to her flowers at his censure of her praise. He watched her crouching, sipping the flowers with fervid kisses.
> 'Why must you always be fondling things!' he said irritably.
> 'But I love to touch them', she replied, hurt.
> 'Can you never like things without clutching them as if you wanted to pull the heart out of them? Why don't you have a bit more restraint, or reserve, or something?'
> She looked up at him full of pain, then continued slowly to stroke her lips against a ruffled flower. Their scent, as she smelled it, was so much kinder than he; it almost made her cry.
> 'You wheedle the soul out of things,' he said. 'I would never wheedle – at any rate, I'd go straight.'
> He scarcely knew what he was saying. These things came from him mechanically. She looked at him. His body seemed one weapon, firm and hard against her.
> 'You're always begging things to love you', he said, 'as if you were a beggar for love. Even the flowers, you have to fawn on them –'
> Rhythmically, Miriam was swaying and stroking the flower with her mouth, inhaling the scent which ever after made her shudder as it came to her nostrils.
> 'You don't want to love – your eternal and abnormal craving is to be loved. You aren't positive, you're negative. You absorb, absorb, as if you must fill yourself up with love, because you've got a shortage somewhere.'
> She was stunned by his cruelty, and did not hear. He had not the faintest notion of what he was saying. It was as if his fretted, tortured soul, run hot by thwarted passion, jetted off these sayings like sparks from electricity.   (pp. 273–4)

The shortage is in Paul; and she fondles the flowers so warmly because they offer solace from his ruthless rejection of her natural being. Her closeness to flowers throughout the book shows her as an innocent Persephone who needs only to be carried away by the power that Paul might possess if he were a whole man. But he is not. He is a child, with a child's limited outlook. His mother's influence has reduced all other human beings to unreality. This the narrator makes plain in one of his rare moments of illumination:

> He had come back to his mother. Hers was the strongest tie in his life. When he thought round, Miriam shrank away. There was a vague, unreal feel about her. And nobody else mattered. There was one place in the world that stood solid and did not melt into unreality: the place where his mother was. Everybody else could grow shadowy, almost non-existent to him, but she could not. It was as if the pivot and pole of his life, from which he could not escape, was his mother.   (p. 278)

So then for Paul the warm reality of Miriam must fade away into spirituality and soulfulness, and she must suffer the cruel accusation summed up in the falsely composed letter that he writes at the end of the chapter, 'Defeat of Miriam' – a letter of stilted, inflated rhetoric, false in every way:

> 'May I speak of our old, worn love, this last time. It, too, is changing, is it not? Say, has not the body of that love died, and left you its invulnerable soul? You see, I can give you a spirit love, I have given it you this long, long time; but not embodied passion. See, you are a nun. I have given you what I would give a holy nun – as a mystic monk to a mystic nun. Surely you esteem it best. Yet you regret – no, have regretted – the other. In all our relations no body enters. I do not talk to you through the senses – rather through the spirit. That is why we cannot love in the common sense. Ours is not an everyday affection. As yet we are mortal, and to live side by side with one another would be dreadful, for somehow with you I cannot long be trivial, and, you know, to be always beyond this mortal state would be to lose it. If people marry, they must live together as affectionate humans, who may be common-place with each other without feeling awkward – not as two souls. So I feel it.'   (p. 309)

So she feels it too, and the hopeless rejection of her true character gives a death-blow to her inner vitality. '"You are a nun – you are a nun." The words went into her heart again and again. Nothing he ever had said had gone into her so deeply, fixedly, like a mortal wound.'

After such a wound, his later effort to carry on sexual relations with her is bound to be a failure. She tries, as she always has tried, but her inner life is ebbing. This is not the marriage that she yearns for, not the union that he needs. Paul hardly knows that she is there, as a person; indeed he does not want to know her as a human being. 'He had always, almost wilfully, to put her out of count, and act from the brute strength of his own feelings' (p. 352). The title of the chapter, 'The Test on Miriam', is bitterly ironic, for what the chapter presents is the test on Paul's ability to free himself from the imprisonment which he feels, but does not understand. This is clear from Paul's stream of consciousness at the very outset of the chapter: 'There was some obstacle; and what was the obstacle? It lay in the physical bondage. He shrank from the physical contact. But why? With her he felt bound up inside himself. He could not go out to her' (p. 339). His only refuge is to turn towards a sort of mindless evasion of his torments, a rejection of his own humanity:

> He courted her now like a lover. Often, when he grew hot, she put his face from her, held it between her hands, and looked in his eyes. He could not meet her gaze. Her dark eyes, full of love, earnest and searching, made him turn away. Not for an instant would she let him forget. Back again he had to torture himself into a sense of his responsibility and hers. Never any relaxing, never any leaving himself to the great hunger and impersonality of passion; he must be brought back to a deliberate, reflective creature. As if from a swoon of passion she called him back to the littleness, the personal relationship. (pp. 345-6)

So Paul, near the end of this chapter, is reduced to pitiful, even contemptible, littleness. Miriam, in her violent despair, at last cries out the essential truth: 'It has been one long battle between us – you fighting away from me' (p. 259). His response is shock and utter amazement: in his self-absorption he had never even begun to see it from her point of view. And he turns at once towards a painful series of self-justifications, throwing the blame on her: 'He was full of a feeling that she had deceived him. She had despised him when he thought she worshipped him. She had let him say wrong things, and had not contradicted him. She had let him fight alone ... She had not played fair' (p. 260). Yet at the very end of the chapter, the bitter truth of what he has done to her emerges poignantly out of his self-deception:

> 'She never thought she'd have me, mother, not from the first, and so she's not disappointed.'
> 'I'm afraid', said his mother, 'she doesn't give up hopes of you yet.'
> 'No', he said, 'perhaps not.'
> 'You'll find it's better to have done', she said.

'*I* don't know', he said desperately.

'Well, leave her alone', replied his mother.

So he left her, and she was alone. Very few people cared for her, and she for very few people. She remained alone with herself, waiting.   (p. 363)

III

Now all the tension of that doomed affair is over, and for the last four chapters of the book the method of the objective narrator may be resumed. With the opening of chapter 12 everything comes back into clarity and firmness. Paul is making progress with his designs, he believes in his work, and the clear tone of this conclusion is struck at once as we read: 'He was twenty-four when he said his first confident thing to his mother' about his art. Had Lawrence been a more conventional craftsman, he might have put the heading 'Part III' at the top of this chapter, so that we could see clearly the essential structure of the book, that of a triptych, with the major scene of suffering in the centre, and two smaller scenes on either side, focusing our eyes towards the centre of the drama.

The portrait of Clara Dawes is not in any way designed to rival that of Miriam. Clara is second-best, and second-hand, for all her beauty. 'Some part, big and vital in him, she had no hold over; nor did she ever try to get it, or even to realise what it was. And he knew in some way that she held herself still as Mrs Dawes' (p. 428). Their physical passion is significant, not for itself, but for the clari-fying, purgatorial effect upon both of them, leading them to find a truth that lies beyond those times when they 'included in their meeting the thrust of the manifold grass-stems, the cry of the peewit, the wheel of the stars' (p. 421). This sort of immersion in mindlessness plays an essential part in Lawrence's later philosophy of love; but it is only a part, and it is here shown to be utterly insufficient. For Paul, the immediate result of the affair is the feeling that Clara is 'not much more than a big white pebble on the beach'. 'What does she mean to me, after all?' he asks. 'She represents something, like a bubble of foam represents the sea. But what is *she*? It's not her I care for' (pp. 425–6).

It has been, from the beginning, a flawed relationship, with un-pleasant overtones of the mother-substitute.[9] During that trip to Lincoln with his mother, we recall, Paul had complained bitterly of his mother's ageing: 'Why can't a man have a *young* mother?' he cries

(p. 299). So now he has her, in Clara, only six or seven years older than he, a woman married, like his mother, to a rough workman who has, she says, treated her badly. There is a striking resemblance between Baxter Dawes and Paul's father – their use of dialect, their roughness, and their collapse into drunkenness and apathy, with out-bursts of violence. Clara is 'reserved' and 'superior', like his mother; and she has the mother's deep discontent, her independent spirit, her sharp tongue, her bitterness against life and against men. This is an affair which, as the ominous flower ritual has prophesied, carries in itself the sources of its own death; and the affair dies as the mother is dying: 'She [Clara] was afraid of the man who was not there with her, whom she could feel behind this make-believe lover: somebody sinister, that filled her with horror. She began to have a kind of horror of him. It was almost as if he were a criminal. He wanted her – he had her – and it made her feel as if death itself had her in its grip' (p. 456). For Paul, at its best, the affair has been a blind rushing, an escape from thought, like being swept away in the torrent of the Trent: 'Gradually, the little criticisms, the little sensations, were lost, thought also went, everything borne along in one flood. He became, not a man with a mind, but a great instinct' (p. 432).

Yet the result of this immersion is a new clarity of vision in Paul and a consequent clarity and precision in the remarks of the narrator. The whole effect is summed up in the remarkable self-understanding that Paul displays in chapter 13, in the luminous conversation with his mother about his feeling for Clara: 'You know, mother, I think there must be something the matter with me, that I *can't* love ... I feel sometimes as if I wronged my women, mother.'

> 'How wronged them, my son?'
> 'I don't know.'
> He went on painting rather despairingly; he had touched the quick of the trouble.
> 'And as for wanting to marry', said his mother, 'there's plenty of time yet.'
> 'But no, mother. I even love Clara, and I did Miriam; but to *give* myself to them in marriage I couldn't. I couldn't belong to them. They seem to want *me*, and I can't ever give it them.'
> 'You haven't met the right woman.'
> 'And I never shall meet the right woman while you live', he said.
> She was very quiet. Now she began to feel again tired, as if she were done.   (p. 418)

His growth in understanding, his realisation of the importance, the bigness of the human relationship, is shown in his sympathy for Dawes, in his deepened understanding of the basic relationship between his mother and father (p. 381), and in his final reconciliation of Clara and her husband. In this way, perhaps, he can make amends to his father, by reconciling the surrogates of father and mother. And finally, the superb clarity of the whole objective vision now is shown in the long passage of the mother's dying, where she becomes in death a youthful bride in Paul's eyes, and Paul says his long farewell to his only love.

But for Miriam, nothing can be done, as we see in that last sad interview, after the mother's death: 'Still, the curls were fine and free, but her face was much older, the brown throat much thinner. She seemed old to him, older than Clara. Her bloom of youth had quickly gone. A sort of stiffness, almost of woodenness, had come upon her' (p. 488). She is the walking ghost of her former self. He knows what he has done to her, but he cannot help her, for she no longer attracts him. The mother's influence has stifled the vitality in Miriam that once drew them together. Inevitably, he rejects her pathetic proposal with the mother's reasoning: 'But – you love me so much, you want to put me in your pocket. And I should die there smothered' (p. 489).

'"Mother!" he whimpered – "mother!"' we read on the book's last page. It is the clearest judgement of the book. For *whimpered* is precisely the right word[10] to describe the bondage that has held him from Miriam. Yet there remains in him his mother's tough, unyielding will; maimed and damaged as he is, 'he would not give in'. The phrase has been three times applied to the mother in her fatal illness, and the words are perfectly in line with the whole tragic story. Whatever happens to others, he will survive: his mother's will drives him on into a pilgrimage of pain. But there is no reason to feel that his pilgrimage, however painful to him, will always be only destructive to others. His growth in self-knowledge offers a better hope. Paul has within himself a vital, creative spark; when that energy is frustrated, the results are bitterly destructive; but when, however briefly, that energy can be released, the results may be beneficent and beautiful. He has still, potentially, an artist's vision that can bring all things into harmony:

'What a pity there is a coal-pit here where it is so pretty!' said Clara.

'Do you think so?' he answered. 'You see, I am so used to it I
should miss it. No; and I like the pits here and there. I like the rows
of trucks, and the headstocks, and the steam in the daytime, and the
lights at night. When I was a boy, I always thought a pillar of cloud
by day and a pillar of fire by night was a pit, with its steam, and its
lights, and the burning bank, – and I thought the Lord was always at
the pit-top.'   (p. 320)

From *Imagined Worlds: Essays on Some English Novels and
Novelists in Honour of John Butt*, ed. Maynard Mack and Ian
Gregor (London, 1968), pp. 342–68.

NOTES

[In some respects, Louis Martz's classic account of the narrative method of
Sons and Lovers looks back to assumptions which dominated Anglo-
American criticism in the mid-century. This is particularly noticeable at the
close when he reads *Sons and Lovers* as a conventional novel of maturing
personal development. But other aspects of his essay have been influential
on more recent thinking. His analysis of why the narrative voice cannot be
considered neutral has been taken up by many subsequent commentators
and has suggested a number of important general considerations. The pene-
tration of Paul's point-of-view into the narrative language seems to undermine any simple sense we might have of the novel's realism, for example.
At the same time Martz reveals how the customary understanding of
Miriam's character is coloured by Paul's interests. Though Martz draws no
political conclusions from this, the perspective he opens up has been explored since by feminists. Perhaps the best way of understanding his essay,
therefore, is as a point of transition from older assumptions to ones which
have dominated much recent debate about the novel. Page references to
Sons and Lovers are incorporated into the text and are to the Penguin
edition edited by Keith Sagar (1981). Ed.]

1. Mark Spilka, *The Love Ethic of D. H. Lawrence* (Bloomington, IN,
   1955), pp. 45, 51, 56, 66. A notable exception to this view is presented
   by Graham Hough, *The Dark Sun: A Study of D. H. Lawrence*
   (New York, 1956), pp. 39–47, where Hough sees the 'co-presence in
   the Paul and Miriam parts of *Sons and Lovers* of two different kinds of
   experience – more or less simple recollections, checked and assisted by
   Jessie Chambers; and a later interpretation of the whole sequence of
   events'. The very early Freudian interpretation by Alfred Booth
   Kuttner also shows clearly the way in which Paul is being unfair to the
   character of Miriam: see the reprint of this essay of 1916 in the valuable collection edited by E. W. Tedlock, Jr, *D. H. Lawrence and Sons*

and Lovers: Sources and Criticism (New York, 1965); see especially pp. 81–6. For the later Freudian study by Daniel Weiss, see note 8 below.

2. This important line is omitted in the current texts of the Modern Library and Compass Books.

3. Julian Moynahan, *The Deed of Life: The Novels and Tales of D. H. Lawrence* (Princeton, NJ, 1963), p. 17.

4. Mark Schorer, 'Technique as Discovery', in *The Modern Critical Spectrum*, ed. Gerald and Nancy Goldberg (Engelwood Cliffs, NJ, 1962), pp. 76–7; the essay originally appeared in *The Hudson Review* (1948). See also the interesting essay by Seymour Betsky in *The Achievement of D. H. Lawrence*, ed. Frederick J. Hoffman and Harry T. Moore (Norman, OK, 1953), esp. pp. 138–40.

5. The phrase is applied to Miriam by Dorothy Van Ghent on the later occasion when Miriam is caressing the daffodils and draws down Paul's harshest charges: see *The English Novel: Form and Function* (New York, 1953), p. 256.

6. Spilka, *Love Ethic*, pp. 51–3.

7. Many editions read 'stream'.

8. Daniel A. Weiss, *Oedipus in Nottingham: D. H. Lawrence* (Seattle, 1962), p. 53. Though Weiss sees Miriam primarily as 'a static figure ... the Ophelia, the virginal side of the maternal image' (p. 82), his book is excellent for the light it throws on the causes of Paul's misunderstanding.

9. Weiss's book is excellent on this point too, particularly in its treatment of the significance of the similarity between Clara's husband and Paul's father. See especially pp. 26–37.

10. The current Modern Library, Compass and Penguin texts all erroneously read 'whispered': see the comment on this textual crux by Harry T. Moore in Tedlock's collection, p. 63. (The older printings in the Modern Library and in Compass Books, however, retain the plates that read 'whimpered'.) [In the latest Penguin edition, edited by Keith Sagar in 1981, this error has been corrected. Ed.]

5

Sexual Politics in
Sons and Lovers

KATE MILLETT

In a letter to Edward Garnett written in 1912, Lawrence provided
his own description of *Sons and Lovers*:

> A woman of character and refinement goes into the lower class, and
> has no satisfactions in her own life. She has had a passion for her
> husband, so the children are born of passion, and have heaps of vi-
> tality. But as her sons grow up, she selects them as lovers – first the
> eldest, then the second. These sons are *urged* into life by their recip-
> rocal love of their mother – urged on and on. But when they come to
> manhood, they can't love, because their mother is the strongest
> power in their lives, and holds them... As soon as the young men
> come into contact with women there is a split. William gives his sex
> to a fribble, and his mother holds his soul. But the split kills him,
> because he doesn't know where he is. The next son gets a woman
> who fights for his soul – fights his mother. The son loves the mother
> – all the sons hate and are jealous of the father. The battle goes on
> between the mother and the girl, with the son as object. The mother
> gradually proves the stronger, because of the tie of blood. The son
> decides to leave his soul in his mother's hands, and like his elder
> brother, go for passion. He gets passion. Then the split begins to tell
> again. But, almost unconsciously, the mother realises what is the
> matter and begins to die. The son casts off his mistress, attends to his
> mother dying. He is left in the end naked of everything, with the drift
> toward death.[1]

In the same letter Lawrence assured Garnett this would be a great
book. Both the précis and the boast have truth, but the latter has

74

more of it. *Sons and Lovers* is a great novel because it has the ring of something written from deeply felt experience. The past remembered, it conveys more of Lawrence's own knowledge of life than anything else he wrote. His other novels appear somehow artificial beside it.

Paul Morel is of course Lawrence himself, treated with a self-regarding irony which is often adulation: 'He was solitary and strong and his eyes had a beautiful light' (p. 423); 'She saw him, slender and firm, as if the setting sun had given him to her. A deep pain took hold of her, and she knew she must love him' – and so forth (p. 216). In the précis, Lawrence (and his critics after him) have placed all the emphasis in this tale of the artist as an ambitious young man, upon the spectral role his mother plays in rendering him incapable of complete relations with women his own age – his sexual or emotional frigidity. That the book is a great tribute to his mother and a moving record of the strongest and most formative love of the author's life, is, of course, indisputable. For all their potential morbidity, the idyllic scenes of the son and mother's walking in the fields, their excited purchases of a flower or a plate and their visit to Lincoln cathedral, are splendid and moving, as only *Sons and Lovers*, among the whole of Lawrence's work, has the power to move a reader. But critics have also come to see Mrs Morel as a devouring maternal vampire as well, smothering her son with affection past the years of his need of it, and Lawrence himself has encouraged this with the self-pitying defeatism of phrases such as 'naked of everything', 'with the drift toward death', and the final chapter heading 'Derelict'.[2]

The précis itself is so determinedly Freudian, after the fact as it were,[3] that it neglects the two other levels at which the novel operates – both the superb naturalism of its descriptive power,[4] which make it probably still the greatest novel of proletarian life in English, but also the vitalist level beneath the Freudian diagram. And at this level Paul is never in any danger whatsoever. He is the perfection of self-sustaining ego. The women in the book exist in Paul's orbit and to cater to his needs: Clara to awaken him sexually, Miriam to worship his talent in the role of disciple and Mrs Morel to provide always that enormous and expansive support, that dynamic motivation which can inspire the son of a coal miner to rise above the circumstances of his birth and become a great artist. The curious shift in sympathy between the presentation of Mrs Morel from the early sections of the novel where she is a woman tied by poverty to a man she despises, 'done out of her rights' (p. 105) as a human being, compelled, despite her education and earlier aspirations, to accept the tedium of poverty and child-bearing in cohabitation with a man for whom she no longer feels any sympathy and whose alcoholic brutality repels and enslaves her, to the possessive matron guarding her beloved son from matu-rity – is but the shift of Paul's self-centred understanding. While a boy, Paul hates his father and identifies with his mother; both are emotionally crushed and physically afraid before the paternal tyrant. The identification is real enough. When Walter Morel locks his pregnant wife out of the house in a boozy rage, it is Paul with whom she is pregnant, and the scene derives its conviction from the outraged prose of the precious burden himself. When Morel beats her and draws blood, it is Paul's snowy baby clothes that are stained with the sacrifice. As Mrs Morel cowers, sheltering the infant, a bond is sealed that will last past other attachments.

The book even provides us with glimpses of the Oedipal situation at its most erotic: 'I've never had a husband – not really... His mother gave him a long fervent kiss' (p. 268).[5] At this critical junc-ture Walter Morel walks in, justifiably annoyed, to mutter 'at your mischief again'. Thereupon the two rivals square off and nearly fight it out. But Walter is beaten anyway, and one foresees that Paul is a son who will have much to atone for: 'The elderly man began to unlace his boots. He stumbled off to bed. His last fight was fought in that home' (p. 267).

But the Oedipus complex is rather less a matter of the son's passion for the mother than his passion for attaining the level of power to which adult male status is supposed to entitle him. Sexual possession of adult woman may be the first, but is hardly the most impressive manifestation of that rank. Mrs Morel (in only one short passage of the novel is she ever referred to by her own name – Gertrude Coppard) has had no independent existence and is utterly deprived of any avenue of achievement. Her method of con-tinuing to seek some existence through a vicarious role in the success she urges on her sons, is, however regrettable, fairly under-standable. The son, because of his class and its poverty, has per-ceived that the means to the power he seeks is not in following his father down to the pits, but in following his mother's behest and going to school, then to an office, and finally into art. The way out of his dilemma lies then in becoming, at first, like his mother rather than his father.

We are frequently told that Lawrence made restitution to his father and the men of his father's condition in creating Mellors and others like him.[6] Such, alas, is not the case. Mellors is as one critic observes, 'really a sort of gentleman in disguise',[7] and if the portrait of the broken drunkard in *Sons and Lovers* is cruel, and it is undeniably, it is less cruel than converting this victim of industrial brutality into a blasé sexual superman who is too much of a snob to belong to either the working or the middle classes. The late Lawrentian hero is clearly Lawrence's own fantasy of the father he might have preferred. In the same way, Lady Chatterley is a smartened-up version of his mother herself. Like his own wife Frieda von Richthofen, she is a real lady, not that disappointed little woman of the mining village with chapped red hands who fears her clothes are too shabby to be seen in Lincoln cathedral. Yet Mrs Morel is a brave, even a great woman, though waitresses in tea-houses snub her when she can only order custard, too poor to pay for a full meal. *Sons and Lovers* gives us Lawrence's parents without the glamour with which his snobbishness later invested them. All the romances of his later fiction are a reworking of his parents' marriage, and of his own too, modelled on theirs, but a notable advance in social mobility. For Lawrence saw his course, saw it with a Calvinistic sense of election, as a vocation to rise and surpass his origins.

When Paul's ambition inspires his escape from identical circumstances it will be upon the necks of the women whom he has used, who have constituted his stepping-stones up into the middle class. For Paul kills or discards the women who have been of use to him. Freud, another Oedipal son, and a specialist in such affairs, predicted that 'he who is a favourite of the mother becomes a "conqueror"'.[8] Paul is to be just that. By adolescence, he has grown pompous enough under the influence of maternal encouragement to proclaim himself full of a 'divine discontent' (p. 458) superior to any experience Mrs Morel might understand. And when his mother has ceased to be of service, he quietly murders her. When she takes an unseasonably long time to die of cancer, he dilutes the milk she has been prescribed to drink: '"I don't want her to eat... I wish she'd die"... And he would put some water with it so that it would not nourish her' (pp. 458, 462). By a nice irony the son is murdering her who gave him life, so that he may have a bit more for himself: he who once was fed upon her milk now waters what he gives her to be rid of her. Motherhood, of the all-absorbing variety, is a dangerous vocation. When his first plan doesn't work, he tries morphine poisoning: 'That evening he got all the morphia pills there were, and took them downstairs. Carefully, he crushed them to powder' (p. 464). This too goes into the milk, and when it doesn't take hold at once, he considers stifling her with the bed-clothes.

A young man who takes such liberties must be sustained by a powerful faith. Paul is upheld by several – the Nietzschean creed that the artist is beyond morality; another which he shares with his mother that he is an anointed child (at his birth she has the dream of Joseph and all the sheaves in the field bow to her paragon); and a faith in male supremacy which he has imbibed from his father and enlarged upon himself. Grown to man's estate, Paul is fervid in this piety, but Paul the child is very ambivalent. Despite the ritual obser-vances of this cult which Paul witnessed on pay night[9] and in his father's feckless irresponsibility toward family obligations, he was as yet too young to see much in them beyond the injustices of those who hold rank over him as they did over his mother. Seeing that his father's drinking takes bread from his young mouth, he identifies with women and children and is at first unenthusiastic about mas-culine prerogative. When a crony comes to call for his father, Paul's vision makes us aware of the man's insolence: 'Jerry entered unasked, and stood by the kitchen doorway... stood there coolly asserting the rights of men and husbands' (p. 55).

Lawrence later became convinced that the miner's life and the curse of industrialism had reduced this sacred male authority to the oafishness of drinking and wife- and child-beating. Young Paul has been on the unpleasant end of this sort of power, and is acute enough to see that the real control lies in the bosses, the moneyed men at the top. Under industrialism, the male supremacy he yearns after is, in his eyes, vitiated by poverty and brutality, and it grants a noisy power over all too little. This is part of the unfortunately more ignoble side of Lawrence's lifelong hatred for industrialism. In his middle period he was to concentrate his envy upon the capitalist middle classes, and in his last years he championed primitive soci-eties, where he was reassured male supremacy was not merely a social phenomenon all too often attenuated by class differences, but a religious and total way of life.

The place of the female in such schemes is fairly clear, but in Lawrence's own time it was already becoming a great deal less so. As in *The Rainbow*, this novel's real contrasts are between the older women like his mother, who know their place, and the newer breed, like his mistresses, who fail to discern it. Mrs Morel has her traditional vicarious joys: 'Now she had two sons in the world. She could think of two places, great centres of industry, and feel she had put a man into each of them, that these men would work out what she wanted; they were derived from her, they were of her, and their works would also be hers' (pp. 143–4). When Paul wins a prize for a painting at Nottingham castle, she crows 'Hurrah, my boy! I knew we should do it!' (p. 311). For the rest, she is an eager devotee: 'He was going to alter the face of the earth in some way which mattered. Wherever he went she felt her soul went with him. Whatever he felt her soul stood by him, ready, as it were, to hand him his tools' (p. 278). She irons his collars with the rapture of a saint: 'It was a joy to her to have him proud of his collars. There was no laundry. So she used to rub away at them with her little convex iron, to polish them till they shone from the sheer pressure of her arm' (p. 94).[10] Miriam's mother, Mrs Leivers, also goes a way toward making a god of the young egoist: 'She did him that great kindness of treating him almost with reverence' (p. 279). Lawrence describes with aplomb how Miriam idolises Paul; even stealing a thrush's nest, he is so superior that she catches her breath: 'He was concentrated on the act. Seeing him so, she loved him; he seemed so simple and sufficient to himself. And she could not get to him' (p. 280). Here we are treated not only to idealised self-portraiture but to a preview of the later godlike and indifferent Lawrentian male.

Paul is indeed enviable in his rocklike self-sufficiency, basking in the reverence of the bevy of women who surround him, all eager to serve and stroke – all disposable when their time comes. Meredith's *Egoist*[11] is comic exposure; Lawrence's is heroic romance. When Paul first ventures forth into the larger male world, it is again the women who prepare the way for his victories. In a few days he is a favourite of all the 'girls' at Jordan's Surgical Appliances. 'The girls all liked to hear him talk. They often gathered in a little circle while he sat on a bench and held forth to them, laughing' (p. 153). We are told that 'they all liked him and he adored them' (p. 153).[12] But as Paul makes his way at the factory the adoration is plainly all on their side. They give him inordinately expensive oil colours for his birthday and he comes more and more to represent the boss, ordering silence, insisting on speed and, although in the time-honoured manner of sexual capitalism, he is sleeping with one of his underlings, he insists on a rigid division between sex and business.[13]

The novel's centre of conflict is said to lie in Paul's divided loyalty to mother and mistresses. In *Fantasia of the Unconscious*, one of two amateur essays in psychoanalysis in which Lawrence disputes with Freud, he is very explicit about the effect of doting motherhood:

> The son gets on swimmingly... He gleefully inherits his adolescence and the world at large, mother-supported, mother-loved. Everything comes to him in glamour, he feels he sees wondrous much, understands a whole heaven, mother-stimulated. Think of the power which a mature woman thus infuses into her boy. He flares up like a flame in oxygen.

'No wonder they say geniuses mostly have great mothers'.[14] 'They mostly have sad fates,' he immediately adds with the same sort of self-pity one detects in the précis. About its negative effects on sons, he is equally explicit, for there comes a time when the mother becomes an obstacle: 'when faced with the actual fact of sex-necessity', the young man meets with his first difficulty:

> What is he actually to do with his sensual, sexual self? Bury it? Or make an effort with a stranger? For he is taught, even by his mother, that his manhood must not forego sex. Yet he is linked up in ideal love already, the best he will ever know... You will not easily get a man to believe that his carnal love for the woman he has made his wife is as high a love as that he felt for his mother or sister.
>
> (*Fantasia*, pp. 169–70)

What such a sceptic will do instead is outlined fairly succinctly in Freud's 'The Most Prevalent Form of Degradation in Erotic Life', he will make a rigid separation of sex from sensibility, body from soul; he will also develop a rationale to help him through this trying schizophrenic experience. The Victorians employed the lily–rose dichotomy; Lawrence appeared to have invented something new in blaming it on his mother. But the lily/rose division, which Lawrence is so harsh in excoriating in Hardy,[15] is also a prominent feature of *Sons and Lovers*. Miriam is Paul's spiritual mistress, Clara his sexual one – the whole arrangement is carefully planned so that neither is strong enough to offset his mother's ultimate control. Yet the mother too is finally dispensable, not so that Paul may be free to find a complete relationship with either young woman, but simply because he wishes to be rid of the whole pack of his female supporters so that he may venture forth and inherit the great masculine world which awaits him. Therefore the last words of the book are directed, not at the self-sorrowing of Paul's 'nuit blanchs', his 'dereliction' and 'drift towards death', but at the lights of the city, the brave new world which awaits the conqueror.

When Paul wonders incoherently aloud – 'I think there's something the matter with me that I can't... to give myself to them in marriage, I couldn't,... something in me shrinks from her like hell' – just as when Miriam reproaches him, 'It has always been you fighting me off', the reader is expected to follow the précis and the critics and understand that this is all part of the young man's unfortunate Oedipal plight. Lawrence himself attempts to provide a better clue to Paul's type of fixation:

> ... the nicest men he knew... were so sensitive to their women that they would go without them forever rather than do them a hurt. Being the sons of women whose husbands had blundered rather brutally through their feminine sanctities, they themselves were too diffident and shy. They could easier deny themselves than incur any reproach from a woman; for a woman was like their mother, and they were full of the sense of their mother...   (p. 340)

Yet all this well-intentioned puritanism dissolves before the reader's observation of the callowness with which Paul treats both Miriam and Clara. The first girl is, like Paul himself, a bright youngster restless within the narrow limitations of her class and anxious to escape it through the learning which has freed Paul. Less privileged than he, enjoying no support in a home where she is bullied by her brothers and taught the most lethal variety of Christian resignation by her mother, she retains some rebellious hope despite her far more discouraging circumstances. Having no one else to turn to, she asks Paul, whom she has worshipped as her senior and superior, to help her eke out an education. The scenes of his condescension are some of the most remarkable instances of sexual sadism disguised as masculine pedagogy which literature affords until Ionesco's memorable *Lesson*.

Paul has grandly offered to teach her French and mathematics. We are told that Miriam's 'eyes dilated. She mistrusted him as a teacher' (p. 204). Well she might, in view of what follows. Paul is explaining simple equations to her:

> 'Do you see?' she looked up at him, her eyes wide with the half-laugh that comes of fear. 'Don't you?' he cried... It made his blood boil to

see her there, as it were, at his mercy, her mouth open, her eyes
dilated with laughter that was afraid, apologetic, ashamed. Then
Edgar came along with two buckets of milk.

'Hello!' he said. 'What are you doing?'

'Algebra,' replied Paul.

'Algebra!' repeated Edgar curiously. Then he passed on with a
laugh.   (p. 206)

Paul is roused by the mixture of tears and beauty; Miriam is beautiful
to him when she suffers and cringes: 'She was ruddy and beautiful.
Yet her soul seemed to be intensely supplicating. The algebra-book
she closed, shrinking, knowing he was angered' (p. 206).

As she is self-conscious and without confidence (Miriam's sense
of inferiority is the key to her character), she cannot learn well:
'Things came slowly to her. And she held herself in a grip, seemed
so utterly humble before the lesson, it made his blood rouse'
(p. 206). Blood roused is, of course, the Lawrentian formula for
sexual excitement and an erection; the algebra lesson is something
of a symbol for the couple's entire relationship. The sight of Miriam
suffering or humiliated (she later gives Paul her virginity in a delir-
ium of both emotions) is the very essence of her attractiveness to
him, but his response is never without an element of hostility and
sadism. His reaction here is typical: 'In spite of himself, his blood
began to boil with her. It was strange that no one else made him in
such a fury. He flared against her. Once he threw the pencil in her
face. There was a silence. She turned her face slightly aside'
(p. 207). Of course, Miriam is not angry, for one does not get angry
at God. 'When he saw her eager, silent, as it were, blind face, he felt
he wanted to throw the pencil in it... and because of the intensity
with which she roused him, he sought her' (p. 207). The reader is
made uncomfortably aware that 'pencil' is etymologically, and
perhaps even in the author's conscious mind as well, related to
'penis' and both are instruments which have here become equated
with literacy and punishment.

Miriam's aspirations are not respected; her failures are understood to be due to inferiority of talent. There are also a great many
explanations provided the reader that she is frigid, and everything
in her situation would seem to confirm this. Her mother's literal
Victorian repugnance toward sexuality is the most plausible explanation, even without our knowledge of Miriam's debilitating inse-
curity. When she thinks of giving herself to Paul, she foresees
beforehand that 'he would be disappointed, he would find no satis-

faction, and then he would go away'. The chapter where Paul finally brings her to bed is entitled, 'The Test on Miriam'. Needless to say, she does not measure up, cannot pass his demanding examination. So her prediction comes true and Paul throws her away and takes up Clara. Yet the situation is somehow not this simple; even within the muddled explanations of Lawrence's text, it is several times made clear that Paul withholds himself quite as much as does Miriam (p. 339). Her famous frigidity appears to be his excuse. In the classic dilemma of the lily/rose choice Paul has been provided with an alibi which passes responsibility on to his mother.

While the first half of *Sons and Lovers* is perfectly realised, the second part is deeply flawed by Lawrence's overparticipation in Paul's endless scheming to disentangle himself from the persons who have helped him most. Lawrence is so ambivalent here that he is far from being clear, or perhaps even honest, and he offers us two contrary reasons for Paul's rejection of Miriam. One is that she will 'put him in her pocket'. And the other, totally contradictory, is the puzzling excuse that in their last interview, she failed him by not seizing upon him and claiming him as her mate and property.

It would seem that for reasons of his own, Lawrence has chosen to confuse the sensitive and intelligent young woman who was Jessie Chambers[16] with the tired old lily of another age's literary convention. The same discrepancy is noticeable in his portrait of Clara,[17] who is really two people, the rebellious feminist and political activist whom Paul accuses of penis envy and even man-hating, and who tempts him the more for being a harder conquest, and, at a later stage, the sensuous rose, who by the end of the novel is changed once again – now beyond recognition – into a 'loose woman' whom Paul nonchalantly disposes of when he has exhausted her sexual utility. Returning her to her husband, Paul even finds it convenient to enter into one of Lawrence's Blutbruderschaft bonds with Baxter Dawes, arranging an assignation in the country where Clara, meek as a sheep, is delivered over to the man she hated and left years before. The text makes it clear that Dawes had beat and deceived his wife. Yet, with a consummate emotional manipulation, Paul manages to impose his own version of her marriage on Clara, finally bringing her to say that its failure was her fault. Paul, formerly her pupil in sexuality, now imagines he has relieved Clara of what he smugly describes as the 'femme incomprise' quality which had driven her to the errors of feminism. We are given to understand that through the sexual instruction of this novice, Clara was granted feminine 'fulfilment'. Paul is now pleased to make a gift of Clara to her former owner fancying, that as the latter has degenerated through illness and poverty (Paul has had Dawes fired) he ought to be glad of salvaging such a brotherly castoff.

Even before it provides Paul with sexual gratification, the affair offers considerable opportunities for the pleasure of bullying:

> 'Here, I say, you seem to forget I'm your boss. It just occurs to me.'
> 'And what does that mean?' she asked coolly.
> 'It means I've got a right to boss you.'
> 'Is there anything you want to complain about?'
> 'Oh, I say, you needn't be nasty,' he said angrily.
> 'I don't know what you want,' she said, continuing her task.
> 'I want you to treat me nicely and respectfully.'
> 'Call you "sir", perhaps?' she asked quietly.
> 'Yes, call me "sir". I should love it.' (pp. 325–6)

The sexual therapy Clara affords to Paul is meant to be a balm to his virulent Oedipal syndrome, but is even more obviously a salve to his ego. Only in the fleeting moments of the orgasm can the egoist escape his egotism, but Lawrence's account fails to confirm this:

> She knew how stark and alone he was, and she felt it was great that he came to her, and she took him simply because his need was bigger than either her or him, and her soul was still within her. She did this for him in his need, even if he left her, for she loved him.
> (pp. 420–1)

This is a dazzling example of how men think women ought to think, but the book is full of them. By relieving his 'needs' with a woman he rigidly confines to a 'stranger in the dark' category, Paul has touched the great Lawrentian sexual mystery and discovered 'the cry of the peewit' and the 'wheel of the stars' (p. 421).

Having achieved this transcendence through Clara's offices, he finds it convenient to dismiss her. While watching her swim far out at sea during a holiday they have taken together, Paul converts himself into a species of god in the universe before whom Clara dwindles to the proportions of microscopic life:

> 'Look how little she is!' he said to himself. 'She's lost like a grain of sand in the beach – just a concentrated speck blown along, a tiny white foam-bubble, almost nothing among the morning... She represents something, like a bubble of foam represents the sea. But what is *she*. It's not her I care for. (pp. 425–6)

This is an impressive demonstration of how subject diminishes object and having, through his sexual magnetism, reduced this once formidable, independent woman to the level of quivering passion, Paul cannot help but find her a nuisance. What if their affair were discovered at work? We are told that 'She invariably waited for him at dinner-time for him to embrace her before she went' (p. 422). Paul reacts to such attentions like the bumptious young clerk he has become:

> 'Surely there's a time for everything... I don't want anything to do with love when I'm at work. Work's work –'
> 'And what is love?' she asked. 'Has it to have special hours?'
> 'Yes, out of work hours.'...
> 'Is it only to exist in spare time?'
> 'That's all, and not always then.'   (p. 423)

It is Paul's habit to lecture his mistresses that, as women, they are incapable of the sort of wholehearted attention to task or achievement that is the province of the male and the cause of his superiority.

> 'I suppose work can be everything to a man... But a woman only works with a part of herself. The real and vital part is covered up.'
> (p. 487)

The idea seems to be that the female's lower nature, here gently phrased as her 'true nature', is incapable of objective activity and finds its only satisfactions in human relationship where she may be of service to men and to children. Men in later Lawrence novels, men such as Aaron, constantly ridicule trivial female efforts at art or ideas.

Given such views, it is not very surprising that Paul should make such excellent use of women, Clara included, and when they have outlived their usefulness to him, discard them. As Clara is a creature of the double standard of morality, the woman as rose or sensuality, he invokes the double standard to get rid of her, declaring sententiously that 'after all, she was a married woman, and she had no right even to what he gave her' (p. 420). He finally betakes himself to a fustian view of the indissolubility of marriage, decrees that she is completely Dawes's property, and with a sense of righteousness, returns her, no worse, indeed much the better, for wear.

Having rid himself of the two young women, time-consuming sex objects, who may have posed some other threat as well, possibly one of intellectual competition, Paul is free to make moan over his mother's corpse, give Miriam a final brushoff, and turn his face to the city. The elaborate descriptions of his suicidal state, however much they may spring from a deep, though much earlier, sorrow over the loss of his mother, appear rather tacked on in the book itself, as do certain of the Freudian explanations of his coldness as being due to his mother's baneful influence. Paul is actually in brilliant condition when the novel ends, having extracted every conceivable service from his women, now neatly disposed of, so that he may go on to grander adventures. Even here, the force of his mother, the endless spring of Lawrence's sacred font, will support him: 'She was the only thing that held him up, himself amid all this. And she was gone, intermingled herself' (p. 492). But Paul has managed to devour all of mother that he needs; the meal will last a lifetime. And the great adventure of his success will henceforward be his own. 'Turning sharply, he walked toward the city's gold phosphorescence. His fists were shut, his mouth set fast' (p. 492). Paul may now dismiss his mother's shade with confidence; all she had to offer is with him still.

From Kate Millett, *Sexual Politics* (London, 1977), pp. 245–57. First published 1969.

NOTES

[Kate Millett's *Sexual Politics*, from which this account of *Sons and Lovers* is taken, was one of the pioneering texts of Anglo-American feminist criticism. The book became an international bestseller in the early seventies and spurred what has probably been the most far-reaching of modern critical developments. Feminist approaches to literature have evolved in different ways since, as the essays by Diane Bonds and Hilary Simpson in this collection demonstrate, but Millett's was a crucial early voice in discussion of an area which previous generations of critics had noticed sporadically if at all. With hindsight it may be objected that there are aspects of the argument which some readers now question (for an indication of these, see the general Introduction). But her contribution has all the merits of provocation and contains a disturbing account of the ways in which sexual power infiltrates the relations between men and women and the ways in which texts by male writers are organised around their own desires. This selection is extracted from a somewhat longer chapter on Lawrence's work in general. Page references to *Sons and Lovers* are incorporated into the text and are to the Penguin edition edited by Keith Sagar (1981). Ed.]

1. D. H. Lawrence, *The Letters of D. H. Lawrence*, ed. Aldous Huxley (New York, 1932), pp. 78–9.

2. One of the most influential essays on *Sons and Lovers* is Van Ghent's article which describes Paul as the victim of scheming and possessive women. Dorothy Van Ghent, *The English Novel: Form and Function* (New York, 1953).

3. Lawrence rewrote the book at least twice. The final version, like the précis, was done after Frieda had 'explained' Freudian theory to Lawrence.

4. The narrative of William's funeral, especially the moment when the coffin is brought into the house, the class honesty of the Christmas parties, and the daily life of Mrs Morel, are, in my opinion, the most convincing and poignant prose Lawrence ever wrote.

5. 'I was born hating my father: as ever as I can remember, I shivered with horror when he touched me ... This has been a kind of bond between me and my mother. We have loved each other, almost with a husband and wife love ... We knew each other by instinct.' From a letter to Rachel Annand Taylor, 3 Dec. 1910. From the *Collected Letters of D. H. Lawrence*, ed. Harry T. Moore (New York, 1962), vol. 1, pp. 69–70.

6. [Oliver Mellors is the gamekeeper-hero in Lawrence's last novel *Lady Chatterley's Lover* (1928). Ed.]

7. Graham Hough, *The Dark Sun: A Study of D. H. Lawrence*, (New York, 1956), p. 31.

8. Alfred Kazin, 'Sons, Lovers and Mothers,' in the *Viking Critical Edition of Sons and Lovers*, ed. Julian Moynahan (New York, 1968), p. 599.

9. The miners divide their money out of the presence of the women, who are thereby prevented from interfering on the behalf of household and child-rearing expenses.

10. *Portnoy's Complaint* is a healthy antidote to this sort of thing. [A celebrated novel by Philip Roth (1969). Ed.]

11. [George Meredith, *The Egoist* (1879) – a famous satirical study of male selfishness. Ed.]

12. In Lawrence's day, as in ours, it is customary in business to refer to all low-status female employees, i.e. the vast majority of women workers, as 'girls', whatever their age, and some of Paul's co-workers were twice or thrice his age. The custom bears a curious resemblance to that whereby black men are addressed as 'boy' right through to senility.

13. Julian Moynahan, '*Sons and Lovers*: the search for form', in the Viking critical edition of *Sons and Lovers*, p. 569. Like much else in

the novel, Paul's phenomenal success with the factory women appears to be an instance of wish-fulfilment. Lawrence quit a similar factory job 'after a few weeks because the factory girls jeered at him and one day removed his trousers in a dark corner of the storerooms'.

14. D. H. Lawrence, *Fantasia of the Unconscious* (1922) (New York, 1960), p. 159.

15. D. H. Lawrence, 'A Study of Thomas Hardy', reprinted in *Phoenix: The Posthumous Papers of D. H. Lawrence* (New York, 1936).

16. See Jessie Chambers, *D. H. Lawrence: A Personal Record, by 'E.T.'*, 2nd, revised edition (New York, 1965).

17. Actually, Clara is nobody at all. Tradition has it that Lawrence's initiatrix was a Mrs Dax who simply took pity on the lad: 'She took him upstairs one afternoon because she thought he needed it.' Julian Moynahan, *'Sons and Lovers*: the search for form', p. 569.

6

Narrative Evasion in *Sons and Lovers*: A Metaphysical Unsettling

DIANE S. BONDS

One point at which *Sons and Lovers* discloses its dominant metaphysic is the scene in which Paul Morel explains to Miriam Leivers why she likes one of his sketches so much: '"It's because – it's because there is scarcely any shadow in it; it's more shimmery, as if I'd painted the shimmering protoplasm in the leaves and everywhere, and not the stiffness of the shape. That seems dead to me. Only this shimmeriness is the real living. The shape is a dead crust. The shimmer is inside really"' (pp. 202–3). The opposition between an outer dead crust and an inner vitality, between form and substance, presupposes the notion of essence; and Paul's speech grants value to immediacy, spontaneity, vitality – to temporal and spatial presentness. Direct presentation of the 'shimmering' protoplasmic essence of things, were it possible, would be the artistic aim of Lawrence's youthful hero: it is not pine trunks at sunset that Paul paints in another picture, but '"red coals, standing up pieces of fire"', '"God's burning bush ... that burned not away"' (p. 203).

THE FLAME OF IMMEDIACY

The values implied by Paul's speech are kept before the reader of *Sons and Lovers* through the pervasive imagery of light, warmth, and glowing colour.[1] Walter Morel's 'sensuous flame of life, that

89

flowed off his flesh like the flame from a candle' (p. 45), for example, appears to be an index to his full presence to himself and others; in the form of a ruddy glow, the flame permeates those scenes where he works happily at some domestic chore like mending boots: 'he hammered the soft, red-glowing stuff on his iron goose, and made the shape he wanted. Or he sat absorbed for a moment, soldering. Then the children watched with joy as the metal sank suddenly molten, and was shoved against the nose of the soldering-iron, while the room was full of a scent of burnt resin and hot tin, and Morel was silent and intent for a moment' (p. 103).

The powerful association that Part I forges between fire imagery and the 'real living' quality in Morel, the vividness and warmth that inspire such joy in his children, is especially well exemplified by the admirable passage describing Morel's breakfast routine:

> He went downstairs in his shirt and then struggled into his pit-trousers, which were left on the hearth to warm all night. There was always a fire, because Mrs Morel raked. And the first sound in the house was the bang, bang of the poker against the raker, as Morel smashed the remainder of the coal to make the kettle, which was filled and left on the hob, finally boil. His cup and knife and fork, all he wanted except just the food, was laid ready on the table on a newspaper. Then he got his breakfast, made the tea, packed the bottom of the doors with rugs to shut out the draught, piled a big fire, and sat down to an hour of joy. He toasted his bacon on a fork and caught the drops of fat on his bread; then he put the rasher on his thick slice of bread, and cut off chunks with a clasp-knife, poured his tea into his saucer, and was happy.   (p. 63)

Morel's activities centre about the fire, which seems to illumine each object he uses, each action he performs, in turn. As in the passage where Morel mends his boots, 'joy' is a focal word, the confluence of streams of sensory, emotional, and mental details – or to use Lawrence's own words from his definition of 'the art-symbol or art term' – of the 'emotional and passional, spiritual and percep-tional, all at once'.[2] The term 'joy' scarcely registers itself as ab-stract because of the way in which the passage bolsters it with the fond delineation of specific detail. We might in fact expect Mr Morel to sit down to an hour of toast and tea; when he sits down to 'an hour of joy' our delight derives from the unexpected precision of the abstract phrase. And by virtue of its position at the end of a sequence of parallel phrases presenting specific actions and concrete objects, the phrase 'was happy' assumes some of the substance and radiance of the objects themselves.

Part I of *Sons and Lovers* presents us with analogous passages in which the mother's presence makes itself powerfully felt as she engages in domestic tasks that centre about the fire:

> She liked to do things for [William]: she liked to put a cup for his tea and to iron his collars, of which he was so proud. It was a joy to her to have him proud of his collars. There was no laundry. So she used to rub away at them with her little convex iron, to polish them till they shone from the sheer pressure of her arm.   (p.94)

> She spat on the iron, and a little ball of spit bounded, raced off the dark, glossy surface. Then, kneeling, she rubbed the iron on the sack lining of the hearth-rug, vigorously. She was warm in the ruddy firelight. Paul loved the way she crouched and put her head on one side.   (pp. 105–6)

As in the passage describing Mr Morel's breakfast routine, the concrete seems to absorb the abstract, and the abstract seems to absorb the concrete. Emotive terms like 'love' and 'joy' have the force of sensory detail, and concrete terms have the force of symbol. The shine produced by Mrs Morel's proud labour, her warmth in the ruddy firelight – these are physical and emotional at once.

The coalescence of concrete and abstract in such passages might be viewed as the stylistic correlative of presence. The pervasive imagery of heat and light in such passages constitutes an index to the value of the immediate, full emotional presence of the parents. Lawrence is not, however, investing a particular emotion like love with value; rather he is privileging an emotional intensity that betokens immediacy. The value of such intensity becomes plain in an episode like the one in which Mr Morel shears William's baby curls:

> Mrs Morel lay listening, one Sunday morning, to the chatter of the father and child downstairs. Then she dozed off. When she came downstairs, a great fire glowed in the grate, the room was hot, the breakfast was roughly laid, and seated in his arm-chair, against the chimney-piece, sat Morel, rather timid; and standing between his legs, the child – cropped like a sheep, with such an odd round poll – looking wondering at her; and on a newspaper spread out upon the hearthrug, a myriad of crescent-shaped curls, like the petals of a marigold scattered in the reddening firelight.   (p. 50)

The episode presents a violation of Mrs Morel in which the child is shorn of the mother's influence, the 'myriad of crescent-shaped curls, like the petals of a marigold scattered in the reddening firelight'; *her* child, 'cropped like a sheep', is a sacrifice to the father's need to assert himself, to affirm his masculinity by making sure nobody mistakes *his* boy for a 'wench'. The great fire, the excessive heat, the reddening firelight all intimate the emotional conflagration to follow: '[Mrs Morel] gripped her two fists, lifted them, and came forward. Morel shrank back. "I could kill you, I could!" she said. She choked with rage, her two fists uplifted' (p. 50). The light in the scene operates as a kind of textual spotlight, drawing our attention to the scene's significance. Mrs Morel 'remembered *the scene* all her life, as one in which she had suffered *the most intensely*' (p. 51 emphasis added).

In these and many other passages in *Sons and Lovers*, especially in Part I, the coalescence of sensory detail and emotional import, of concrete and abstract, further endorses the values communicated through the imagery of heat and light: the values of immediacy, spontaneity, and presence. Now it is important to recognise that this stylistic trait corresponds to a belief in the symbolic nature of language: a belief in the possibility of a seamless unity of language and truth, image and idea, signifier and signified. Such a belief appears to animate those earnest, 'struggling, abstract speeches' of the adolescent Paul Morel. But when he talks to Miriam about his painting, he does so in a context where the light imagery makes significant counterstatements to the implications of his speech.

Ultimately the scene, which I quote at length, suggests a problematic relation between language and reality, especially reality defined as the 'real living':

> [T]he girl gradually sought him out. If he brought up his sketchbook, it was she who pondered longest over the last picture. Then she would look up at him. Suddenly, her dark eyes alight like water that shakes with a stream of gold in the dark, she would ask:
> 'Why do I like this so?'
> Always something in his breast shrank from these close, intimate, dazzled looks of hers.
> 'Why *do* you?' he asked.
> 'I don't know. It seems so true.'
> 'It's because – it's because there is scarcely any shadow in it; it's more shimmery, as if I'd painted the shimmering protoplasm in the leaves and everywhere, and not the stiffness of the shape. That seems

dead to me. Only this shimmeriness is the real living. The shape is a
dead crust. The shimmer is inside really.'

And she, with her little finger in her mouth, would ponder these
sayings. They gave her a feeling of life again, and vivified things
which had meant nothing to her. She managed to find some meaning
in his struggling, abstract speeches. And they were the medium
through which she came distinctly at her beloved objects.

(pp. 201–2)

The passage constitutes an implicit claim that Paul apprehends
things directly – intuitively and immediately; he sees into the heart
of things, the passage seems to argue, while Miriam is scarcely
capable of seeing what is right in front of her eyes: she needs Paul's
'struggling, abstract speeches' to clarify her world for her and to
enable her to come 'distinctly at her beloved objects'.

But *does* Miriam need to be enlightened by Paul's speeches? The
imagery of light associated with her eyes creates a peculiar ambiguity which unsettles the narrative's implicit claims, an ambiguity as to
the source of light in the scene, the location of the fire. Do her 'dark
eyes alight like water that shakes with a stream of gold' merely
reflect the shimmer in the painting she scrutinises or are they lighted
from within, giving Paul (and us) a glimpse of the 'shimmering protoplasm' of her being? Are her 'dazzled looks' a sign of the fire
within or of her staring too fixedly at a fire without (Paul or his
painting)? Where is 'the real living' – the vital presence – signified by
the imagery of light? The possibility 'that Miriam represents the
"shimmeriness" that is "the real living"'[3] would seem to counter the
claim that she needs Paul's speeches to give her 'a feeling of life'.

But the text says that they 'gave her a feeling of life *again*' (emphasis added). The curious qualification added by *again* opens two
possibilities. It may be that the 'feeling of life' reflected in Miriam's
eyes can only be hers through mediation. She needs Paul's words
not only to grasp the world, but also to come into contact with
herself, to apprehend the flame of life within her or to have that
flame 'kindled'. Or it may be that Paul's speeches actually deaden
Miriam's initial lively intuitive response to the painting (she
ponders his words dumbly with 'her little finger in her mouth').
Then it would be by her own reanimating of the dead husks of his
pronouncements – in other words, by her own imaginative effort –
that things which had meant nothing to her are revivified or given
meaning ('She managed to find some meaning in his struggling, abstract speeches').

The text does not enable us to decide between these two possibilities, but in the case of the second possibility it is worth noticing that Miriam would end up doing what the passage claims Paul does for her: vivifying things that had 'meant' nothing to her. And she would end up doing so in spite of the obstacle that Paul's words (abstract meanings) had posed for her. The passage can be said to differ with itself not only in this suggestion but also in Paul's shrinking from Miriam's 'close, intimate, dazzled looks', an action that contradicts the values implied by his speech, values endorsed by much of the imagery of the novel. In art, the 'real living' essence is what Paul wishes to uncover, but in life, apparently, too close an approach to the 'protoplasm', the 'inside', is a threat. Because he feels threatened, Paul's speech is actually a duplicity: it is a response to Miriam that attempts to evade her, to distract him from her disturbing presence.

In its ambivalence as a verbal gesture, Paul's speech encompasses a dichotomy that characterises the representation of verbal intercourse throughout the novel. On the one hand, the verbal relations of the characters in the novel suggest the power of language to create meaning and unity: the power of language for communication and communion. On the other hand, they also dramatise the ways in which language can be used to subvert communication and prevent intimacy.

NARRATIVE EVASION AND THE EXILE FROM PRESENCE

The text urges us to believe, for example, in the power of speech to create a sense of 'real living' in the Morel family. The Morel children depend upon talk with their mother: 'Nothing had really taken place in them until it was told to their mother' (pp. 101–2). In turn, Mrs Morel depends upon talk with her children, especially Paul, for her sense of having a 'real' life. Each evening after returning from work at Jordan's, Paul tells her the events of his day: 'His life-story, like an Arabian Nights, was told night after night to his mother. It was almost as if it were her own life' (p. 156). And Mrs Morel secures her tie to Paul through talk: 'She waited for his coming home in the evening, and then she unburdened herself of all she had pondered, or of all that had occurred to her during the day. He sat and listened with his earnestness. The two shared lives' (p. 158). Mrs Morel and her children create a common reality through talk.

In Part II of *Sons and Lovers*, sexual metaphors urge the reader to believe in the fecundity of speech between Paul and Miriam. Paul takes 'the most intense pleasure in talking about his work to Miriam. All his passion, all his wild blood, went into this intercourse with her, when he talked and conceived his work. She brought forth to him his imaginations. She did not understand, any more than a woman understands when she conceives a child in her womb. But this was life for her and for him' (p. 256). Miriam not only stimulates Paul's imagination but also leads him to fuller consciousness, to understanding of his intuitions: 'He was conscious only when stimulated. A sketch finished, he always wanted to take it to Miriam. Then he was stimulated into knowledge of the work he had produced unconsciously. In contact with Miriam he gained insight; his vision went deeper' (p. 208).

These passages seem to attribute to Miriam a role similar to that attributed to Paul in the passage where we learn that his 'struggling, abstract speeches', his 'sayings', give Miriam 'a feeling of life' and vivify 'things which had meant nothing to her'. But the suggestion that Paul's speeches beget her vision of the world ultimately subverts our sense of a mutually sustaining or 'fertilising', creative interdependency between the two adolescents. An obvious irony in their intercourse is that it is utterly chaste for much of the novel. In shaping Miriam's vision of the world, Paul also urges her toward a particular view of herself, one dictated by his own psychological requirements. A clinical view of those requirements is likely to conclude that Paul needs Miriam to remain non-sexual, virginal.[4] His efforts to protect her virginity account for Paul's use of speech to avoid communication and to prevent intimacy.

Lawrence uses non-human, almost brutal metaphors to characterise some of Paul's unacknowledged efforts to put words between himself and the ripening Miriam: 'Miriam was the threshing-floor on which he threshed out all his beliefs. While he trampled his ideas upon her soul, the truth came out for him. She alone was his threshing floor. She alone helped him towards realisation' (pp. 283–4). Miriam has good reason for feeling 'as if he were using her unconsciously as a man uses his tools at some work he is bent on' (pp. 284), but despite appearances to the contrary, the pursuit of truth is not Paul's work here. Rather it is the evasion of intimacy on which he is 'bent'.

One never learns much about the religious conflict that Paul is supposed to be suffering, or if or how he resolves it; but one easily recognises that Paul's discomfort as he reads from the Bible has a sexual, not an intellectual, cause: 'he began to falter and get self-conscious. And when he came to the verse, "A woman, when she is in travail, hath sorrow because her hour is come", he missed it out. Miriam had felt him growing uncomfortable. She shrank when the well-known words did not follow' (p. 284). Paul's omission hints that his Bible reading and expounding are calculated to put a distance between him and Miriam – or to distract him from the sexual possibilities thrust upon him by her appearance in this scene: 'She wore a large white hat with some pinkish flowers. It was a cheap hat, but he liked it. Her face beneath was still and pensive, golden-brown and ruddy' (p. 284). She is virginal but tempting.

Paul's most characteristic strategy for avoiding intimacy is not, however, to discuss religion, but rather to make pronouncements about Miriam's personality and feelings. In this respect, at least, *Sons and Lovers* seems accurately to reflect Lawrence's relationship with Jessie Chambers, who writes in *D. H. Lawrence: A Personal Record*, about Lawrence's tendency to 'label' her:

> He declared I was like Emily Brontë, which I resented, feeling it was a false short-cut to understanding me, like sticking a label on. To all my protests he merely shook his head.

> Finally he told me I had no sense of humour, and it occurred to me that if it were so I should be too angry to listen to him ... I could only reveal myself to him by what I was, and his crude groping into the recesses of my personality confused me and made me shut up tight.

> Lawrence had found a new name for me. I was no longer Emily Brontë. I was a pre-Raphaelite woman. I disliked the new label even more than the old one. It made me feel that for him I was becoming less and less of a suffering, struggling human being, and more and more of a mental concept, a pure abstraction.[5]

Paul Morel, of course, labels Miriam, tells her who or what she is, sometimes in terms approximating those mentioned by Jessie Chambers. Paul's claim that Miriam '"is never jolly, or even just all right"' (p. 202) corresponds, for example, to Lawrence's claim that Jessie Chambers 'had no sense of humour'. But furthermore Paul's attempts to give names to Miriam's personality traits and feelings follow a pattern that resembles the one adumbrated in *D. H. Lawrence: A Personal Record*: Paul makes an assertion about Miriam; if she replies, she denies the assertion; Paul then reaffirms his initial statement; even if Miriam has previously attempted to argue, she may now 'shut up tight' – be quieted by chagrin, confusion, or frustration; if she should attempt to argue again, Paul changes the subject.

The following interchange between Paul and Miriam illustrates both the pattern to which I am referring and its Oedipal motivation:

> 'I wish you could laugh at me just for one minute – just for one minute. I feel as if it would set something free.'
>
> 'But' – and she looked up at him with eyes frightened and struggling – 'I do laugh at you – I do.'
>
> 'Never! There's always a kind of intensity. When you laugh I could always cry; it seems as if it shows up your suffering. Oh, you make me knit the brows of my very soul and cogitate.'
>
> Slowly she shook her head despairingly.
>
> 'I'm sure I don't want to', she said.
>
> 'I'm so damned spiritual with you always!' he cried.
>
> She remained silent, thinking, 'Then why don't you be otherwise'. But he saw her crouching, brooding figure, and it seemed to tear him in two.
>
> 'But there, it's autumn', he said, 'and everybody feels like a disembodied spirit then.'   (p. 241)

Paul's need to be so spiritual with Miriam may partly be explained by noting that 'her crouching, brooding' presence recalls a vivid image of his mother that Paul registered as a child: 'kneeling, she rubbed the iron on the sack lining of the hearth-rug vigorously. She was warm in the ruddy firelight. Paul loved the way she crouched and put her head on one side' (pp. 105–6). In the later scene Miriam crouches in the firelight: 'she crouched on the hearth-rug near his feet. The glow was warm on her handsome, pensive face as she kneeled there like a devotee' (p. 239). The parallels in imagery of course provoke the idea that Miriam reanimates one of Paul's revered images of his mother. Whether such a reanimation would lead him to identify Miriam with his mother or to be reminded of his primary loyalty to Mrs Morel, Miriam's crouching on the hearth likely insists upon the young woman's untouchability for him. Yet he blames Miriam for his being 'so damned spiritual with [her] always'.

The coincidence of images suggests the possibility of another reawakening in Paul of childhood memories. In the firelight, his mother made his heart 'contract with love': 'When she was quiet, so she looked brave and rich with life, but as if she had been done out of her rights' (p. 105). In the later scene Paul may feel torn in two because he knows that in a sense Miriam is being done out of her rights. He has devoted his talk, earlier in this scene, to the subject of Clara Dawes, commenting on '"her mouth – made for passion – and the very setback of her throat"' and pointedly admiring '"her skin and the texture of her – and … a sort of fierceness somewhere in her"' (p. 240). No wonder if there is some suffering in Miriam's laughter here. Paul has avoided intimacy with her by anatomising Clara's sensual charms.

Miriam's silent challenge of Paul's judgement of her here – that she is humourless or too serious and too spiritual – provokes from him an evasive generalisation as response. The pattern repeats itself a few scenes later, where he becomes so intense discussing Michelangelo that 'his voice gradually filled her with fear, so level it was, almost inhuman, as if in a trance' (p. 247). Paul rejects Miriam's attempts to curtail his speech, insisting to her that his talk is what her 'unconscious self' really wants from him no matter what her conscious self may say. He continues in 'his dead fashion' '"If only you could want *me*, and not what I can reel off for you"' (p. 247). To Miriam's bitter contradiction – '"I! Why, when would you let me take you?"' – Paul replies with an insincere gesture of defeat: '"Then it's my fault", he said, and, gathering himself together, he got up and began to talk trivialities' (pp. 247–8).

Such a scene repudiates Paul's notion that Miriam wants 'to draw all of him into her' (p. 247), that belief being a reflection of his mother's fear that Miriam '"is one of those who will want to suck a man's soul out till he has none of his own left"' (p. 211).[6] Rather than encouraging Paul's spiritual intensity, his baring of his soul, Miriam tells him to be quiet, to save himself. How remarkable are the deadness and automatism with which he persists in his notions about Miriam, and then his willingness to give up his pursuit of truth as soon as she threatens, with her questions, to spoil his illusions about her!

One could of course cite scenes in which Paul is more overtly manipulative and even abusive. In discussing the scenes in which Paul 'condescends' to teach Miriam, for example, Kate Millett has written that the passages represent 'some of the most remarkable instances of sexual sadism disguised as masculine pedagogy which literature affords until Ionesco's memorable *Lesson*'.[7] But even more disquieting than Paul's verbal behaviour in scenes like those I have discussed and those to which Millett refers is that the pattern of manipulative and ultimately destructive verbal behaviour represented by those scenes not only governs Paul's conversations with Miriam but also more subtly seems to direct the narrative procedure of those sections of Part II that focus on Paul's relationship with Miriam. The specific pattern is this: the narrator makes certain assertions about Miriam; Miriam's dramatised behaviour may constitute an implicit challenge to those assertions, but narrative commentary of a reductive sort repeatedly reasserts the thesis-like statements about Miriam's character or personality. Miriam, like Jessie Chambers, tends to 'shut up tight', and her actions are frequently ambiguous. Consequently, by the end of the novel, the narrator's assertions about her may well hold sway in the reader's mind *even though the text provides evidence enough for a counterinterpretation of her character*.[8]

The narrator presents his major assertions about Miriam's personality in the lengthy 'description' of her that occurs at the beginning of Part II:

> The girl was romantic in her soul. Everywhere was a Walter Scott heroine being loved by men with helmets or with plumes in their caps. She herself was something of a princess turned into a swine-girl in her own imagination. And she was afraid lest this boy, who, nevertheless, looked something like a Walter Scott hero, who could paint and speak French, and knew what algebra meant, and who went by train to Nottingham every day, might consider her simply as the swine-girl, unable to perceive the princess beneath; so she held aloof.
>
> Her great companion was her mother. They were both brown-eyed, and inclined to be mystical, such women as treasure religion inside them, breathe it in their nostrils, and see the whole of life in the mist thereof. So to Miriam, Christ and God made one great figure, which she loved tremblingly and passionately when a tremendous sunset burned out the western sky, and Ediths, and Lucys, and Rowenas, Brian de Bois Guilberts, Rob Roys, and Guy Mannerings, rustled the sunny leaves in the morning, or sat in her bedroom aloft, alone, when it snowed. That was life to her. For the rest she drudged in the house, which work she would not have minded had not her clean red floor been mucked up immediately by the trampling farm boots of her brothers. She madly wanted her little brother of four to let her swathe him and stifle him in her love; she went to church reverently, with bowed head, and quivered in anguish from the vulgarity of the other choir-girls and from the common-sounding voice of the curate; she fought with her brothers, whom she considered brutal louts; and she held not her father in too high esteem because he did not carry any mystical ideals cherished in his heart, but only wanted to have as easy a time as he could, and his meals when he was ready for them.   (pp. 191–2)

As Gavriel Ben-Ephraim has written, 'The commentary is deft, but we should be wary of it – its tone is a bit too confident, its revelations too categorical. Lawrence employs the absolutes he disbelieved in when he portrays the farmgirl whose life is all make-believe and idealisation ...'[9] The passage anticipates a number of assertions about Miriam that are made more pointedly and negatively later in the text: she is overly religious, overly romantic, and overly sensitive; discontented with her lot and not completely in touch with reality, she has an abnormal craving for affection but is unable to get along with others.

When we state the implications of the passage this bluntly, it is easier to see that, as Louis L. Martz has shown, the view of Miriam presented by the narrator at the opening of Part II finds *substantiation* only through the obviously blurred vision of Paul.[10] Before this passage, Miriam appears in the novel only once, in the episode where Paul visits Willey Farm with his mother. The attention there to the girl's ruddiness – to her 'rosy dark face' her 'beautiful warm colouring' (pp. 169–70) – suggests that she, like Walter Morel, embodies 'the dusky, golden softness' of the 'sensuous flame of life' (p. 45). Furthermore, her effort in that introductory episode to overcome her fear of feeding chickens directly from her hand surely suggests that life is really more to her than the trembling passion with which she supposedly indulges in her romantic daydreams: Miriam would like to be considered more 'ordinary' than others consider her, more normal. She is not necessarily 'something of a princess turned into a swine-girl in her own imagination'; quite possibly she is something of a swine-girl turned into a princess by the imaginations of others – her mother, her brothers, and Paul.

Nothing in the text really *dramatises* the excessive religiosity imputed to Miriam. She goes to chapel regularly, as does Paul. She has a picture of Saint Catherine on her bedroom wall, a picture she admires for its dreamy quality. On at least one occasion she wears a rosary that Paul has given her; on another, at age sixteen, she falls to her knees in frightened prayer when she realises that she loves Paul.

These indications of an inclination toward mysticism in Miriam are far outweighed by abundant evidence of mysticism in Paul. He is first attracted to the Leivers family by the mother's religious intensity: 'Everything had a religious and intensified meaning when he was with her. His soul, hurt, highly developed, sought her as if for nourishment' (p. 197). Mrs Leivers's way of exalting 'everything –

even a bit of housework – to the plane of a religious trust' (p. 196) exerts a 'subtle fascination' on him and in effect levels the distinctions he sees when he is with his mother, who is 'logical' (p. 196). Much later in Paul's relationship with Miriam, she finds occasion to be frightened by his mysticism. After first making love with Miriam, Paul lapses from ordinary consciousness into a state where 'life seemed a shadow', where 'night, and death, and stillness, and inaction ... seemed like *being*... . The highest of all was to melt out into the darkness and sway there, identified with the great Being' (p. 348).

Some critics have taken Miriam's horror at the mystic in Paul here as a sign of her supposed sexual repression, but Daniel A. Weiss convincingly argues that Paul's desire to lose individuality through sexual intercourse implies a need for 'the ultimate regression to the child's status with its mother': 'It is Miriam's refusal to allow him to regress to the Nirvana, the paradisal state of the infant, her insistence that he recognises her, that fills him with anguish' and accounts for his breaking off their relationship.[11] It is thus a projection when Paul attributes the torment and ultimate failure of their sexual relationship to Miriam's spirituality; he 'spiritualises' their sexual relationship to satisfy his own psychological needs.

It is not merely by means of narrative commentary that the narrator endorses or recommends Paul's view. The organisation and narrative procedure of some sections of Part II subtly but illegitimately insist upon the truth of certain undramatised generalisations about Miriam. The portion of the narrative treating Paul's relationship with Mrs Leivers illustrates this point. The focus on relationship between Paul and Miriam's mother soon broadens to include Miriam, and to identify the girl with her mother – 'Miriam was her mother's daughter' (p. 197). But the drama that follows only partly justifies the identification.

The scene in which Paul and the two women discover a jenny wren's nest illustrates a cycle of creative interaction that characterises his early relationship with both mother and daughter: both apparently stimulate him into opening his eyes to his surroundings, which he then sketches in words or water colours, thus bringing the object of representation into clearer focus or fuller being for his companions. The pattern is confirmed by a second brief episode in which Paul, accompanied by Miriam, notices some 'celandines, scalloped splashes of gold, on the side of the ditch' (p.198). After

Paul explains to Miriam what he likes about the flowers, the narrator makes the following remarks:

> And then the celandines ever after drew her with a little spell. Anthropomorphic as she was, she stimulated him into appreciating things thus, and then they lived for her. She seemed to need things kindling in her imagination or in her soul before she felt she had them. And she was cut off from ordinary life by her religious intensity which made the world for her either a nunnery garden or a paradise, where sin and knowledge were not, or else an ugly, cruel thing.
> So it was in this atmosphere of subtle intimacy, this meeting in their common feeling for something in Nature, that their love started.
> (p. 198)

In general, before closing with its hazy generality about their common love for nature, the narrative unit moves from an emphasis on the nourishment that Paul receives from Mrs Leivers to a greater emphasis on the nourishment that Miriam receives from Paul – from the 'spell' that the mother casts on Paul to the 'spell' that Paul casts on the daughter.

This movement is characteristic of the presentation of Miriam throughout in that any *exposure* of Paul's needs is usually balanced or outweighed by *analysis* of Miriam's. The summation – 'she stimulated him into appreciating things thus, and then they lived for her' – seems irreproachable since the pattern has been dramatised twice in swiftly succeeding scenes. Yet why the apparently irrelevant insistence that Miriam is anthropomorphic? Nothing that preceeds this sentence indicates how she is anthropomorphic (and in fact it is slightly unclear whether she stimulates Paul *because* she is anthropomorphic or *even though* she is). Paul, one might argue, has taken an *anthropomorphic* view of the flowers in observing that they seem '"to be pressing themselves at the sun"' (p. 198), but applied to Miriam the term seems a label designed to certify in advance Paul's accusations that Miriam is always wheedling the soul out of things, begging them to love her (p. 274) – in other words, that she wants to possess things and to possess them on her own limited, personal terms. But this view is most likely dictated by Paul's attachment to his mother.[12] So is much else in the paragraph that I have quoted.

If Miriam needs 'things kindling in her imagination or in her soul' before she feels she 'has' them, so does Paul, as the next paragraph but one reveals: 'But Mrs Leivers and her children were almost his disciples. They kindled him and made him glow to his work, whereas his mother's influence was to make him determined, patient, dogged, unwearied' (p. 198). Perfectly characteristic of the narrator's 'shiftiness' in this section of the novel is the way in which similar conditions or needs in Paul and in Miriam are presented in terms of an opposition; the emphasis on Miriam's passive need as a contrast to Paul's inspired activity subtly prepares the way for one of Paul's cruellest accusations: '"You aren't positive, you're negative. You absorb, absorb ... because you've got a shortage somewhere"' (p. 274). Again, Mrs Morel's view.

What I have called the narrator's shiftiness also emerges in the way in which action trails off into summation which, in turn, shades off into commentary only superficially related to the preceding drama. The transitions in the paragraph that presents Miriam as anthropomorphic, needy, excessively religious, hypersensitive and alienated ('And then ... and then ... And she was... .') may create the effect that facts are being related in terms of causality; but actually they are a clue to the looseness of the connections that the paragraph proposes. The narrator here mimes Paul's verbal behaviour by piling assertion upon assertion, each one less concretely objectified than the preceding one and therefore insisted upon all the more strongly; when the narrator turns from the subject of Miriam's isolation in her 'religious intensity' to conclude, 'So it was in this atmosphere of subtle intimacy, this meeting in their common feeling for something in Nature, that their love started' (p. 198), what we hear is something like the voice of Paul: the Paul who, torn in two by Miriam's brooding presence, trails lamely off, '"But, there, it's autumn ... and everybody feels like a disembodied spirit then "' (p. 241). Yet it is very important to recognise that because narrative commentary of the sort I have been analysing here *precedes* those conversations where Paul most blatantly fails to respond to Miriam's timid confrontations, his failures, when they do occur, are the less noticeable: they do not necessarily seem failures at all because they repeat a pattern of discourse familiar to the reader from exposure to ostensibly reliable narrative.

The narrative may in other ways deflect the reader's attention from an alternate picture of Miriam that emerges from the action. There is, for example, the abruptness with which the narrator, who can change the subject as fast as Paul can, shifts scenes. A sequence from 'Lad-and-Girl Love' will illustrate this point. In one scene Miriam shows Paul a swing in the cow shed. Fascinated by the spectacle of his swinging, she is still frightened when he swings her. The sexual yearning that lies beneath Miriam's fear becomes pronounced when she watches Paul swing one more time and realises that she 'could never lose herself so... . It roused a warmth in her. It were almost as if he were a flame that had lit a warmth in her whilst he swung in the middle air' (p. 201).

At this point, in a manner that merely mimes a genuine transition, the narrator abruptly shifts the focus from Miriam's incipient sexuality to Paul's intimacy with the rest of the family: 'And gradually the intimacy ... concentrated for Paul on three persons – the mother, Edgar, and Miriam... . [T]o Miriam he more or less condescended, because she seemed so humble' (p. 201). The next scene, the one in which Paul makes his 'struggling, abstract speech' about the 'shimmeriness' of the painting that she admires, seems calculated to illustrate Miriam's humility, the inferiority of her perceptions, and her consequent willingness to defer to Paul's opinion. But the exposure of the 'real living' quality in Miriam, through the light imagery in the passage, may account for the fact that the next scene comes across almost as a revision of the preceding one, as a new version designed to insist more effectively on Miriam's liabilities.

There Paul preaches to Miriam about another of his paintings – and about herself: she is '"never jolly, or even just all right"'; she is '"different inside"', not '"ordinary"' (pp. 202–3). While Paul argues, he finds that Miriam gets 'so near him' that he experiences 'a strange roused sensation' (p. 202). The emotional logic of the rather abrupt transition to the next scene – 'Then sometimes he hated her' (p. 202) – is clear; the words present a fair summary of Paul's reaction to any situation where he begins to respond sexually to Miriam. Yet the reader may not fully apprehend the logic, for the scene introduced by these words attempts to forward the idea that Miriam has an abnormal craving for love. When she kneels and folds her little brother in her arms, she provokes Paul to 'suffering because of her extreme emotion': 'Her intensity, which would leave no emotion on a normal plane, irritated the youth into a frenzy' (p. 203).

It is of course ironic that Paul should become frenzied because of her intensity, but the text acknowledges the irony of his overreaction only by a sudden shift to commentary about the lack of flexibility and life in Miriam's body. It is as if the narrator realises that he has revealed Paul's fear of the intensity and openness of Miriam's emotions and attempts to cover – or at least compensate for – the exposure by changing the subject. But in so doing, the narrator contradicts the judgement implied by the scene he has left behind. There Paul wishes that Miriam possessed 'his mother's reserve' (p. 203); here she is subtly indicted because '[t]here was no looseness or abandon about her' (p. 203). The scene that 'illustrates' Miriam's restraint shows Paul teaching her to overcome her fear of jumping over stiles. Yet she learns relatively easily while Paul is 'frightened' not only by 'a kind of ecstasy' that blazes in her eyes as they run down the fields, but also by the 'wild "Ah!" of pain' with which she precedes her safe landing on the other side of the stile. Once again the scene shifts, this time to one introduced by the words 'She was very much dissatisfied with her lot' (p. 204). The narrator revives the princess-turned-swine-girl thesis.

Thus the narrative both does and does not allow the action to reveal character. Scene after scene presents evidence of Paul's limitations and Miriam's potentialities, but shifts in the focus of the narrative are conducted in such a way that they may prevent the reader from assimilating and judging the evidence, evidence that contradicts the narrator's *assertions* about Miriam.[13] Such a failure is especially likely since the lengthy dissection of Miriam's character which appears at the beginning of Part II may predispose the reader to accept Paul's view of Miriam. That predisposition may in turn continually be reinforced by narrative commentary of a reductive, simplifying sort: 'He was now about twenty-three years old, and, though still virgin, the sex instinct that Miriam had over-refined for so long now grew particularly strong' (p. 310). One might call this the view of a self-deceived neurotic couched in the language of an objective, authoritative onlooker who has access to all the facts.

By means of this pose of authority the narrator of *Sons and Lovers* attempts to shape the reader's view of Miriam much as Paul, in his conversations with her, attempts to shape her view of herself. The view proposed is that Miriam is passive and non-sexual – undesiring and undesirable. In closing his eyes to Miriam's sensuous appeal and embracing this view of her, Paul forfeits 'the glow', 'the shimmer', the 'real living' quality in her. To the extent that Miriam allows herself to assent to this view, she allows herself to be victimised by Paul. And to the extent that readers allow this view to command their unquestioning assent, they allow themselves to be victimised by the narrator of *Sons and Lovers*.

The narrative procedures I have scrutinised here may be viewed as constituting a psychological 'game' of the sort that contemporary psychologists have categorised and anatomatised, a game of the sort in which we find only three basic game roles: victim, persecutor, and rescuer.[14] One might argue that critics of *Sons and Lovers* have played all three roles. The most prominent of the 'persecutors' is Mark Schorer, whose response to the narrative difficulties of the novel is not merely the claim (in his famous essay, 'Technique as Discovery') that Lawrence failed to master the past through 'technique', but also a more general judgement that is telling in its harshness: 'The handling of the girl, Miriam, if viewed closely, is pathetic in what it signifies for Lawrence, both as man and artist.'[15]

Other critics have attempted to 'rescue' the novel from such charges by giving the problems Schorer saw names like 'technique' and 'form'. One such rescuer, Louis L. Martz, argues that ambiguities and contradictions in the presentation of Miriam constitute a successful 'technique' for rendering the ambivalence of the protagonist.[16] Though Martz is surely correct in much of his carefully detailed treatment of Miriam, one must question his smooth way of disposing of the novel's presentation of that character by claiming that 'it works'. After all, for many perspicacious readers who have accepted the narrator's view as accurate and objective – Keith Sagar, Dorothy Van Ghent, Mark Spilka, and even at times Kate Millett – that presentation does not 'work' in the way Martz means: it does not succeed in reflecting the patterns of the hero's distorted consciousness.[17]

In a more recent essay than Martz's, Daniel R. Schwarz has argued that 'the discrepancies between the narrator's interpretations and ours create a tension that becomes an intrinsic part of the novel's form.'[18] To justify this view, Schwarz must emphasise the value of the reader's participation 'in the agonising but wonderfully exciting *aesthetic* process by which an author tries to give shape and unity to his recent past'. But *Sons and Lovers* does not really invite the kind of participation that Schwarz mentions; the text in many ways – for example through the narrator's pose of authority – discourages and frustrates any such participation as well as readers' attempts to counterpoise their own interpretations to the narrator's.

A striking feature of the articles by Martz and Schwarz is the poor fit between their highly insightful analyses of detail and their dubious generalisation, a problem that curiously duplicates the narrative split that is a central concern here. The difficulty seems to arise in these two articles – as does Schorer's almost moralising judgement of *Sons and Lovers* – from viewing the novel in formalistic terms. The formalistic demand for unity or organic wholeness may lead critics, on the one hand, to make harsh, moralising judgements about a book that they may on many grounds love to read and teach; or it may tempt them, on the other hand, to smooth over the jagged edges of Lawrence's treatment of the past, in the process stretching notions of form and technique beyond recognition in an effort to make them fit the often recalcitrant facts of the novel.

If, as Calvin Bedient has suggested, the 'burgeoning of psychology into metaphysics is the hidden drama of *Sons and Lovers*',[19] then a more just appreciation of the novel may arise from suspending formalistic preconceptions about fiction and viewing the novel in epistemological terms. From such a perspective, the text may be seen as one in which the point of view reflects a belief in the possibility of truth and in the power of language to uncover the truth; at the same time, however, the narrative 'facts' presented in the text undermine those beliefs. That is, the story the narrator undertakes to tell deconstructs the belief in an unambiguous relation between language and truth. Like Paul's story, the narrator's quest for truth dramatises an exile from a world of clarity, immediacy, and presence to one of obscurity, deferment, and absence.

From Diane S. Bonds, *Language and the Self in D. H. Lawrence* (Ann Arbour, MI, 1988), pp. 29–44.

NOTES

[There are a number of influential developments in modern criticism which run through Diane S. Bonds' account of the narrative method and sexual politics of *Son and Lovers*, and her argument can be understood as developing from that of Louis Martz in essay 4 and Kate Millett in essay 5. Like Martz, Bonds is interested in the ways in which the narrative voice is infiltrated by Paul's biases. But she is more far-reaching in her conclusions. Whereas Martz sees *Sons and Lovers* as a text which recovers its balance in Chapter 12, for Bonds the novel is, in this respect, unstable throughout. As a result, though she accepts Millett's political outlook, she rejects her way of seeing *Sons and Lovers* as a schematic, chauvinist fable. For Bonds, the instability of the novel's language makes it a much more complex and contradictory text and her analysis of this is guided by the the poststructuralist philosopher Jacques Derrida, as indicated in the general Introduction. This selection is extracted from a somewhat longer chapter. Page references to *Sons and Lovers* are incorporated into the text and are to the Penguin edition edited by Keith Sagar (1981). Ed.]

1. In writing of 'the glow of something wonderful and lost, remembered vividly', John A. Taylor singles out this feature of the novel as a source of the book's power over readers: 'The Greatness of *Sons and Lovers*', *Modern Philology*, 71 (1974), 382.

2. Quoted in Arnold Armin, *D. H. Lawrence and America* (London, 1958), p. 40.

3. Daniel R. Schwarz, 'Speaking of Paul Morel: Voice, Unity and Meaning in *Sons and Lovers*', *Studies in the Novel*, 8 (1976), 264.

4. Daniel A. Weiss's psychoanalytic discussion of 'Miriam's contribution to the composite mother image' leads to this conclusion as does Shirley Panken's discussion of Paul's 'fear of separation from and loss of his mother'. See Weiss, *Oedipus in Nottingham: D. H. Lawrence* (Seattle, 1962), pp. 48–9, and Panken, 'Some Psychodynamics in *Sons and Lovers*: A New Look at the Oedipal Theme', *Psychoanalytic Review*, 61 (1974–5), 580.

5. Jessie Chambers, *D. H. Lawrence: A Personal Record by 'E.T.'* (New York, 1965), pp. 130, 132, 145.

6. See Louis L. Martz, 'Portrait of Miriam', in *Imagined Worlds*, ed. M. Mack and I. Gregor (London, 1968), pp. 342–68. [Reprinted in this volume, pp. 49–73. Ed.] Also Weiss argues that in such passages Paul attributes to Miriam 'his [own] infantile need for love' (Weiss, *Oedipus in Nottingham*, p. 52).

7. Kate Millet, *Sexual Politics* (New York, 1969), p. 253. [Reprinted in this volume, p. 81. Ed.]

8. Martz's essay presents that counterinterpretation at length. Though Gavriel Ben-Ephraim does not cite Martz, his reading overlaps with Martz's – and mine – in a number of details. See Gavriel Ben-Ephraim, *The Moon's Dominion: Narrative Dichotomy and Female Dominance in Lawrence's Earlier Novels* (London, 1981).

9. Ben-Ephraim, *The Moon's Dominion*, p. 90.

10. Martz 'Portrait of Miriam', see above pp. 54–7.

11. Weiss, *Oedipus in Nottingham*, p. 53.

12. Martz, 'Portrait of Miriam', see above p. 59.

13. Cf. Ben-Ephraim, 'The careful examination of narrative dichotomy in Lawrence reveals that the function of the teller is to subvert the integrated identity of woman and evade the failed autonomy of man' (p. 23).

14. Claude M. Steiner, *Scripts People Live: Transactional Analysis of Life Scripts* (New York, 1975), pp. 181–5.

15. *Hudson Review*, 1 (1948), 77. Less harsh in his judgement of Lawrence is Emile Delavenay, whose criticisms of *Sons and Lovers* and whose defences of Jessie Chambers place him in the same camp as Schorer. See Delavenay, *D. H. Lawrence: The Man and His Work: The Formative Years: 1885–1919*, trans. Katherine M. Delavenay (Carbondale, 1972), pp. 119–21, and 'D. H. Lawrence and Jessie Chambers: The Traumatic Experiment', *D. H. Lawrence Review*, 12 (1979), 305–25.

16. Martz, 'Portrait of Miriam', see above p. 57.

17. See, for example, Dorothy Van Ghent, *The English Novel: Form and Function* (New York, 1967), pp. 298, 309–10; Mark Spilka, *The Love Ethic of D. H. Lawrence* (Bloomington, IN, 1955), pp. 45, 51, 56, 66; Keith Sagar, *The Art of D. H. Lawrence* (Cambridge, 1966), pp. 25–32; Millett, *Sexual Politics*.

18. Schwarz, 'Speaking of Paul Morel', 255.

19. Calvin Bedient, *Architects of the Self: George Eliot, D. H. Lawrence, and E. M. Forster* (Berkeley, CA, 1972), pp. 118. The 'metaphysics' Bedient has in mind, however, centres on an ideal of 'mythic self-dispersal' in 'a universe of apotheosised feeling' (p. 118) which enters Lawrence's writing with this novel.

7

Lawrence and Feminism in *Sons and Lovers*

HILARY SIMPSON

Lawrence's views on the suffragist movement are most clearly set out in the *Study of Thomas Hardy*. He admires the crusading spirit of the suffragists – 'certainly the bravest, and, in the old sense, most heroic party amongst us' – and sees their aims as 'worthy and admirable'.[1] But for Lawrence they are only measures to patch up a social system which is already rotten at the core. He is committed to complete social and spiritual revolution, not piecemeal reform, 'Law can only modify the conditions, for better or worse, of that which already exists' (p. 405). And for Lawrence the revolution must start with the individual. He locates the sickness of the twentieth century 'in the heart of man, and not in the conditions' (p. 406).

> Is there any great sickness in the body politic? Then where and what is it? Am I, or your suffragist woman, or your voting man, sex-whole and money-healthy, are we sound human beings? Have we achieved to true individuality and to a sufficient completeness in ourselves? Because, if not – then, physician, heal thyself. (p. 405)

The language and imagery are traditional, almost identical to Matthew Arnold's in *Culture and Anarchy*, the opposition between the organic and the mechanical being central to Lawrence's argument. Law is a 'very, very clumsy and mechanical instrument' which cannot 'empower the poppy to flower' (p. 405). The poppy is Lawrence's chosen symbol throughout the Hardy study for the full achievement of individuality and wholeness, bursting into a flame-coloured flower that serves no utilitarian purpose, but somehow connects us with the unknown, 'the colour and shine of being' (p. 406). Lawrence declares that, if the women's movement aligned itself with spiritual revolution rather than with mechanical reform, 'I should be glad, and the opposition would be vital and intense, instead of just flippantly or exasperatedly static'. Then 'the woman's movement would be a living human movement' (p. 405). This position towards the suffrage movement was a common one. Wyndham Lewis's *Blast*, for example, praised the suffragists' energy – 'You and artists are the only things (you don't mind being called things?) left in England with a little life in them'[2] – but it too questioned the goal of legal reform that the suffrage movement set itself. It was also a view shared by many women. The *Freewoman's* contributors and readers would have sympathised with Lawrence's stance.

In Lawrence's early work there are several characters, some major, others minor, who consciously identify themselves or are identified by others as feminists. (Their actual connection to one of the suffrage organisations may be tenuous or even non-existent, but because of the contemporary predominance of the suffragists they tend to be associated with them.) But the issues raised by feminism are reduced to personal problems to which individual answers must be sought. *The White Peacock* stresses the inability of the individual to do anything about social injustice or misery. When, towards the end of the novel, George taxes Lettie with 'the monstrous denial of life to the many by the fortunate few', she replies: 'Of course ... I have read Mr Wells and Mr Shaw ... But what can I do? I think the rich have as much misery as the poor, and of quite as deadly a sort. What can I do?'[3] George persuades Lettie into a brief flirtation with socialism and feminism but she confesses to her brother Cyril that 'at the bottom, you know, ... I don't care for anything very much except myself'.

> I have had such a lark. Two or three times I have been to the Hollies; to socialist meetings. Leslie does not know. They are great fun. Of course, I am in sympathy with the socialists, but I cannot narrow my eyes till I see one thing only. Life is like a large, rather beautiful man who is young and full of vigour, but hairy, barbaric, with hands hard and dirty, the dirt ingrained. I know his hands are very ugly, I know his mouth is not firmly shapen, I know his limbs are hairy and brutal: but his eyes are deep and very beautiful. That is what I tell George.
>
> (pp. 377–8)

Lettie makes the usual objections to the people involved in the socialist and feminist movements; they are comic, narrow-minded,
over-earnest and cannot see life whole.

> The people are so earnest, they make me sad. But then they are so di-
> dactic, they hold forth so much, they are so cock-sure and so narrow-
> eyed, they make me laugh. George laughs too. I am sure we made
> such fun of a straight-haired goggle of a girl who had suffered in
> prison for the cause of women, that I am ashamed when I see my
> 'Women's League' badge. (p. 378)

Socialism and feminism remain abstract notions in *The White
Peacock* because the situations which might show why they are
necessary are missing from the novel. The brief tour of the London
slums in Part 3 which is supposed to inspire George's socialism is
hardly convincing; Lettie's discontent is shown to have something
to do with her role as a woman, her lack of any real occupation,
her choice of husband and her self-abnegation in marriage and
motherhood, but this is left vague. The only strategy for coping
with these discontents that is implied in the novel is Emily's escapist
return, through her marriage to a solid farmer, to the simple life.

> Emily had at last found her place, and had escaped from the torture
> of strange, complex modern life. She was making a pie, and the flour
> was white on her brown arms. She pushed the tickling hair from her
> face with her arm, and looked at me with tranquil pleasure, as she
> worked the paste in the yellow bowl. (p. 404)

In the portrayal of Mrs Morel and Clara in *Sons and Lovers*, on the
other hand, many of the material conditions of women's oppression which inspired the women's movement are revealed. The close
attention to detail and the faithful rendering of the texture of everyday existence give us a vividly accurate picture of working-class life.
But the predominant note is still the personal one. Miriam's
reflection on land nationalisation is typical of the novel's emphasis
on individualism: 'After all ... if the land were nationalised, Edgar
and Paul and I would be just the same' (pp. 207–8). Organisations
which exist to promote social change come to be seen as irrelevant;
it is suggested that the problems with which they are concerned can
be solved on a personal level.

Feminism first enters *Sons and Lovers* in the form of the
Women's Guild to which Mrs Morel belongs. The details are those
of Mrs Lawrence's own life.

> When the children were old enough to be left, Mrs Morel joined the Women's Guild. It was a little club of women attached to the Co-operative Wholesale Society, which met on Monday night in the long room over the grocery shop of the Bestwood 'Co-op'. The women were supposed to discuss the benefits to be derived from co-operation, and other social questions. Sometimes Mrs Morel read a paper.
>
> (pp. 89–90)

Mrs Morel enjoys these meetings; they give her an opportunity to use her intelligence and her sharp tongue in discussion, and she gains a new stature in the eyes of her children: 'It seemed queer to the children to see their mother, who was always busy about the house, sitting writing in her rapid fashion, thinking, referring to books, and writing again. They felt for her on such occasions the deepest respect' (p. 90). The Guild is, however, resented by many of the men.

> The Guild was called by some hostile husbands, who found their wives getting too independent, the 'clat-fart' shop – that is, the gossip-shop. It is true, from off the basis of the Guild, the women could look at their homes, at the conditions of their own lives, and find fault. So the colliers found their women had a new standard of their own, rather disconcerting.[4]   (p. 90)

The Guild no doubt served a useful purpose in raising the political awareness of ordinary women. But the whole of the first part of *Sons and Lovers* proclaims that to the problem of Mrs Morel's life the Co-operative Women's Guild can at best be only a very superficial answer; as John Goode says, 'She has her own ways out – significantly through the moral vitality of the chapel and the feminist emancipation of the Women's Guild, but these are only consolatory'.[5] The novel itself, however, portrays with unusual clarity the economic basis of women's oppression. In Chapter 1, pregnant with her third child, Mrs Morel reflects that 'she could not afford to have this third. She did not want it' (p. 40). The first quarrel between the Morels centres on Mr Morel's financial deceit; he has not paid for the furniture, and rents the house in which they live rather than owning it as Mrs Morel has been led to believe. Mrs Morel is constantly at a disadvantage because of her lack of financial independence. Logically, she cannot even upbraid her husband for stealing money from her purse when she is totally dependent on him to give her that money in the first place. In their battles Morel exploits this position as breadwinner and Mrs Morel's essential powerlessness is revealed.

'The house is filthy with you,' she cried.

'Then get out on it – it's mine. Get out on it!' he shouted. 'It's me as brings th' money whoam, not thee. It's my house, not thine. Then ger out on't – ger out on't!'

'And I would,' she cried, suddenly shaken into tears of impotence. 'Ah, wouldn't I, wouldn't I have gone long ago, but for those children.' (p. 58)

But despite her poverty, Mrs Morel will not stoop to being exploited by the out-work which the other women of her area undertake: 'I'd starve before I'd sit down and seam twenty-four stockings for twopence ha'-penny' (p. 66).

There is little that Mrs Morel can do to change the fundamental condition of her life. With Clara the position is different. Being childless, she has been able to leave her husband and work for her living, and feminism has given her the support she needs to do this. At first it seems as if the fact of Clara's feminism is going to be of some importance in the novel. In the end it is not – but its fate is interesting. Clearly, some important areas of Clara's character, including her feminism, are based on Alice Dax, who recognised herself in the character.[6] For example, Clara's indifference to Paul's art reflects the lack of support for his writing that Lawrence sensed in Mrs Dax, who was in favour of strict naturalism. 'How can a woman whose feelings flow in such straight canals follow me in my threadings, my meanderings, my spurts and my sleepings!' he complained.[7] On the other hand, Clara's blonde statuesque beauty seems to be inspired by Frieda, and Jessie Chambers asserted that at least one incident in the novel, the visit of Paul and Clara to the theatre, was based on an outing that Lawrence and Frieda made to see Shaw's *Man and Superman* in Nottingham.[8] But this episode could just as easily have been based on a visit that he and Alice Dax made to see *Electra* at Covent Garden, after which he wrote to Jessie saying that he had 'very nearly' been unfaithful to her.[9]

Clara has left her husband because of his cruelty and unfaithfulness. She is an 'advanced woman', a suffragette who 'talks on platforms', having been in the women's movement before her marriage and remained active in it for ten years. Through her, Paul gets 'into connexion with the Socialist, Suffragette, Unitarian people in Nottingham' (p. 317). But Clara is an individualist too, and her feminism has led her, not to identify with other women, but to separate herself from them – 'she considered herself as a woman apart, and particularly apart, from her class' (p. 323) – a stance based to some extent on the education she has been able to obtain through the women's movement. Her feminism begins by intriguing Paul, but later it comes to seem an irrelevance, and towards the end of the novel we hear less about it. Eventually the novel implies that Clara's dissatisfaction has nothing to do with women's oppression, but concerns only her own sexuality and the necessity for her to come to terms with it; she has only to 'sort herself out', not to try to change society. Her affair with Paul is a kind of therapy, enabling her finally to return to her husband. Because the novel betrays little appreciation of the relationship between the personal and the political, the character of Clara lacks coherence; her feminism, one of the major characteristics through which she is first defined for us, ultimately has no real function. Kate Millett has remarked on the shifting centre of Clara's character:

> Clara ... is really two people, the rebellious feminist and political activist whom Paul accuses of penis envy and even man-hating, and who tempts him the more for being a harder conquest, and, at a later stage, the sensuous rose, who by the end of the novel is changed once again – now beyond recognition – into a 'loose woman' whom Paul nonchalantly disposes of when he has exhausted her sexual utility.[10]

The contradictory attitudes towards Clara can be examined in more detail. When Paul first meets Clara she is out walking with Miriam, and he is struck by her confident assertiveness, which contrasts strongly with Miriam's shrinking manner. Clara is a 'striking woman', the way she holds herself is 'defiant', she is tall, with 'handsome shoulders', and (most provocative of all) she is not in the least interested in Paul. Miriam notices the response to this apparent challenge: 'The girl saw his masculine spirit rear its head' (p. 237). As Clara remains indifferent to Paul, his perception of her becomes more complex. We get a closer picture of her, moving in to her face. Her grey eyes are still only 'scornful', but Paul becomes conscious of her sensual appeal – 'a skin like white honey' – and then, in observing her mouth, uses the sensuality to cast doubt upon the integrity of the scornfulness, implying that Clara is out of touch with her body and its needs: 'a full mouth, with a slightly lifted upper lip that did not know whether it was raised in scorn of all men or out of eagerness to be kissed, but which believed the former' (p. 237). Paul obviously believes the latter, and the implication that Clara should be concerned with her own unacknowledged sexuality rather than with a spurious feminism is already present. We are then distanced from Clara again: we are told that she is dressed in simple clothes, the sort of thing, one imagines, that Alice Dax used to wear, inspired by the Dress Reform movement; but these are not to Paul's taste, and again he casts doubts upon Clara's motives in choosing them, suggesting that it is an affectation: 'a sort of slightly affected simple dress that made her look rather sack-like' (p. 237). Paul then dismisses her economic status and her aesthetic sense – 'she was evidently poor, and had not much taste' – reminding himself that 'Miriam usually looked nice' (p. 237).

It is only when Paul has parted from the two women that he remembers that 'Mrs Dawes was separated from her husband, and had taken up Women's Rights. She was supposed to be clever' (p. 238). This interests Paul, and the next time he and Miriam meet they discuss Clara. Miriam sympathises with her feminism and thinks her a 'fine woman', but Paul refuses to call her 'fine' except in so far as her physical traits are concerned. He praises the 'fight' and aggressiveness he sees in her face, her 'fierceness', 'her skin and the texture of her'. 'Look at her mouth – made for passion – and the very set-back of her throat' (p. 240). For Paul, Clara's assertiveness and her physical presence are an indication of *sexual* energy.

After a quarrel, Miriam invites Paul to meet Clara at Willey Farm. Miriam has already concluded that Paul's interest in Clara is physical, and has arranged a test (a parallel to his 'Test on Miriam') to see whether he will succumb to what she views as the temptation offered by the older woman. This time Paul starts by meeting Clara on her own ground: 'You were at Margaret Bonford's meeting the other evening' (p. 286). The discussion about Margaret Bonford – who is obviously Margaret Bondfield, at that time president of the Adult Suffrage League[11] – is a good example of the way in which Paul consistently ignores the larger implications of feminism and reduces it to a series of personal issues.

> 'I think she's a lovable little woman,' said Paul.
> 'Margaret Bonford!' exclaimed Clara. 'She's a great deal cleverer than most men.'
> 'Well, I didn't say she wasn't,' he said, deprecating. 'She's lovable for all that.'
> 'And, of course, that is all that matters,' said Clara witheringly.
>
> (p. 287)

Paul and Clara are talking about different women. Clara is talking about Margaret Bonford the public figure, while Paul can only see

Margaret Bonford the character, the individual, the human phenome-non, divorced from any political or social context. Both points of view are equally limited, and while it has been argued that Clara's is a 'rigid, egocentric isolation which has cut her off from all warm contact with others, leaving her with minimal verbal, intellectual, po-litical, and commercial relationships only',[12] Paul's individualism and emphasis on 'character' tend to blind him to any larger relationships than the personal. He cannot see why Clara speaks 'as if he were responsible for some deprivation which Miss Bonford suffered' (p. 287), because of his failure to grasp that he exists not only as an individual but also as a member of various social groups and classes.

> 'Well,' he said, 'I thought she was warm, and awfully nice – only too frail. I wished she was sitting comfortably in peace –'
> '"Darning her husband's stockings,"' said Clara scathingly.
> 'I'm sure she wouldn't mind darning even my stockings,' he said. 'And I'm sure she'd do them well. Just as I wouldn't mind blacking her boots if she wanted me to.' (p. 287)

Paul thus reduces the larger issue of women's rights to the level of domestic give-and-take (he obviously has in mind his relationship with his mother). Clara will not answer him and he, offended, escapes to meet Edgar, with whom he debates the question of whether Clara is really a man-hater.

Later Mrs Leivers makes some allusions to Clara's personal life and her separation from her husband. Paul, although he character-istically chooses to be left with the women instead of going out with the men, deflates the intimate, serious mood of their conversation.

> After tea, when all the men had gone but Paul, Mrs Leivers said to Clara:
> 'And you find life happier now?'
> 'Infinitely.'
> 'And you are satisfied?'
> 'So long as I can be free and independent.'
> 'And you don't *miss* anything in your life?' asked Mrs Leivers gently.
> 'I've put all that behind me.'
> Paul had been feeling uncomfortable during this discourse. He got up.
> 'You'll find you're always tumbling over things you've put behind you,' he said. Then he took his departure to the cowsheds. He felt he had been witty, and his manly pride was high. He whistled as he went down the brick track. (pp. 289–90)

One of the principal ways in which Paul avoids the issues raised by feminism is by appealing to the principle of chivalry. He has already shown a tendency to cope with the world of the factory by romanticising it:

> Connie, with her mane of red hair, her face of apple-blossom, her murmuring voice, such a lady in her shabby black frock, appealed to his romantic side.
> 'When you sit winding,' he said, 'it looks as if you were spinning at a spinning-wheel – it looks ever so nice. You remind me of Elaine in the "Idylls of the King".' (p. 153)

Knowing that one reminds the office boy of a medieval heroine does not necessarily make factory work any more pleasant, and when, later, Paul sees Clara, now back at Jordan's, as a Penelope at her loom, she is impatient. 'Would it make any difference?' she retorts (p. 235).

Paul explicitly sets up this chivalric attitude in opposition to Clara's feminism. On the day of Clara's visit to Willey Farm, when he and Clara and Miriam are out walking, he remarks:

> 'What a treat to be a knight ... and to have a pavilion here.'
> 'And to have us shut up safely?' replied Clara.
> 'Yes,' he answered, 'singing with your maids at your broidery. I would carry your banner of white and green and heliotrope. I would have "W.S.P.U." emblazoned on my shield, beneath a woman rampant.'
> 'I have no doubt,' said Clara, 'that you would much rather fight for a woman than let her fight for herself.'
> 'I would. When she fights for herself she seems like a dog before a looking-glass, gone into a mad fury with its own shadow.'
> 'And *you* are the looking-glass?' she asked, with a curl of the lip.
> 'Or the shadow,' he replied. (p. 290)
> [White, green and purple were the WSPV colours.]

The tone here is light and jocular, but two different concepts are discernible. Paul suggests that in setting themselves up against men, women gain nothing, since the lots of the two sexes are bound up with each other – man is woman's own 'shadow'. Clara takes his reference to the mirror differently, suggesting that what he really means is that man is the mirror in which woman must seek her true self.

It is when Clara reveals emotion or weakness that Paul starts to feel attracted towards her and not merely interested. After the above exchange, he looks at her and sees that 'the upward lifting of her face was misery and not scorn' and 'his heart grew tender' (p. 291). Paul's reaction is not unlike that of Everard Barfoot in *The Odd Women* or Basil Ransome in *The Bostonians*. It is one of the stock responses to an emancipated woman – a desire to experience the thrill of seeing a strong and independent person betray her vulnerability. When Paul visits Clara's home and sees her jennying lace, he reflects that 'she seemed denied and deprived of so much. And her arm moved mechanically, that should never have been subdued to a mechanism, and her head was bowed to the lace, that never should have been bowed' (p. 321). When Paul asks her about her work – 'Is it sweated?' – Clara tries to make a general point: 'More or less. Isn't *all* women's work? That's another trick the men have played, since we force ourselves into the labour market' (p. 320). But Paul sees it as an individual problem that he can solve by getting Clara back to Jordan's. When Clara's mother reveals that Clara would in fact like to return to the factory but is too proud to ask, Paul experiences 'a thrill of joy, thinking that she might need his help' (p. 321), and when she is back at work he asserts his rights as her supervisor in order to break down her aloofness and reserve.

Not only does Paul want to see Clara betray her vulnerability; he also wants her to acknowledge that her feminism is misguided and that what she really needs is sexual fulfilment. When Paul, Miriam and Clara, still on their walk, encounter Miss Limb and her horse, Paul gets the hint for which he has been waiting. The three discuss Miss Limb's eccentricity and her obsessive attachment to her stallion. Clara suddenly says, 'I suppose ... she wants a man', which silences the other two (p. 293). This comment amounts to an admission from Clara that she is aware of the consequences of sexual deprivation, and it arouses Paul's excitement. Later, speaking about Clara to Miriam, he uses the same phrase that the three of them had previously used about Miss Limb – 'something's the matter with her' (p. 294) – implying that the answer in Clara's case is the same: she too wants a man. From this point onwards Clara's aggressive feminism, which had previously intrigued Paul, is less important. In his eyes it comes increasingly to signify that she is not bound by traditional sexual morality. When Mrs Morel asks 'Won't people talk?' about his liaison with Clara, he says: 'They know she's a suffragette, and so on ... she lives separate from her husband, and talks on platforms; so she's already singled out from the sheep, and, as far as I can see, hasn't much to lose' (pp. 377–8).

Much has been written about Paul's 'baptism of fire in passion' with Clara and the relative success or failure of this relationship and the relationship ,with Miriam. In fact the relationships are similar in many crucial respects and both can be said to 'fail' for essentially the same reasons. Paul conceives of sexual desire as something impersonal: 'a sort of detached thing, that did not belong to a woman' (p. 235), 'the great hunger and impersonality of passion' (p. 346). With Miriam, who is reluctant and apprehensive about their love-making, 'he had always, almost wilfully, to put her out of count, and act from the brute strength of his own feelings' (p. 352). Paul resents the fact that Miriam insists on calling him back to 'the littleness, the personal relationship' (p. 346). Clara is more sexually experienced, and not afraid of physical passion in the way that Miriam is; and for a brief spell it seems as if she and Paul experience what he calls 'the something big and intense that changes you when you really come together with somebody else' (p. 381). This crucial epiphany is usually located in the scene of their love-making by the canal, when the following famous passage occurs.

> He lifted his head, and looked into her eyes. They were dark and shining and strange, life wild at the source staring into his life, stranger to him, yet meeting him; and he put his face down on her throat, afraid. What was she? A strong, strange, wild life, that breathed with his in the darkness through this hour. It was all so much bigger than themselves that he was hushed. They had met, and included in their meeting the thrust of the manifold grass-stems, the cry of the peewit, the wheel of the stars.   (p. 421)

Lawrence writes: 'It was for *each of them* an initiation and a satisfaction ... There was a verification which they had had *together*' (p. 421; my emphasis). But the text itself gives the lie to this, for the satisfaction is Paul's; the impersonal satisfaction of an impersonal urge, the only difference being that Clara has not resisted in the way that Miriam did.

> But then Clara was not there for him, only a woman, something he loved and almost worshipped, there in the dark. But it was not Clara, and she submitted to him ... she took him simply because his need was bigger either than her or him, and her soul was still within her.
>   (pp. 420–1)

On the very next page it is admitted that 'Clara was not satisfied' (p. 421). From this point on Paul begins to feel more and more that 'his experience had been impersonal, and not Clara', while she feels the need for a more personal intimacy, needs to feel surer of Paul the individual – 'he might leave her' (p. 422). The relationship in effect reaches the same impasse that the relationship with Miriam had reached. Paul complains, 'Love should give a sense of freedom, not of prison. Miriam made me feel tied up like a donkey to a stake. I must feed on her patch, and nowhere else. It's sickening.' To Clara's retort, 'And would *you* let a *woman* do as she likes?', Paul says 'Yes' (p. 428). He is genuinely unconcerned about the double standard of morality. He does not expect his women to be 'pure'. In fact, Paul's concept of sexual love, which originates as a way of coping with his own psycho-sexual problems but ends up as a *desideratum*, really *requires* that both partners should be equal, free to plunge together into the baptism of fire. Yet this theory ignores the facts – the fact, for example, that women have traditionally had a larger stake in love and marriage than men, and that society expects the sexual relationship to be a woman's principal mode of self-definition. Clara tells Paul that she feels as if she has been asleep all her adult life (p. 334); but instead of helping her to wake up, Paul consigns her to further unconsciousness. At one point in the novel he says, 'To be rid of our individuality, which is our will, which is our effort – to live effortless, a kind of conscious sleep – that is very beautiful, I think' (p. 349). In one sense Paul's rejection of the double standard is a radical gesture, but on the other hand it displays considerable insensitivity to the real position of women in society. Talking of the fact that Clara's husband is living openly with another woman, Miriam says to Paul:

> 'Don't you think a position like that is hard on a woman?'
> 'Rottenly hard!'
> 'It's so unjust!' said Miriam. 'The man does as he likes –'
> 'Then let the woman also,' he said.
> 'How can she? And if she does, look at her position!'
> 'What of it?'
> 'Why, it's impossible! You don't understand what a woman forfeits –'
> 'No, I don't. But if a woman's got nothing but her fair fame to feed on, why, it's thin tack, and a donkey would die of it!' (p. 380)

At times it almost seems as though feminism must be kept in the background of the novel as much as possible because continual reference to it would remind the reader that the sexes are *not* equally placed in society, and this in turn would upset Paul's theory of sexuality.

Clara's return to her husband at the end of the novel is singled out by Kate Millett as a particularly glaring example of *Sons and Lovers'* anti-feminism.

> Returning her to her husband, Paul even finds it convenient to enter into one of Lawrence's Blutbruderschaft bonds with Baxter Dawes, arranging an assignation in the country where Clara, meek as a sheep, is delivered over to the man she hated and left years before. The text makes it clear that Dawes had beat and deceived his wife. Yet, with a consummate emotional manipulation, Paul manages to impose his own version of her marriage on Clara, finally bringing her to say that its failure was her fault. Paul, formerly her pupil in sexuality, now imagines he has relieved Clara of what he smugly describes as the 'femme incomprise' quality which had driven her to the errors of feminism. We are given to understand that through the sexual instruction of this novice, Clara was granted feminine 'fulfilment'. Paul is now pleased to make a gift of Clara to her former owner fancying, that as the latter has degenerated through illness and poverty (Paul has had Dawes fired) he ought to be glad of salvaging such a brotherly castoff.[13]

As usual in Millett's criticism, there is much of a certain kind of truth in this savage account of the end of the novel. But the text also makes it clear that Clara has never really abandoned her commitment to Baxter. She refuses to divorce him, and 'in some way ... she held herself still as Mrs Dawes' (p. 428). It is clear that this is because in the relationship with Baxter, he is the dependent one, he needs her, and she is therefore in control. When Paul asks her about her husband, 'Do you feel as if you belonged to him?', she replies, 'No ... I think he belongs to me' (p. 427). Like Miriam, Clara will not, in the last issue, submit to Paul, will not choose the relationship in which she would have to be the subordinate partner.

> She did not love Dawes, never had loved him; but she believed he loved her, at least depended on her ... She had received her confirmation; but she never believed that her life belonged to Paul Morel, nor his to her ... They would have to part sooner or later. Even if they married, and were faithful to each other, still he would have to leave her, go on alone, and she would only have to attend to him when he came home. But it was not possible. Each wanted a mate to go side by side with.   (pp. 428–9)

This account of the dissolution of her affair with Paul seems to me convincing enough. The real blow to feminism in *Sons and Lovers* lies in Lawrence's failure to connect the personal world of individual development to the larger material forces which have a part in shaping it. Because it has no anchor in the material world, Clara's feminism comes to seem merely an extraneous detail, as though Lawrence had given her a squint. The personal world of feeling is explored so well in *Sons and Lovers* that we are liable to forget that there is any other; that, although we see Clara at work, we never see her 'talking on platforms' or doing any of the other things that we are assured she takes part in as a suffragist.

From Hilary Simpson, *D. H. Lawrence and Feminism* (London, 1982), pp. 26–37.

NOTES

[Hilary Simpson's account of *Sons and Lovers*, taken from a longer chapter on representations of 'The Suffragist' in his fiction, is an example of another direction taken by feminist criticism. She is interested in the attention *Sons and Lovers* gives to topical feminist issues in the period of the campaign to gain women the vote. In particular, Simpson focuses on Clara, whose feminism Paul finds a stimulating provocation and who has been relatively neglected in recent work. Simpson establishes the historical situation and brings out Lawrence's ambivalent attitudes towards feminist and other political issues. Her analysis complicates judgements about gender issues in the novel by asking us to understand what happens in an historical context somewhat different from our own. Her partial revision of some other feminist accounts of Paul, for example that of Kate Millett, opens up the discussion of this important dimension of the novel. Page references to *Sons and Lovers* are incorporated into the text and are to the Penguin edition edited by Keith Sagar (1981). Ed.]

1. D. H. Lawrence, *Phoenix: The Posthumous Papers of D. H. Lawrence*, ed. Edward D. MacDonald (London, 1936), p. 404.

2. *Blast*, 1, 20 June 1914, p. 151.

3. D. H. Lawrence, *The White Peacock*, ed. Alan Newton (Harmondsworth, 1982), pp. 375–6. Subsequent page references will appear in the text.

4. Cf. 'Sometimes my husband rather resented the teachings of the Guild ... The Guild, he said, was making women think too much of themselves.' *Life As We Have Known It, by Cooperative Working Women*, ed. Margaret Llewelyn Davies (London, 1931), p. 48.

5. John Goode, 'D. H. Lawrence' in *The Sphere History of English Literature: The Twentieth Century*, ed. B. Bergonzi (London 1970). [Reprinted in this volume – see p. 127 Ed.]

6. Emile Delavenay, *D. H. Lawrence: L'Homme et la genèse de son oeuvre*, 2 vols (Paris, 1969), vol. 2, p. 671.

7. Letter to Blanche Jennings, 13 May 1908, *The Collected Letters of D. H. Lawrence*, ed. Harry T. Moore (London, 1962), vol. 1, p. 53.

8. Delavenay, *D. H. Lawrence*, vol. 2, p. 671.

9. Ibid., p. 703.

10. Kate Millett, *Sexual Politics*. (New York, 1969). [Reprinted in this volume, p. 83. Ed.]

11. In 1923 Margaret Bondfield became one of the first women MPs and in 1929 the first woman cabinet member.

12. Charles Rossman, '"You are the Call and I am the answer": D. H. Lawrence and Women', *D. H. Lawrence Review*, 8 (1975), 266.

13. Millet, *Sexual Politics*. See above, pp. 83–4.

8

Individuality and Society in *Sons and Lovers*

JOHN GOODE

It is not until we reach *Sons and Lovers* that the complexities we have already noted[1] can be made coherent through the extension of consciousness within the protagonists so that they become subjects of these complexities and not merely objects. It is, of course, an auto-biographical novel based on Lawrence's own early life, but he was right, I think, to describe it as 'impersonal'. It is impersonal in the sense that the subjectivity portrayed in the novel belongs to the characters and not to the narrator. Paul Morel's experience is fully coherent with the world realised in the novel so that its coincidence with Lawrence's own is only a matter of curiosity. The more so since the subjectivity of Paul is a highly representative one in that it is responsive to the most salient features of the historical world which the novel imitates. Of course, Paul is, like Lawrence himself, very exceptional, but it is only possible to realise the whole truth of a social world in fictional terms through the exceptional man; the character who is realised as 'average' in a novel can only, obviously, embody part of the truth. *Sons and Lovers* is a portrait of the artist as a young man, but the portrait can stand for the landscape of a whole epoch. In the particular case, it is the only way in which the epoch can be recorded since it is an epoch in which the working class emerges not as a *class* but as separate individuals nurtured and uprooted by the new aspirations and opportunities offered by the post-Forsterian 'democracy'.

This is not merely a matter of content but of the very form of the novel. We are to witness the working-class boy emerge as the bourgeois hero, and whereas *The White Peacock* fails because Lawrence tries to engraft an impersonal range of experience onto a personal form, *Sons and Lovers* is a great novel because it *transforms* a bourgeois fictional structure. It is a structure in which the education of the hero is achieved by exile from the sanctity of childhood and a search for values 'in the world' which will accommodate his integrity and aspirations. The major instances in English are *Tom Jones* and *Great Expectations*, but in them the hero's exile is external: neither Tom nor Pip have a family. *Sons and Lovers* is a radical transformation because the exile cannot be referred to that particularity; on the contrary, Paul's exile takes place from within the family because the family itself is changing. We are aware, above all, not of personal and moral alienation from a static ideal, but of a series of cultural dislocations which create and demand a particular kind of personal integrity.

The first of the major cultural dislocations is within the marriage of Paul's parents. Mrs Morel has been drawn into her marriage by the need for an experience which is outside the narrow confines of her puritan upbringing. But it is not simply an atavistic reaction against her father's middle-class values: the 'dusky, golden softness' of Morel's 'sensuous flame of life' belongs to his working-class vitality but she sees it in terms of expansion, 'something wonderful, *beyond her*' (p. 45), so that as soon as it is seen, socially, as a contraction of possibilities, she becomes alien to their relationship. She can only relate to Morel subjectively, trying to change him into her own image: 'His nature was purely sensuous, and she strove to make him moral, religious. She tried to force him to face things. He could not endure it – it drove him out of his mind.' The verbs, 'strove', 'tried to force' are verbs of an imposed will bent on assimilating their relationship to the social reality, and later in the chapter, we have 'She was almost a *fanatic* with him... she tortured him... she destroyed him.' Lawrence later felt that he had been unfair to Morel, but the reservations are clearly there. It is not that the novel is unbiased – it cannot be because it is to be about Paul's experience, and Paul is given his identity by his mother – it is that the bias is registered as a socially specific mode of consciousness. For Mrs Morel's vision of the family is culturally specialised: she sees it as an agent of social mobility. In a significant glimpse into her past, Lawrence relates how she rebuked her middle-class lover,

John Field, for not going into the ministry because of his father's pressure to go into business with 'But if you're a *man?*' But she now recognises that being a man is not enough, and it is significant that she calls Barker, Morel's colleague, more of a man than her husband although he is physically inferior – she can admire Barker for his ability to do his wife's chores when she is in childbirth. She sublimates a primarily physical relationship into a socially efficient one. Of course, Morel *is* a failure and it is to sentimentalise the novel to see him as the embodiment of 'organic' values. Nevertheless through him we are alerted to other possibilities of family life. Paradoxically, the most fully realised moment is immediately after he has been definitively placed in relation to his own family: 'He was an outsider. He had denied the God in him' (p. 102). The phrase adumbrates a kind of social Calvinism – through his irresponsibility he has cut himself off from grace, from the elect in a world of social mobility (it comes after he has found out that Paul has won a prize). But immediately after this we see him inaugurating a Ruskinian idyll in which he unites the whole family through their participation in craftsmanship. This is followed by Paul's most transparently unfair rejection of Morel during his illness. Lawrence is not being inconsistent here. Morel *can* achieve an organic relationship with his family, but it is only vestigial: through his lack of moral rigour in a world of social hardship, he is beyond redemption. But so too is the kind of familiar order his craftsmanship memorialises, for it is marginal to his real social life as a miner. We are in a world in which the only meaningful social unit is Mrs Morel's vision of the family.

It is this vision which gives Paul his identity. The process of individuation for Mrs Morel is through her family. She has her own ways out – significantly through the moral vitality of the chapel and the feminist emancipation of the Women's Guild, but these are only consolatory. The very naming of Paul is an act of self-realisation. She takes the baby to the cricket field, a pastoral island in the urban prison of her marriage, and thinks of her child as a future Joseph, an exile who was to save a nation and his own family. Momentarily, she offers him up to the sun, to the impersonal world from whence he came, but immediately she clutches him to her bosom, to the particular individuality of his origin. And she names him Paul, after the only theologian her father had felt sympathy with, so that it means a recommitment to his narrow individualistic values – St Paul, of course, is not, like Joseph, the hero of social salvation, but of personal salvation. Paul's exile is not to be that of the leader, but of the isolate self. After she has settled Paul in his first job, Mrs Morel thinks proudly of her two sons: 'Now she had two sons in the world. She could think of two places, great centres of industry, and feel that she had put a man into each of them' (pp. 143–4). 'In the world', in this context, is a cliché of the self-made man, and when Paul tells her about his work, it is like a tale from the *Arabian Nights* to her: she discovers her 'beyond' in the modern social structure, the centre of industry.

Of course, the realisation of Paul's relationship with his mother is much more profound than such an analysis suggests. It is not just the product of the social order, it is the creation of a cultural world, a new human group. Soon after Morel has asserted his relatedness through craftsmanship, we have a glimpse of a pastoral communion between Mrs Morel and Paul when she brings home a small cornflower dish from the market – it is a reminder that Mrs Morel is not just putting sons into the world, but creating a home for them to return to. But there is a very significant difference between this moment and the vestigial communal sense created by Morel: the latter has to do with work, the former with a possession. It is as though the tenor of the relationship between Paul and his mother were communal, but its inevitable vehicle of expression acquisitive. What most immediately identifies Paul as separate from the environment he confronts, is the class-based social mediation which has been granted to him by his mother's aspiration (Mr Braithwaite drops his 'h' 's, Mr Jordan is 'common'). It is this context which we should bear in mind when we consider the quality of their relationship. Inevitably it has been seen as Oedipal, and certainly it is very close: they sleep together, Mrs Morel fights bitterly to prevent Paul from being taken from her by Miriam, and Paul finally has to kill her to release himself from her possessive will. But the most overtly Oedipal moments in the novel, when they both go to Paul's interview, and when they go for the first time to Leiver's farm are surely too conscious to suggest repression: 'She was gay, like a sweetheart' (p. 134); 'You *are* a fine little woman to go jaunting out with' (p. 166). Moreover, the language, 'sweetheart', 'jaunting', suggests less sexual love than the *social appearance* of sexual love. And the episodes in which it occurs confirm this: both are scenes in which Paul, through his mother, establishes emancipation from the world of Morel. In the first he is going to get a job which takes him out of the mining community, and, in the second, mother and son are going to re-establish a friendship made through the chapel in the rural world beyond the industrial reality of Bestwood (we note that Mr Leivers is another of the men Mrs Morel feels she could have been a good wife to). The texture of Paul's relationship with his mother is one of an intimacy so close that the only adequate means of expression are sexual, but its structure is throughout one of social aspiration. The texture is determined by the distortion of family relationships caused by the cultural dislocation between the working man and his aspiring wife. When Morel is ill because of an accident caused by his own irresponsibility, Paul talks of himself as the man in the house. Later, when Mrs Morel complains that her husband is giving her less money because Paul is working, Paul grows angry because she still cares about Morel's responsibility when he feels that it is a role that he himself can fill. Whatever quasi-sexual relationship there is between Paul and his mother, is thus determined by the changing structure of the family. The Morel family is neither an organic cultural unit because of the father's inability to establish its unity, nor is it straightforwardly an agent of social mobility because Mrs Morel cannot establish her own kind of relationship with Morel, and has to replace it first by her relationship with William and then with Paul. And Paul becomes so meaningful because he is able, like Barker and like John Field, to be, for his mother, more than a man – a domestic help-meet (the bread-baking emphasises this, and when Paul burns the bread it is the first crisis in the break-up of the relationship) and a social success. We shall only make the mistake of devaluating Mrs Morel if we trivialise her social aspiration with a word like snobbery. Lawrence knows better, and he is able to dramatise the deep inner pressure towards individuation in terms of the social structure with such force that it is right to say, as Keith Sagar puts it, that Paul is 'kindled into life by his mother'. But we shall not make sense of the rest of the novel unless we are aware as well that this does not mean that Mrs Morel's values are a moral norm. For it is a particular mode of life that she kindles Paul into – one determined by the Congregational Chapel and the bourgeois vitality of her father. And it is a mode that Paul has to grow beyond to rediscover his manhood.

This is a simplifying formula and the process which the novel records involves a more complex evolution than it suggests. In the first place, we have a second cultural dislocation, between Paul and his mother, which is dramatised through his relationship with

Miriam, the girl he meets at the farm to which his mother takes him. It is predicted already on their walk to the farm. Paul rhapsodises over the pit in the distant landscape while his mother remains utilitarian about it. Paul's response is aesthetic and humanist – 'There's a feel of men about trucks' (p. 167) – and it is the kind of romanticism which only those who are already emancipated from the social world of the colliery can afford. The individuality conferred on Paul by his mother and his job takes him beyond both, into the realm of the ideal. The exact process is made clear by a comment on his art: 'From his mother he drew the life-warmth, the strength to produce; Miriam urged this warmth into intensity like a white light' (p. 208). The distinction here is not very different from the distinction Arnold makes between Hebraic and Hellenic qualities which differentiate middle-class and cultured virtues – the distinction between energy and light. At the climax of the quarrel with his mother about Miriam, Paul overtly defines his estrangement in cultural terms: '*You* don't care about Herbert Spencer' (p. 266). Unlike the dislocation between Paul's parents, however, this is not one of class but of generation: 'You're old, mother, and we're young.' The movement from Mrs Morel to Miriam, and the shift of interest from the work at Jordan's to the pastoral world of the farm, is a development from one phase of middle-class aspiration to another – from a desire for self-realisation by 'facing' the world (society) to a desire for self-realisation in a world that the self shapes, a movement, in the vocabulary Lawrence knew from Schopenhauer, from will to idea.

It is a move to an inevitable but expendable phase in Paul's individuation. The relationship with Miriam is doomed because it does not release Paul from his mother's subjectivity but merely offers a rival imposed image, more narrowly subjective because it is more atrophied from reality. Miriam remains coiled up against reality and she uses Paul to mediate with the world without coming to terms with it. In scene after scene we see that Miriam relates only to a specialised image of Paul, always having to make allowance for a 'lower' (physical and societal) self which has nothing to do with her. Finally she has to hand over this lower self to Clara Dawes, and it is after Paul has showered Clara with flowers in a dionysiac ritual which transcends Miriam's dualistic being that Paul begins to grow free of his mother in more than intellectual terms. He takes her to Lincoln Cathedral and there realises that his 'woman' is old, and cannot share his life any more. At the end of the same chapter the Morel family disintegrates – Paul's sister gets married, his younger brother finds a sweetheart and Paul begins to feel that he must leave. After this, the novel becomes a painful record of Paul's search for a total self which is neither his mother's nor Miriam's.

Nor Clara's. Through her he finds 'a baptism of fire in passion', but this is a single rite which is unrepeatable and transitional. Their relationship is simply, for Paul, a release from other subjectivities. It involves, above all, a descent from the other-created self into oblivion: 'She wanted to soothe him into forgetfulness' (p. 420). During their first walk together, they watch the landscape merge into a oneness which obliterates all the individual life of Paul into indistinctness. Only an impersonal relationship can release him from personality. But, of course, Clara is a person – 'About *me* you know nothing' (p. 430) – and as soon as she demands a personal relationship, he has to retreat into the dualism of a day-time world of work, and a night-time of love. The womanliness of Clara gives Paul his manhood, makes possible for him the kind of vitality that had once existed between his parents and that had momentarily flickered up again in the scene immediately before Paul's quarrel with his mother about Miriam as a reminder both of what the parents might have achieved and of what Paul's relationship with Miriam necessarily leaves out of account. But Clara has to return to her husband for a permanent relationship, and, indeed, it is only through her husband that Paul can discover his manhood as an isolate being. Fighting him, he becomes aware of himself as a machine, and after the fight, Lawrence habitually calls him not Paul, but Morel. In a more meaningful sense than before he has become the man in the house, for he has learnt the physical intimacy and separateness which is part of the vitality of manhood but which for the collier is confined to the mine. Clara and Baxter give Paul not a new self, but a knowledge of the impersonality and separateness that a truly self-created being must take account of. Both his mother and Miriam remain to be fully rejected in the closing pages of the novel. And, paradoxically, in releasing himself from their subjectivities through a brutal self assertion, he becomes more nakedly bourgeois than either – a kind of Robinson Crusoe figure, stripped of everything but the shut fist and the clenched mouth, turning his back on the proffered oblivion in his mother's death 'towards the faintly humming, glowing town'. For all that it is a journey towards self discovery, there is no discovery at the end of *Sons and Lovers*, for Paul asserts his selfhood, not like Robinson

Crusoe in an unknown land, but in the old world of men and the city: it is merely a renewed determination to go on 'quickly' without the mediating relationships offered by the subjectivities around him. And this takes us to the heart of the Lawrencean moral agony: for in the escape from the dualistic 'personality' which transforms its vitality into an energy within the social machine or tries to hold it apart in mystic evasion, the hero has to recognise more radically his own apartness. The intensity and completeness with which this agony is realised seem to me to make *Sons and Lovers* a very great novel indeed, and although we must see *The Rainbow* and *Women in Love* as necessary progressions following it, it is surely a futile and academic exercise to try to arrange a hierarchy of value between the three.

From John Goode, 'D. H. Lawrence' in *The Sphere History of English Literature: The Twentieth Century*, ed. Bernard Bergonzi (London, 1970), pp. 117–24.

NOTES

[This extract from John Goode's long essay on Lawrence's whole career pursues arguments which have been influential in recent discussion of *Sons and Lovers* by critics interested in what the novel has to say about social issues. Relating a reading of the novel's unsettled form to what many take to be an ambivalence on Lawrence's part towards Paul's fortunes, Goode argues that the novel does not establish a consistent formal pattern: it is sometimes grittily realistic, sometimes turbulently symbolic, sometimes delicately pastoral and so on. This instability reflects Paul's dislocating journey from the community of Bestwood to different cultural territory. In this, there is perhaps a gain in education and independence but, in another and perhaps dominant sense, the novel also presents an experience of isolation and loss. Like Graham Holderness (essay 9) and Scott Sanders (essay 10), Goode's analysis is influenced by the work of Raymond Williams and all of these critics see the historical significance of *Sons and Lovers* as one in which experiences of transition are described and explored. Page references to *Sons and Lovers* are incorporated into the text and are to the Penguin edition edited by Keith Sagar (1981). Ed.]

1.   [In an earlier part of his essay, Goode argued that Lawrence's fiction before *Sons and Lovers* is beset by a number of problems and complexities including the lack of an authentic narrative voice and the contradiction between the pastoral idiom of *The White Peacock* and its occasional scenes of urban realism and 'unassimilated violence'. Ed.]

9

Language and Social Context in *Sons and Lovers*

GRAHAM HOLDERNESS

Sons and Lovers (1913) is known familiarly as an autobiographical or a biographical novel. The descriptions have different implications: (1) that the novel is Lawrence's autobiography, a narrative based on the events of his life and designed to interpret that life; (2) that the novel is primarily a work of fiction, which takes its form from the conventions of biography; a novel composed around the life of an individual character, rather than the series or group of characters which had been the norm of Victorian novels. Both these implications are true, but need to be clearly separated. It is too easy to think of *Sons and Lovers* as a direct transcription of Lawrence's life, which has no purpose other than to make sense of that life. Lawrence thought of the book in this way: 'One sheds one's sicknesses in books – repeats and presents again one's emotions, to be master of them.'[1] Considered in this light, the novel is a kind of 'confessional autobiography in the third person'; and the extensive biographical writing on Lawrence tends to treat *Sons and Lovers* in this theoretically naïve and reductive way. It is true that the events of the novel are very close indeed to the circumstances of Lawrence's childhood and adolescence, but the novel still has to be considered as a work of fiction which has some of the 'impersonality' and deliberate, calculated construction of art. In fact while working on the first draft (while the novel was still *Paul Morel*) Lawrence described it in this way: 'It will be a novel – not a florid prose poem, or a decorated idyll running to seed in realism – but a restrained, somewhat impersonal novel.'[2] This combination of intensely personal material with an impersonal manner of presentation is probably the best way of characterising *Sons and Lovers*. Keith Sagar defines the issue well:

> The autobiographical and intensely personal subject-matter contributes much.... But *Paul Morel* will be a 'somewhat impersonal novel' – not an autobiography, however well done. There is ample evidence in *Sons and Lovers* that Lawrence is now mature enough to create the real, without being slavishly naturalistic; that form is more important to him than autobiographical accuracy; and that his distinctive use of imagery carries a great deal of the novel's significance. Too close a concentration on the autobiographical, the personal problem, has persistently led critics away from the novel's value as a work of art towards its interest as a case-history.[3]

The combination can be seen in the novel's opening sequence. Gāmini Salgādo has described this introduction as a conventional opening – the description of a familiar and intimately known landscape, common in George Eliot, Hardy and elsewhere.[4] But apart from the fact that the landscape is one that hadn't figured very prominently in the English novel before Lawrence – certainly not at such close quarters – the manner of presentation is strikingly new. The newness can be seen in this language; and this feature has been ably demonstrated by Richard Hoggart in a comparison between the openings of *Sons and Lovers* and E. M. Forster's *A Passage to India*.[5] Whereas Forster's passage, like the majority of nineteenth-century writing, 'expresses the manners and tones of the educated middle class', Lawrence's voice is rather that of a working-class man who has become articulate and who, instead of acquiring speech rhythms foreign to his own ways of feeling, has kept the rhetoric of his people:

> 'The Bottoms' succeeded to 'Hell Row'. Hell Row was a block of thatched, bulging cottages that stood by the brookside on Greenhill Lane. There lived the colliers who worked in the little gin-pits two fields away. The brook ran under the alder-trees, scarcely soiled by these small mines, whose coal was drawn to the surface by donkeys that plodded wearily in a circle round a gin. And all over the countryside were these same pits, some of which had been worked in the time of Charles II, the few colliers and the donkeys burrowing down like ants into the earth, making queer mounds and little black places among the corn-fields and the meadows. And the cottages of these

coalminers, in blocks and pairs here and there, together with odd farms and homes of the stockingers, straying over the parish, formed the village of Bestwood. (p. 35)

In comparison with the Forster passage, Hoggart notes that the writing is more direct, has more 'attack', and is more concrete, dramatic and demonstrative; and that emotions are more plain and exposed, and placed directly in front of the reader. In general the language doesn't suggest that 'several centuries of civilised discourse have given a texture, a variety, a weight, an obliquity and irony' to the prose; in fact it sounds less like prose than speech. It recreates, in Hoggart's words, 'some of the experience of how working-class people live'.

In fact both these methods of describing a human landscape – that of direct presentation, and that of ironical, impersonal distance – were available to Lawrence; and he used the latter himself in the opening of *The Lost Girl*:

Take a mining townlet like Woodhouse, with a population of ten thousand people, and three generations behind it. This space of three generations argues a certain well-established society. The old 'County' has fled from the sight of so much disembowelled coal, to flourish on mineral rights in regions still idyllic. Remains one great and inaccessible magnate, the local coal-owner: three generations old, and clambering on the bottom step of the 'County', kicking off the mass below. Rule him out.

A well-established society in Woodhouse, full of fine shades, ranging from the dark of coal-dust to grit of stone-mason and sawdust of timber-merchant, through the lustre of lard and butter and meat, to the perfume of the chemist and the disinfectant of the doctor, on to the serene gold-tarnish of bank-managers, cashiers for the firm, clergymen and such-like, as far as the automobile refulgence of the general manager of all the collieries. Here the ne plus ultra. The general manager lives in the shrubberied seclusion of the so-called Manor. The genuine Hall, abandoned by the 'County', has been taken over as offices by the firm.

Here we are then: a vast substratum of colliers; a thick sprinkling of tradespeople inter-mingled with small employers of labour and diversified by elementary schoolmasters and nonconformist clergy; a higher layer of bank-managers, rich millers and well-to-do iron-masters, episcopal clergy and the managers of collieries: then the rich and sticky cherry of the local coal-owner glistening over all.

Such the complicated social system of a small industrial town in the Midlands of England, in this year of grace 1920. But let us go back a little. Such it was in the last calm year of plenty, 1913.[6]

The word 'townlet' itself implies a stance of metropolitan sophisti-
cation on the part of the narrator (Bestwood, by contrast, is a
'village'). The manner of approach suggested by the breezy imperative 'Take a mining townlet' is characteristic: the author 'takes', the
reader 'takes', the community itself is easily and lightly held in
the ironical consciousness for curious contemplation. The tone
throughout is ironical and sophisticated: 'argues a certain well-
established society' could be Forster's phrase. The writing aims delicately to suggest 'fine shades' of social discrimination, and the
fineness of perception is suggested by the overtly 'poetic' descriptions of the various trades. The approach throughout, culminating
in the brisk and casual, no-nonsense 'Such the complicated social
system of a small industrial town', suggests distance, impersonality,
irony and wit, and an easy and graceful command of the society by
the refined, sophisticated sensibility of the narrator.

It is not simply that Lawrence started (as Hoggart implies) with
the common language of the community and then worked it into a
creative language. On the contrary his first two novels were written
in a more conventional manner. He was not only conscious of the
necessity of fighting against the weight of that tradition; he knew
also that it was not enough simply to substitute some naïve directness and spontaneity for impersonality and detachment. It was
necessary rather to develop a *new* kind of impersonality which
could be much more closely in touch with the experience presented,
and yet capable also of detachment and an open perspective.

The opening of *Sons and Lovers* offers a distinction between the
'detached' and the 'direct' perspectives on the mining community
which is the location of Paul's birth and upbringing. The novelist's
approach is first a distant one, almost an 'aerial' view:

> To accommodate the regiments of miners, Carston, Waite and Co.
> built the Squares, great quadrangles of dwellings on the hillside of
> Bestwood, and then, in the brook valley, on the site of Hell Row,
> they erected the Bottoms.
> The Bottoms consisted of six blocks of miners' dwellings, two
> rows of three, like the dots on a blank-six domino, and twelve houses
> in a block. (p. 36)

Then the perspective moves closer, but it is still the perspective of
the superficial observer, as both the view and the syntax suggest:

> The houses themselves were substantial and very decent. One could
> walk all round, seeing little front gardens with auriculas and sax-

ifrage in the shadow of the bottom block, sweet-williams and pinks in the sunny top block; seeing neat front windows, little porches; little privet hedges, and dormer windows for the attics.   (p. 36)

Appropriate to this 'estate-agent's view' is the impersonal syntax: 'one could walk all round'. Then we have a change of perspective:

> But that was outside; that was the view on the uninhabited parlours of all the colliers' wives. The dwelling-room, the kitchen, was at the back of the house, facing inward between the blocks, looking at a scrubby back garden, and then at the ash-pits. And between the rows, between the long lines of ash-pits, went the alley, where the children played and the women gossiped and the men smoked. So, the actual conditions of living in the Bottoms, that was so well built and that looked so nice, were quite unsavoury because people must live in the kitchen, and the kitchens opened on to that nasty alley of ash-pits.
>
> Mrs Morel was not anxious to move into the Bottoms, which was already twelve years old and on the downward path, when she descended to it from Bestwood. But it was the best she could do. Moreover, she had an end house in one of the top blocks, and thus had only one neighbour; on the other side an extra strip of garden. And, having an end house, she enjoyed a kind of aristocracy among the other women of the 'between' houses, because her rent was five shillings and sixpence instead of five shillings a week. But this superiority in station was not much consolation to Mrs Morel.   (p. 36)

The language of observation, the 'view' from outside, gives way to a language of real existence ('the dwelling-room *was* …') and to verbs of social activity – 'women gossiped … men smoked'. The observer's perspective is contrasted with the participant's knowledge: the fact that the houses 'looked so nice' with the fact that 'people must *live*'. The passage as a whole is the work of a man who can write with directness and precision of the life of a mining community because his own relationship with it has been a close and intimate one and his speech as a writer is being developed in close and intimate relation to the language of the community. But it is also written by a man who could look at that community impersonally, detached, with an appraising and evaluative gaze.

He shows us two kinds of 'impersonality': that which derives from superficial observation or ignorance, and that which derives from the ability to see the life of a mining community with both inward knowledge *and* a wider perspective. There is no basis for believing that Lawrence took Mrs Morel's pretensions to 'aristocracy' with perfect seriousness. Here the word is clearly used with irony; it is used by a man who knew what aristocracy really is (having after all eloped with the daughter of a German baron); and it is used in a clearly defined social context where it implies pretentious and exaggerated claims. But the irony is not destructive or scathing or negative; it combines direct knowledge with detachment; it reveals not only a sympathetic understanding of the desire to feel superior to the deprived and rather squalid lifestyle of the mining village, but also an amused ironical awareness of the absurdity of such pretensions, when they express themselves in trivial details – the end house in the terrace and the extra sixpence a week on the rent.

What we see there in the concrete detail of language and style is a general characteristic of the novel. The individual life which is the novel's subject, that of Paul Morel, began as Lawrence's life; the biography is therefore autobiography, written from the inside. But the life of Paul Morel is also a fictional biography which composes the details of personal experience into an impersonal vision, which is also art.

In *Sons and Lovers* a single life grows and gradually individuates out of a particular family, the life of which is carefully detailed and set in a wider social context of the whole community. As the novel progresses the single life becomes more single, more individual, more isolated. Paul's relationships with other people – apart from his mother and father – are intensely individualistic, intensely close, yet the figures always remain separate, detached, isolated from each other. Miriam, Clara, Baxter Dawes – each figures as a stage in Paul's development towards greater separation, isolation, individuality. At the end of the novel Mrs Morel's death leaves him totally isolated and single; the perfunctory interviews with the three friends in the last two chapters only reinforce the sense of complete individual separateness. This process of individuation arises out of the character of that particular family context, and out of the character of the wider community itself.

Mrs Morel is, of course, a primary instrument in the formation of that process. But it is inadequate to explain that process simply in terms of the peculiar and absorbing passion between mother and son which sets Paul apart from other people. That passion is itself seen as secondary to the primary root cause, which is the conflict in the family. And that conflict is not a purely individual or purely family matter.

Mr Morel is not an unusual or out-of-the ordinary miner. He is in fact very popular, with his sociable drinking and his dancing, his easygoing and cheerful character. But Mrs Morel *is* unusual: she is exceptional, and feels herself to be out of place in the community:

> 'What have *I* to do with it?' she said to herself. 'What have I to do with all this? Even the child I am going to have! It doesn't seem as if *I* were taken into account.' (p. 40)

In the context of the common flow of ordinary experience (the holiday and the fair) Mrs Morel is acutely conscious of herself as an individual, of an isolated and distinctive 'I', separate from the collective life of the community. Morel's existence, on the other hand, is more closely integrated with the society as a whole. Initially the narrator distinguishes the husband and wife in the same way as the miners and their wives are distinguished in Lawrence's essay 'Nottingham and the Mining Country' (1929). He is primarily physical in nature – 'the dusky, golden softness of this man's sensuous flame of life'; she is 'intellectual', 'proud and unyielding', high-principled: 'His nature was purely sensuous, and she strove to make him moral, religious' (p. 49). This fits into Lawrence's later characterisation of his father as a 'pure pagan', representing primitive values of physical existence and unable or unwilling to accept the norms and standards of 'society'. In this context Mrs Morel represents the moral principles and sanctions of 'society', as do the colliers' wives in 'Nottingham and the Mining Country'. But despite Mr Morel's streak of rebelliousness, his 'dislike of authority', he tends to represent certain norms of the community, certain narrow, inflexible, rather limited standards and values, while she stands for the effort to transcend it or improve it. Mr Morel stands for the community, and for the fellowship of the community; but he represents its inadequacies too. He accepts without question the traditional social roles assigned by the community to men, women and children. He expects to be given total personal freedom in exchange for his economic support of the family. He expects his wife to succumb happily to the dreary, oppressive drudgery which most of the colliers' wives obediently accept; and he expects his boys to follow him down the pit. The two characters are not restricted to these roles, although they are the primary and dominant characteristics of each. As Terry Eagleton has pointed out, the mother also possesses a clearer understanding than her children of the 'interrelation of elements within a single texture of life', and the father, in his sullen and stubborn resistance to the exacting disciplines of work and home, shows a selfish individualism which brings into the family a pressure of authoritarian power, reproducing the patterns of dominance structured into the society as a whole.[7]

These contradictions can be illustrated by a well-known early scene from the novel: that in which Morel arrives home from a day's drinking and presents his wife with a coconut (p. 41). Her response to the gift is both mercenary and ungracious: she seems to feel only recrimination and resentment. Morel appears as warm, jovial and 'tender', his wife as unsympathetic and cold. But the real point is that Morel has enjoyed his day at the expense of his wife, who has been left with the drudgery of looking after the children in the 'intolerable' Bottoms. The coconut, for all the 'tenderness' with which it is proferred, is nevertheless a 'thing' which has no relation to the woman's needs and cannot compensate for her dreary, wasted day. On the one hand Morel has derived some tenderness and warmth from enjoyment of that precious margin of freedom accorded him from the brutal discipline of labour in the mine. On the other hand that freedom is denied to Mrs Morel, who is responsible for that other discipline of work, the home. What should be a moment of tender intimacy between husband and wife proves to be a collision of contradictory pressures, of labour and family – a focus of the social contradictions within the working-class community. The presentation here is impersonal; it regards both characters with understanding and openness, and tries to present the nature of the conflict between them in terms of the nature of the whole community which is their life. All the Morel quarrels are really *social* conflicts, as can be seen by close examination of the realistic context in which particular conflicts are realised. The battle between mother and father for possession of the first child is dramatised in these terms:

> William was only one year old, and his mother was proud of him, he was so pretty... . With his little white hat curled with an ostrich feather, and his white coat, he was a joy to her, the twining wisps of hair clustering round his head. Mrs Morel lay listening, one Sunday morning, to the chatter of the father and child downstairs. Then she dozed off. When she came downstairs, a great fire glowed in the grate, the room was hot, the breakfast was roughly laid, and seated in his arm-chair, against the chimney-piece, sat Morel, rather timid; and standing between his legs, the child – cropped like a sheep, with such an odd round poll – looking, wondering at her; and on a newspaper spread out upon the hearthrug, a myriad of crescent-shaped curls, like the petals of a marigold scattered in the reddening firelight.

Mrs Morel stood still. It was her first baby. She went very white, and was unable to speak.

'What dost think o' 'im?' Morel laughed uneasily.

She gripped her two fists, lifted them, and came forward. Morel shrank back.

'I could kill you, I could!' she said. She choked with rage, her two fists uplifted.

'Yer non want ter make a wench on 'im,' Morel said, in a frightened tone, bending his head to shield his eyes from hers. His attempt at laughter had vanished.... . Afterwards she said she had been silly, that the boy's hair would have had to be cut, sooner or later. In the end, she even brought herself to say to her husband it was just as well he had played barber when he did. But she knew, and Morel knew, that the act had caused something momentous to take place in her soul. She remembered the scene all her life, as one in which she had suffered the most intensely.   (p. 50)

Elisio Vivas comments on this scene:

> All one can say, confronted with the writer's statement, is that whether he knew it or not, he was giving us a vivid and living picture of a woman who had an unusual capacity to nurse a slight injury and had a powerful capacity for resentment. But does the writer know what he is presenting us with? Since the novel gives the writer the lie, the answer must be that he does and does not. And we are here faced, not with a contradiction, but with a psychological conflict.[8]

Such an explanation in terms of 'psychological conflict', whether between characters or within the author, fails to recognise that the conflict is one of values, involving traditional, established social roles and identities within a specific community. Mrs Morel's vision of the child is an attempt to set him beyond the community and its conventions; Morel, in cutting the child's hair, is not simply doing something conventional, but asserting his right to do it – to demand that the child conform to the social image of a 'lad'. His nervousness reveals his awareness of the fact that he is doing something more than the 'normal': he is challenging her values. She reacts instinctively with grief and anger: her illusion is shattered – the child now looks like any other miner's child.

The conflict, then, is in fact a very important conflict of values: it shows Mr Morel trying to establish the norms and conventions of the community, and Mrs Morel trying to transcend them by individual appropriation of the child, making him different, isolated from the collective life of the community. Later she acknowledges the justice of the action – but the damage is done.

Mrs Morel was, as I have shown, an exceptional miner's wife. But she is not alone in her desire to transcend the narrow and limited conventions of the community, or to change it for the better. With other colliers' wives she frequents (as Mrs Lawrence did[9]) the Women's Co-operative Guild, an organisation which gives them a new perspective on their lives. The miners react to this with hostility. The following passage will demonstrate how a conflict similar to the one described above – this time over the question of whether the boys should go down the pit or seek non-manual occupation – is set by Lawrence within a general social context, a description of the general cultural life of the community:

> When the children were old enough to be left, Mrs Morel joined the Women's Guild. It was a little club of women attached to the Co-operative Wholesale Society, which met on Monday night in the long room over the grocery shop of the Bestwood 'Co-op.' The women were supposed to discuss the benefits to be derived from co-operation, and other social questions. Sometimes Mrs Morel read a paper... . The Guild was called by some hostile husbands, who found their wives getting too independent, the 'clat-fart' shop – that is, the gossip-shop. It is true, from off the basis of the Guild, the women could look at their homes, at the conditions of their own lives, and find fault. So the colliers found their women had a new standard of their own, rather disconcerting... . Then, when the lad was thirteen, she got him a job in the 'Co-op.' office. He was a very clever boy, frank, with rather rough features and real viking blue eyes.
>
> 'What dost want ter ma'e a stool-harsed Jack on 'im for?' said Morel. 'All he'll do is to wear his britches behind out, an' earn nowt. What's 'e startin' wi'?'
>
> 'It doesn't matter what he's starting with,' said Mrs Morel.
>
> 'It wouldna! Put 'im i' th' pit wi' me, an' 'e'll earn a easy ten shillin' a wik from th' start. But six shilling' wearin' his truck-end out on a stool's better than ten shillin' i' th' pit wi' me, I know.'
>
> 'He is *not* going in the pit,' said Mrs Morel, 'and there's an end of it.' (pp. 89–90)

Like the hair-cutting episode, the disagreement about the children's occupations is a social conflict involving antagonistic values. The family conflict is related to the general cultural life of the community, its organisations and institutions. On this realistic basis the paradox implicit in Mrs Morel's treatment of her children is disclosed: the general social ambition of the women to improve their lives becomes Mrs Morel's *personal* ambition to transcend the community by making her sons middle class. William is, in a sense, a figure destroyed by the tenacity of his ambitions and the intensity of his desire to experience everything the bourgeois world has to offer him. The general social ambition towards 'improvement', translated into the specific desire to transport the children into another class, becomes destructive and futile.

The most significant 'absence' in the realism of *Sons and Lovers* is this suppression of the bourgeoisie. Despite the fact that the novel alludes to the middle class as Mrs Morel's proper home, and points to it as the ultimate goal of social mobility and moral improvement, it is not actually depicted there – not presented, as it is in the *The Rainbow* or *Women in Love* or *Lady Chatterley's Lover*. In *Sons and Lovers* there are miners, but no mine-owners; there is Bestwood, but no Shortlands or Wragby; there is a clear and concrete dramatisation of working-class life, but bourgeois society and culture are firmly excluded from the compass of the novel's social world.

This absence does not call into question the novel's claim to dramatise a comprehensive social totality by the techniques of realism. It is not comparable with the suppression of industry in *The White Peacock*, which leaves the world of the novel to be dominated by a social myth, the purpose of which is to deny history. The society depicted in *Sons and Lovers* does not refuse or resolve social conflict and contradiction, but openly dramatises their confrontation and collision. The suppression of the bourgeoisie makes possible a particular critique and exposure of ideology, which could not be accomplished without that deliberate exclusion, that significant and constitutive absence in the text.

The ideology in question is that of 'social mobility' through education and moral improvement, which operated so powerfully on the young Lawrence, both through his immediate family context and through the conditions of his general historical environment. He escaped his historical function of 'replacement'[10] by becoming a teacher, in a profession expanded and consolidated by the 1870 Education Act; his early career is a classic instance of that pattern of social mobility which involved 'rising' to professional respectability through educational progress and attainment, and thereby transcending the working class. Mrs Morel in the novel typifies this ideological position: her ambitions for her sons take precisely this form. The novel never stands far enough outside its dramatised community to offer an explicit critique or condemnation of this 'self-help' ideology; instead it dramatises a critique of the ideology by creating a social world in which, once the working-class community is left behind, there is precisely nothing 'there'; there is in reality nowhere to go. Individualised entry into the middle class can never constitute a solution to the problems of Bestwood, or of the Morel family.

The mother, in an effort to realise her vision of moral improvement, tries to push her sons into the middle class. In fact, however, she pushes them into isolation, separateness, individuality. The process destroys William and leads Paul into a position of isolated singleness where he is wholly dependent on his mother, so that her death leaves him alone and abandoned, himself drifting towards death. Outside the working-class community there is nothing – a vacuum. When William and Paul are pushed out of the community they find themselves alone and without support, and always close to the kind of death which seems to accompany such isolation. The ultimate end of social mobility through education and individual self-improvement is nothing, a tragic emptiness, death.

The experience of being actively alienated and excluded from the community is enacted in the earlier part of the novel in relation to Mrs Morel herself. Morel comes home drunk, they fight, and he thrusts her out of the house, locking the door behind her. Morel's drinking expedition to Nottingham has been described by the narrator with sympathy and tolerance; but the corollary of that trip is that his wife has been left with the boredom, tedious anxiety and drudgery of a whole day in the Bottoms. So again her reaction to his drunkenness is one of contempt and anger, which provoke him to violence. Thrust out into the garden, Mrs Morel experiences a strange communion with the world outside the house:

> The moon was high and magnificent in the August night. Mrs Morel, seared with passion, shivered to find herself out there in a great white light that fell cold on her, and gave a shock to her inflamed soul....
>
> She became aware of something about her. With an effort she roused herself to see what it was that penetrated her consciousness. The tall white lilies were reeling in the moonlight, and the air was charged with their perfume, as with a presence. Mrs Morel gasped slightly in fear. She touched the big, pallid flowers on their petals, then shivered. They seemed to be stretching in the moonlight. She put her hand into one white bin: the gold scarcely showed on her

fingers by moonlight. She bent down to look at the binful of yellow pollen; but it only appeared dusky. Then she drank a deep draught of the scent. It almost made her dizzy.

Mrs Morel leaned on the garden gate, looking out, and she lost herself awhile. She did not know what she thought. Except for a slight feeling of sickness, and her consciousness in the child, herself melted out like scent into the shiny, pale air. After a time the child, too, melted with her in the mixing-pot of moonlight, and she rested with the hills and lilies and houses, all swum together in a kind of swoon. (pp. 59–60)

She is pregnant with Paul at this point, and the images of the passage recur at two important moments in Paul's life: in Chapter 11 when he decides to 'break off' with Miriam, and again in Chapter 13 when he makes love to Clara. Violently thrust out and pushed beyond 'normality', the shelter of the house, the normal common experiences of the community, the individual has to enter into communion with some alienated 'reality' beyond the common, the ordinary, the collective life of the community. Mrs Morel, in response to these violent discords and contradictions, wants to push her sons beyond the limits of her own life towards something better. The impulse to do this is again initially an impulse towards 'nature', where she seems to find the peace and tranquillity, the resolution of conflict which she craves:

> With Mrs Morel it was one of those still moments when the small frets vanish, and the beauty of things stands out, and she had the peace and the strength to see herself... . The baby was restless on his mother's knee, clambering with his hands at the light... . Once more she was aware of the sun lying red on the rim of the hill opposite. She suddenly held up the child in her hands.
>
> 'Look!' she said. 'Look, my pretty!'
>
> She thrust the infant forward to the crimson, throbbing sun, almost with relief. She saw him lift his little fist. Then she put him to her bosom again, ashamed of her impulse to give him back whence he came. (pp. 73–4)

The bitter irony of this impulse emerges in the life and death of William, where we see that in her desire to offer her child to the beyond, with the hope of vicariously reliving her wasted life, she actually pushes him into isolation, and into the ambition and intensity which cause his death.

In the following scene the child Paul is baptised into violence and horror in a fight between the parents; the family conflict is shown entering into the life of the as yet unconscious, naïve baby. Again the disagreement relates not only to Morel's drunkenness, but to the fact that his wife refuses to 'wait on him', to perform obediently the duties of a submissive wife. Impulsively he strikes her with the dresser drawer, and then in fascination and horror watches the mother and child:

> He was turning drearily away, when he saw a drop of blood fall from the averted wound into the baby's fragile, glistening hair. Fascinated he watched the heavy dark drop hang in the glistening cloud, and pull down the gossamer. Another drop fell. It would soak through to the baby's scalp. He watched, fascinated, feeling it soak in; then, finally, his manhood broke. (p. 77)

The wounding, violent contradictions of the community are not merely external pressures operating on the individual: as the drop of blood 'soaks' into the baby's hair and 'through' to its scalp we see clearly that in this novel 'individuality' can never be separated from the 'community' – from conditions and circumstances of the environment which bear upon and help to compose the individual life.

The true 'autobiographical' character of Sons and Lovers rests in this insistence of the realist method that 'individuality', despite its claim to be an autonomous value, must always be understood in the context of the social forces and pressures which produce it, as an experience and as an ideology. The separateness and isolation of the individual subject is not taken for granted, but traced to its origin within the complex and contradictory totality of the community in which it developed. By means of the realist method Lawrence reaches an understanding of that ideology of individualism which becomes dominant (and damaging) in The Rainbow and Women in Love.

The 'individuality' into which Paul develops is specifically located in the concept of the 'artist'. Maurice Beebe has discussed this question, distinguishing between two kinds of artist: 'the Ivory Tower concept of the artist as an exile from life'; and 'what I call the theme of the Sacred Fount, the view that the artist must experience life in order to depict it in art.... In Sons and Lovers ... Lawrence wrote a portrait-of-the-artist novel of the Sacred Fount type. Yet there is also in the novel a still-unconscious yearning by Lawrence and his hero for the Ivory Tower.'[11] It is the latter suggestion (which Beebe does not develop) that I wish to apply in more detail to Sons and Lovers. In Lawrence's personal life, this ambition or role expressed a deep tension in his relationship with his community, and the figure of the artist as aesthete became a natural part of the language and symbolism used to express that tension, especially in *The Trespasser*. Paul's status as an 'artist' deepens his individualism; but because he, unlike Cyril [in *The White Peacock*] or Siegmund [in *The Trespasser*], has the advantage of a wholly realised social world in which to move and develop, we see him struggling against and finally defeating those impulses which force him to be an individualist, striving to transcend society in his art and in his personal life. Ultimately there is no complete escape from that doom of individuality; but we do see Paul struggling to grasp a symbolic conception of 'wholeness' in experience, which remains trapped in individualism but reaches out towards the life of the community in an effort to retain or restore the broken bond. This process centres on the character of Miriam. The by now familiar Pre-Raphaelite and 1890s imagery collects around the presentation of Miriam, and the rejection of Miriam (which, being a rejection of much more than a personal relationship, seems impersonally cruel) incorporates a formal rejection of that kind of art.

On their first visit to Willey Farm Mrs Morel and Paul take a significant journey from the familiar industrial landscape of Bestwood into a rural landscape of pastoral. The mother and son both observe, and respond to, the human activity in the industrial landscape. The son goes further than this: he sketches it – realises it in art. In search of Willey Farm, the two pass 'over a little bridge' into a completely different world:

> The mother and son went through the wheat and oats, over a little bridge into a wild meadow. Peewits, with their white breasts glistening, wheeled and screamed about them. The lake was still and blue. High overhead a heron floated. Opposite, the wood heaped on the hill, green and still.   (p. 168)

After the visit Mrs Morel responds to the farm with exactly the kind of pastoral longing and nostalgia we would expect:

> A thin moon was coming out. His heart was full of happiness till it hurt. His mother had to chatter because she, too, wanted to cry, with happiness.
> 'Now *wouldn't* I help that man!' she said. '*Wouldn't* I see to the fowls and the young stock! And *I'd* learn to milk, and *I'd* talk with him, and *I'd* plan with him. My word, if I were his wife, the farm would be run, I know!'   (p. 173)

Miriam is discovered in a pastoral world – rural, agricultural, deep in the forest – outside the industrial landscape, by a transition from one world to another. Although Miriam is more than this, and becomes incorporated into the whole world of the novel in a much more complex way, this dimension of her remains important. The pastoral landscape is, of course, revealed to be, in actuality, something quite different – a working farm. But there is in Miriam an idealism which answers to Paul's original preconceptions; and we find that 'transcendent' element of Miriam presented by Lawrence in the language and imagery which he himself had used to express and pursue such transcendence:[12]

> The girl was romantic in her soul. Everywhere was a Walter Scott heroine being loved by men with helmets or with plumes in their caps. She herself was something of a princess turned into a swine-girl in her own imagination... . Ediths, and Lucys, and Rowenas, Brian de Bois Guilberts, Rob Roys, and Guy Mannerings, rustled the sunny leaves in the morning, or sat in her bedroom aloft, alone, when it snowed. That was life to her.   (p. 191)

> Miriam seemed as in some dreamy tale, a maiden in bondage, her spirit dreaming in a land far away and magical. And her discoloured, old blue frock and her broken boots seemed only like the romantic rags of King Cophetua's beggar-maid   (p. 194)

> And she was cut off from ordinary life by her religious intensity which made the world for her either a nunnery garden or a paradise, where sin and knowledge were not, or else an ugly, cruel thing.
>   (p. 198)

> Miriam had nailed on the wall a reproduction of Veronese's 'St Catherine'. She loved the woman who sat in the window, dreaming. Her own windows were too small to sit in. But the front one was dripped over with honeysuckle and virginia creeper, and looked upon the tree-tops of the oak-wood across the yard, while the little back window, no bigger than a handkerchief, was a loophole to the east, to the dawn beating up against the beloved round hills.   (p. 221)

Within the Leivers family in its 'pastoral' setting Paul finds a more sympathetic environment for his art. In the earlier passage where he sketches the pit, his mother 'sits' by, simply observing; she does not share or co-operate in his metaphorical explorations; occasionally she makes non-committal responses or takes a *practical* interest in the subject of her son's artistic vision. The Leivers seem such more directly interested in Paul's *art*:

But even from the seaside he wrote long letters to Mrs Leivers about the shore and the sea. And he brought back his beloved sketches of the flat Lincoln coast, anxious for them to see. Almost they would interest the Leivers more than they interested his mother. It was not his art Mrs Morel cared about; it was himself and his achievement. But Mrs Leivers and her children were almost his disciples. They kindled him and made him glow to his work, whereas his mother's influence was to make him quietly determined, patient, dogged, unwearied.

(p. 198)

With Miriam herself, Paul feels his way towards a conception of art very different from that revealed in the 'pit-sketching' passage.

> But the girl gradually sought him out. If he brought up his sketch-book, it was she who pondered longest over the last picture. Then she would look up at him. Suddenly, her dark eyes alight like water that shakes with a stream of gold in the dark, she would ask:
> 'Why do I like this so?'
> Always something in his breast shrank from these close, intimate, dazzled looks of hers.
> 'Why *do* you?' he asked.
> 'I don't know. It seems so true.'
> 'It's because – it's because there is scarcely any shadow in it; it's more shimmery, as if I'd painted the shimmering protoplasm in the leaves and everywhere, and not the stiffness of the shape. That seems dead to me. Only this shimmeriness is the real living. The shape is a dead crust. The shimmer is inside really.'   (pp. 201–2)

According to this conception of art, 'reality' is located within living things as an internal essence; art can discount the concrete, material substance of reality as 'dead crust' and dispense with any representation of the subject's material relationships with a circumambient context. The opposition between 'living' internal essence and 'dead' external 'crust' was later to become a standard formula in Lawrence's philosophy, and to appear in his fiction at such significant moments as the conclusion to *The Rainbow*. As yet, however, that separation has not been accomplished; the art of the novel in which this statement occurs, the art of *Sons and Lovers*, is predominantly of the *other* kind: the realism which seeks to unite internal and external, subjective and objective, personal and social, private and public, into a complex but cohesive totality.

Miriam is constantly leading Paul towards experiences of a quasi-sexual, religious intensity, experiences which sometimes recall the aesthetic intensities of *The White Peacock* and *The Trespasser*. The incident concerning Miriam's rose-bush (Ch. 7) alludes to a similar structure of feeling:

> 'They seem as if they walk like butterflies, and shake themselves,' he said.
>
> She looked at her roses. They were white, some incurved and holy, others expanded in an ecstasy. The tree was dark as a shadow. She lifted her hand impulsively to the flowers; she went forward and touched them in worship... .There was a cool scent of ivory roses – a white, virgin scent. Something made him feel anxious and imprisoned. The two walked in silence.
>
> 'Till Sunday,' he said quietly, and left her; and she walked home slowly, feeling her soul satisfied with the holiness of the night. He stumbled down the path. And as soon as he was out of the wood, in the free open meadow, where he could breathe, he started to run as fast as he could. It was like a delicious delirium in his veins.
>
> (p. 210)

It would be unwise to simplify the complex emotional atmosphere evoked in this passage: the language of quasi-religious experience; sexual impulses sublimated into 'religious' feeling; an imprisoning and frustrating 'virginity'. But it should be observed that Miriam is leading Paul into an experience in which living natural things – flowers – are being transformed into something 'holy', immortal', capable of worship; living things translated by Miriam's emotional intensity into transcendent objects. Paul resists this process by attributing to the flowers metaphors of living ('They seem as if they walk like butterflies'), while Miriam is concerned to keep them 'immortal': 'They were white, some incurved and holy, others expanded in an ecstasy... . She went forward and touched them in worship.' The experience is isolated; it is incompatible with everyday life (Miriam has to draw Paul away both from his family and from her brothers for this to happen); it takes place deep in the pastoral wood, away from the industrial landscape; it bestows transcendent, religious feelings upon living things, making them into cult-objects (or *objets d'art*); and Paul strives to escape from this 'holy communion' back into real life. It can at least be confidently affirmed that Miriam is offering Paul a kind of fulfilment in his isolation (or even a fulfilment *of* his isolation), and that Paul's rejection of that quality of fulfilment constitutes a resistance to his socially conditioned doom of individuality, and to the kind of art which the isolated individual is likely to produce.

The flower imagery recurs at a moment of decision for Paul:

> A dim white fence of lilies went across the garden, and the air all
> round seemed to stir with scent, as if it were alive. He went across
> the bed of pinks, whose keen perfume came sharply across the
> rocking, heavy scent of the lilies, and stood alongside the white
> barrier of flowers... . And then, like a shock, he caught another
> perfume, something raw and coarse. Hunting round, he found the
> purple iris, touched their fleshy throats and their dark, grasping
> hands. At any rate, he had found something. They stood stiff in the
> darkness. Their scent was brutal... .
> Breaking off a pink, he suddenly went indoors... .
> 'I shall break off with Miriam, mother,' he answered calmly... .
> He put the flower in his mouth. Unthinking, he bared his teeth,
> closed them on the blossom slowly, and had a mouthful of petals.
> These he spat into the fire, kissed his mother, and went to bed.
>
> (pp. 355–6)

The imagery also recalls here the passage where Mrs Morel was
locked out of the house and experienced her transcendental communion with the flowers. Her feeling was of a strongly sexual (or quasi-
sexual) character: 'She touched the big, pallid flowers on their petals,
then shivered. They seemed to be stretching in the moonlight. She
put her hand into one white bin: the gold scarcely showed on her
fingers by moonlight' (see pp. 144–5 above). But in the later passage
Paul seems to be dissatisfied with the quality of experience offered by
the lilies *and* the pinks: he cannot rest content with the 'rocking,
heavy', intoxicating scent of the madonna lilies (his mother) *or* with
the delicate, 'keen perfume' of the pinks (Miriam). He searches for
something more, 'something raw and coarse', the purple iris, with
their 'fleshy throats' and 'dark grasping hands'. He rejects the stupe-
fying power of mother-love and the isolated, purified, transcendent
relationship with Miriam. As a man, Paul will try to incorporate into
his life some sense of wholeness, of completeness, totality of life and
experience. To achieve this necessarily involves the rejection of
Miriam: 'Unthinking, he bared his teeth, closed them on the blossom
slowly, and had a mouthful of petals. These he spat into the fire ...'
Paul rejects Miriam because Miriam is inadequate to his emotional
needs; he cannot rest content with a relationship which seeks to draw
him into an abstract, rarefied, transcendent realm of experience. The
process occurring here as an action within the novel parallels the
process of development undergone by Lawrence's art. The two levels
of experience meet in the character of Miriam, and in the Pre-
Raphaelite and 1890s imagery associated with her.

This incident parallels the passage from *The Trespasser* in which Siegmund finds in the objects of nature an 'objective correlative' for his own problems. There the sunshine and warm sand, the 'white flower of the bay', are like the madonna lilies and pinks, beautiful but inadequate. Siegmund searches deeper, to discover the 'deep mass of cold' which underlies and supports the softness and warmth. Helena (like Miriam, a 'dreaming woman') remains unconscious of such contradiction; she exists purely on a 'transcendent' level of experience. Siegmund tries to embrace the totality of life, and is destroyed by its contradictions. In *The Trespasser* 'romance' and 'reality' were polarised into incompatible levels of experience, incompatible literary styles. Siegmund, the artist within the novel, could not effectively resolve and reconcile those contradictions; Lawrence, the artist creating the novel, could not effectively resolve and reconcile the antithetical styles. But the realist art of *Sons and Lovers* creates and embodies a wholeness of experience which Paul Morel *can* attempt to resolve, though the resolution is not completed within the novel.

One important stage of that resolution is taking place in the above passage from *Sons and Lovers*: Paul rejects the transcendent blossom of Miriam, leaving himself free to strive for connection, for a unification of life's contradictory realities. It is the relationship with Clara that draws Paul into connection with other things, beyond the individual, just as the art of the novel connects the individual with a social reality beyond himself. The imagery of the passage quoted above points, of course, directly to the Paul–Miriam–Clara triangle; and it is in the sexual union with Clara that Paul discovers the possibility of a different kind of transcendence: a quality of experience which does not draw the individual away from the complex reality of life, but puts him into closer touch with it:

> They had met, and included in their meeting the thrust of the manifold grass-stems, the cry of the peewit, the wheel of the stars... . To know their own nothingness, to know the tremendous living flood which carried them always, gave them rest within themselves. If so great a magnificent power could overwhelm them, identify them altogether with itself, so that they knew they were only grains in the tremendous heave that lifted every grass-blade its little height, and every tree, and living thing, then why fret about themselves? They could let themselves be carried by life, and they felt a sort of peace each in the other. (p. 421)

The resolution is partial, precariously balanced and vulnerable. The metaphor of the 'tremendous living flood', and the 'belief in life'

which it embodies, can easily be abstracted into the philosophical an-
tithesis which poses 'life' against social reality. Even after such a tri-
umphant epiphany Paul remains isolated – the irreducible, separate
individual, unable to relate or connect. The connection with another
individual is no substitute for the relation to a community – a community of the kind dramatised in the art of the novel itself.

Man cannot live by 'life' alone. And so *Sons and Lovers* ends
with Paul facing the awful doom of isolation in its most poignant
form, yet determined to resist it:

> Whatever spot he stood in, there he stood alone. From his breast,
> from his mouth, sprang the endless space, and it was there behind
> him, everywhere. The people hurrying along the streets offered no
> obstruction to the void in which he found himself.... Where was he?
> – one tiny upright speck of flesh, less than an ear of wheat lost in the
> field.   (pp. 491–2)

From this limit of experience Paul walks back – towards the town;
back towards relationship, interdependence, social connection; back
towards the community in which alone human life can have
meaning and reality:

> But no, he would not give in. Turning sharply, he walked towards
> the city's gold phosphorescence. His fists were shut, his mouth set
> fast. He would not take that direction, to the darkness, to follow her.
> He walked towards the faintly humming, glowing town, quickly.
>   (p. 492)

Both these examples show that Lawrence's achievement of
realism was a hard-won and precarious achievement, containing
within itself the seeds of its own dissolution. *Sons and Lovers*
shows a realism on the edge of a break, a transition that was to
lead Lawrence's fiction towards more symbolic and mythological
styles, which would offer different ways of presenting his society,
and would imply a different relationship with it.

From Graham Holderness, *D. H. Lawrence: History, Ideology and
Fiction* (Dublin, 1982), pp. 134–58.

NOTES

[Graham Holderness's argument, taken from a longer chapter on 'The
Triumph of Realism' in Lawrence's early work, relates easily to those of John

Goode in the previous essay and Scott Sanders in the next. All three are concerned with *Sons and Lovers* as a text of transition in which Paul's journey mirrors certain representative developments in the period as a whole. As such, Holderness rejects readings of the novel which limit it to 'autobiographical' or 'Oedipal' interpretations. Instead, Paul's story is understood in social context as a searching examination of Edwardian ideologies of self-improvement and social mobility. In addition, Holderness gives a helpfully detailed account of the challenging language Lawrence found for these new experiences and, like many recent critics, he is concerned to assess the strengths and limitations of the novel's realism (for discussion, see the general Introduction). His comments on this topic might be read alongside those of Sanders (essay 10) and Pinkney (essay 11), as well as the discussion of the style and narrative voice of the novel by Kermode (essay 1), Martz (essay 4) and Bonds (essay 6). Page references to *Sons and Lovers* are incorporated into the text and are to the Penguin edition edited by Keith Sagar (1981). Ed]

1. *The Collected Letters of D. H. Lawrence*, ed. Harry T. Moore (London, 1962), p. 234.

2. Ibid., pp. 66–7.

3. Keith Sagar, *The Art of D. H. Lawrence* (Cambridge, 1966), p. 19.

4. Gāmini Salgādo, *D. H. Lawrence: Sons and Lovers* (London, 1966), p. 7.

5. Richard Hoggart, 'A Question of Tone' in *Speaking to Each Other: About Literature* (London, 1970), pp. 194–9.

6. D. H. Lawrence, *The Lost Girl* (Harmondsworth, 1950), p. 11.

7. Terry Eagleton, *Exiles and Emigrés: Studies in Modern Literature* (London, 1970), p. 192.

8. Elisio Vivas, *D. H. Lawrence: The Failure and Triumph of Art* (Bloomington, IN, 1960), p. 181.

9. For Mrs Lawrence's activities in the Women's Co-operative Guild, see Jessie Chambers, *D. H. Lawrence: A Personal Record by 'E.T.'* (London, 1965), p. 40.

10. Raymond Williams, *Culture and Society, 1780–1950* (Harmondsworth, 1961), p. 202.

11. See Maurice Beebe, 'Lawrence's Sacred Fount: The Artist Theme in *Sons and Lovers*', *Texas Studies in Literature and Language*, IV (1962), 539–52.

12. The 'dreaming woman' image recurs here, invoking the earlier contexts in which Lawrence had used it. The descriptions here recall Burne-Jones's painting *King Cophetua and the Beggar Maid*, D. G. Rossetti's *Convent Thoughts*, and the very 'Pre-Raphaelite' picture by Veronese, as well as a general context of Romantic feeling.

10

Society and Ideology in *Sons and Lovers*

SCOTT SANDERS

The difference in speech between Walter and Gertrude Morel, marking as it does their differences in class background and education, corresponds to an underlying conflict in outlook and aspiration. Mrs Morel comes from solid bourgeois stock, stout Congregationalists all. In the memory of her grandfather, a failed lace manufacturer, she possesses an image of lost social eminence that might be regained. From her father, an engineer whose chief concern seems to have been the size of his salary, and who was well-educated and stern-minded, she formed her ideal of manhood. As a young woman she had all but married one John Field, 'the son of a well-to-do tradesman', also an educated man who aspired to the ministry and settled upon merchandising. She is well-educated herself, having taught school for some time. This side of her character emerges in chats with the vicar over starched table-cloths, in her activities with the Women's Guild, and in her promotion of the Morel children's education. Through her sons, for whom she wants middle-class jobs, comfortable homes and 'ladies' to wive, she attempts to regain some of the status which she has lost through marriage to Morel.

Morel on the other hand, who left school at age ten to work in the mine, is barely literate, spelling painfully through the headlines and seeing no value whatsoever in the reading of books. He has no use for Mrs Morel's religion, preferring the pub to chapel, and fails to understand either her highfalutin ideas or Paul's art. Unlike his wife, he does not feel specially pinched by poverty, never dreams of clawing his way into the middle class, nor does he envision a very different future for his children. Little beyond Bestwood attracts him, and little within Bestwood repels him.

Morel clearly does not live up to Mrs Morel's ideal of manhood, and she communicates her judgement to the children... [who] learn from her to mock their father's manners, to belittle his work at the mine, to sneer at his lack of formal education and in general to degrade his manhood. Even though specific grievances often emerge during money squabbles, it is evident that something more basic than customary domestic wrangles over shillings and pence – vital as shillings and pence are – has motivated this total assault upon Morel as father and husband. Of course he scants her budget, but so do the other miners when times are bad. It is far more significant that he does not share her education, religion, social aspirations, aesthetic training, economic motivations, manners, language, moral views or political interests. Their marriage is wrecked by differences that are primarily social rather than personal.

In the scene in Chapter 3 where William's career is at issue, Mrs Morel calls attention to these differences by contrasting herself with Morel's mother: she is not going to put *her* sons down the pit, whatever the old lady had decided to do with the likes of Walter. In the opening chapter these women meet, and from that encounter we learn that while living in a rented house, sitting on mortgaged chairs and eating off mortgaged tables might suit old Mrs Morel, it is far from suiting Gertrude Coppard Morel. Such a cramped financial state pinches her bourgeois soul. She had persuaded herself, we are told, that she was marrying a financially independent man, owner of two houses and a houseful of furniture, possessor of a bank account, a miner with the drive to 'get on'. As it happened she married a man indebted, Marx's classic labourer, owner of nothing but his body.

Her disenchantment with the marriage dates from this experience: 'She said very little to her husband, but her manner had changed towards him. Something in her proud, honourable soul had crystallised out hard as rock.' Because she remains aloof from the other miners' wives, who beard her for having put a stop to Morel's career as dancing master, and by implication for having fettered his free spirit with her puritan scruples, she feels increasingly isolated, 'miles away from her own people'. Her own people, of course, are the ministers, engineers, teachers and the like whom she knew as a girl. We are told that this marks the beginning of their marital battle, a beginning which Lawrence depicts with perfect clarity in social terms. But then what conclusion does he draw?

> She fought to make him undertake his own responsibilities, to make him fulfil his obligations. But he was too different from her. His nature was purely sensuous, and she strove to make him moral, religious. She tried to force him to face things. He could not endure it – it drove him out of his mind.

The narrator has translated social differences into moral and psychological terms: the wife is responsible, aware of obligations, bearing the reformer's burden: the husband is irresponsible, blind to obligations, the crude soil which she is to cultivate; he is sensuous, the body; she is religious, the spirit. Two pages later we read:

> Nevertheless, she still continued to strive with him. She still had her high moral sense, inherited from generations of Puritans. It was now a religious instinct, and she was almost a fanatic with him, because she loved him, or had loved him. If he sinned, she tortured him. If he drank, and lied, was often a poltroon, sometimes a knave, she wielded the lash unmercifully.
>
> The pity was, she was too much his opposite. She could not be content with the little he might be; she would have him the much that he ought to be. So, in seeking to make him nobler than he could be, she destroyed him. She injured and hurt and scarred herself, but lost none of her worth. She also had the children.

Their differences in expectation are translated into valued 'opposites': she has a high moral instinct, he by implication has a low; he sins and she redeems; he is content with mediocrity while she aspires to noble heights; she strives to shape him, he remains the passive clay; although he is destroyed, she, miraculously, loses 'none of her worth'. The passage, like the novel as a whole, assumes Mrs Morel's purpose and standards. Thus concrete differences between particular human beings, differences which are comprehensible in social terms, serve as the basis for constructing a metaphysic which opposes the body to the mind.

Time after time in those early pages Lawrence proffers moral or psychological explanations of incidents which he has already given us evidence for interpreting sociologically. Consider the hair-clipping scene in the opening chapter. Borrowing clothes from her sisters, Mrs

Morel arrays baby William in white coat and hat, complete with ostrich feather, and she lets his hair burgeon in curls to complete this transformation of the miner's son into Little Lord Fauntleroy. One morning Morel takes the boy aside and clips his hair. No son of *his* should be considered a sissy in the village – but this is precisely what Mrs Morel wanted, because the child's appearance was a prop for her performance as lady in the mining community. In his description of the aftermath, however, Lawrence ignores this social dimension, referring to the incident as an 'act of masculine clumsiness'. Morel appears totally cowed, his wife appears the martyr.

Having taken the pledge at the time of his marriage, Morel resumes his drinking after these early battles, but not more heavily than many miners, so we are told, nor anything stronger than beer. In various scenes we learn that the pub offered him a form of community, free from authority, that could be found neither in mine nor home. His pub-sitting was a regular part of the miner's life, a compensation for numbing and back-breaking work, often the only social activity other than chapel (where Noncomformist ministers reconciled an embittered flock to their barren pasture) which was available to an uneducated and exhausted man in an industrial village. Despised by his wife, shut out from his family, Morel has added reason for drinking. But in scene after scene, when he appears drunk and brutal, we hear nothing of his reasons for drinking, but only of his ruin and of his wife's bitter suffering. After these early scenes, which pretend to justify the father's damnation by the mother, and, following her, by the children, Lawrence treats Morel from the outside as a broken man who is responsible for his own ruin, one who is redeemed only in fleeting moments by his singing or tinkering. The narrator's judgement is consistent with that of the mother: 'his manhood broke', 'he broke himself', he became 'more or less a husk', he 'fell into a slow ruin', he 'lapsed slowly', he 'denied the God in him'.

There seems to be a division between the narrator who is compassionately recording the miner's life, and the narrator who is judging that life. After all, the triumph of realism is also Lawrence's triumph as a writer: he conveys a sense of the pressures, deformations and joys of life in that mining community with a loving attention and a vigour of language which is unrivalled in English literature. In a scene midway through the novel Morel observes his own body while bathing, a body prematurely aged, twisted and broken from years of hacking at the coal-face and from scores of accidents, a body scarred blue with coal-dust, and instead of damning the mines which have crippled him, 'he felt the ruin he had made during these years. He wanted to bustle about, to run away from it'. Lawrence simultaneously records a fact and implies a judgement. That Morel *felt* responsible for his own ruin seems convincing and disturbing. But the narrator by his silence at this point appears to accept this judgement, implying that Morel's social fate, a fate shared with millions of labourers, was a sign of personal guilt.

The narrator consistently views the father through the mother's eyes:

> As he bent over, lacing his boots, there was a certain vulgar gusto in his movement that divided him from the reserved, watchful rest of the family. He always ran away from the battle with himself.

Lawrence was later to use the contrast between reserve and gusto as a means of distinguishing the neurotically repressed middle classes from the instinctive and sensuous common people. But here the miner appears 'vulgar', elsewhere we have found him described as a 'knave', 'poltroon', 'nasty' and 'brutal'. When he returns home sweaty and exhausted from the mines, to find the Congregational minister sipping tea over a table-cloth in the kitchen, and when he is treated as a crude beast by his wife, Morel understandably grows furious. The minister is one of Mrs Morel's 'own people', he is an educated man, a spiritual man, possessed of proper manners. He is a reincarnation of John Field, a middle-class substitute for her husband. Enough has passed before to persuade us that Morel appreciates the significance of the minister's presence and of his wife's behaviour; certainly the reader does. Yet the narrator endorses Mrs Morel's opinion that, by fussing and complaining, the miner is just showing off; even young William is made to hate him, 'with a boy's hatred for false sentiment, for the stupid treatment of his mother'. We are told that as Morel ages he acts in increasingly 'dirty and disgusting ways', but all we learn of this behaviour is that 'His manners in the house were the same as he used among the colliers down pit'. Yet what was the determining reality for this miner, cut off from the rest of his family, if it was not that gathering of colliers down pit? His ways were disgusting from Mrs Morel's point of view, according to her middle-class upbringing, and it is this point of view which Lawrence employs throughout the novel, in matters great and small.

Even Morel's lack of education is turned against him. In one important scene Paul reluctantly tells his father of winning a prize in a writing competition for a child's paper:

> Morel turned round to him.
> 'Have you, my boy? What sort of a competition?'
> 'Oh, nothing – about famous women.'
> 'And how much is the prize, then, as you've got?'
> 'It's a book.'
> 'Oh, indeed!'
> 'About birds.'
> 'Hm – hm!'
> And that was all. Conversation was impossible between the father and any other member of the family. He was an outsider. He had denied the God in him.

The breach between father and son appears as an educationally conditioned difference in language. What after all is Morel to say about famous women, resurrected from histories and dressed up in an essay? What conversation is he to make about the prize book which he cannot read? Still a child, Paul has already outstripped his father in formal if not in practical knowledge. Nor is that surprising in view of the miner's upbringing. Yet this demonstration of Morel's educational backwardness (previous scenes have demonstrated his drunkenness, his brutality, his ignorance of bourgeois manners and his indifference to bourgeois culture, his refusal to stand up for his own rights and his inability 'to get on' at work) is made occasion for the judgement that he is *personally* guilty of failing to become a whole human being: 'He had denied the God in him.' Although it is difficult to see how any but an exceptional man could have overcome his disadvantages – poverty, inadequate education and limited class expectations, work that is physically exhausting while mentally undemanding, cramped housing and political impotence – nevertheless Mrs Morel condemns him for failing to achieve precisely this miraculous escape. Paul accepts her class-bound judgement. Lawrence, having himself freshly escaped at the time he wrote the novel, accepted it as well.

In making that judgement Mrs Morel applied what can best be called a 'bourgeois' perspective, wholly consistent with her Protestant ethics, a perspective which treats the individual as the unit of success or failure, without regard to the conditions which shape him, without regard to the collective social reality within which he dwells. Like St Paul, whom her father admired more than any other man, and like the great Reformation theologians who looked to St Paul for their authority, Mrs Morel held the individual responsible for his salvation or damnation. Her individualist perspective dominates the book, as her feelings dominate Paul, as her values dominate the Morel household. Suffering from the capitalist ethic on the job and from the Protestant ethic in his own home, Morel neatly illustrates Max Weber's proposition of a link between the two spheres of ideology. Both the religious and the economic ideology treat mankind as a collection of atomic individuals, each person seeking his own salvation or profit, motivated solely by rational self-interest – according to Adam Smith's formulation – each isolated Robinson Crusoe remaining solely responsible for his worldly condition. Thus both William and Paul make their escape, such as it is, alone, leaving their community unchanged; their alienation would seem to be the natural state of man according to Mrs Morel's individualist perspective.

For Lawrence, writing *Sons and Lovers* between 1910 and 1913, before experiencing the mass insanity of the War, before really understanding his characters' problems as problems of contemporary society, this individualist perspective was convincing. After all, had he not scrambled out of the working class, had he not escaped the industrial system, had he not wooed a lady? Individual autonomy, at least for those who were willing to give a tug at their own bootstraps, seemed to him a proven fact. Enjoying an exile's comparative social independence, he exaggerated man's freedom, since anyone estranged from the conditions and institutions of his society, whether physically exiled like Rousseau, or emotionally like Blake, is prone to stress man's freedom rather than his bondage. Of course the exile is at once the most and the least free of men; his very isolation from all social groups prevents him from effectively acting upon his ideas.[1] Such isolation commonly leads – as has been shown by Emile Durkheim, who named this condition *anomie* – to frustration and disgust, equally with oneself and one's society. Like Swift and Orwell, two other emotional exiles, Lawrence was by spells the aloof yet penetrating observer, and the misanthrope, manifesting by turns the profoundest concern for his countrymen and the most consummate disgust, each alike the fruit of social isolation.

Lawrence's exaggerated sense of individual autonomy led him to distort his representation of reality – especially in *Sons and Lovers*, but to a varying degree in all his novels – by isolating personal existence partly or wholly from social existence. Although *Sons and Lovers* abounds in references to social conditions and historical movements, these are not used to account for the quality, the changes and crises, of individual lives. That is to say, Lawrence explains the problems of his characters psychologically rather than historically, in terms of a personal rather than a collective past. When in a later essay he wrote that 'I feel it is the change inside the individual which is my real concern. The great social change interests me and troubles me, but it is not my field',[2] he posited a dichotomy between individual psychology and social existence which would have seemed alien to George Eliot, Dickens or Austen, and to all of the great Continental realists such as Stendhal, Balzac or Tolstoy. Of course he was entitled to occupy himself primarily with subjectivity, and did so, but when he set himself the task of *explaining* subjectivity, or of passing judgement on individuals, he often failed, as in the case of Morel, to take the social dimension into account.

Morel's failure should be grounds for criticising the industrial and economic system which has maimed him, rather than for criticising the man. Mrs Morel's bitter repudiation of her married state expresses more than class prejudice. Her outrage and Morel's ruin were to be translated by Lawrence into a basic critique of the social order which had produced this humanly degraded way of life. This woman is determined not only to help her children escape the financial straits in which she finds herself, but also to liberate them from the brutal working conditions and from the domestic squalor which the industrial order has imposed upon generations of Morels. To her son she transmits both outrage and frustration, and she teaches him to defend precisely those values which the industrial system – with its associated politics, economics, housing and schools – denies. The son of Mrs Lawrence was to protest – in plays and essays and novels – the evil which had been committed against the human spirit in Eastwood's mines and streets. When Lawrence returned to the same emotional terrain at the end of his life, in *Lady Chatterley's Lover* and 'Nottingham and the Mining Country', he judged his father differently. He had become aware by that time of the larger social forces which had intersected in the lives of the Morels, Leivers and Dawes, and in particular those forces which had mutilated his father.

I have dwelt upon the conflict between Mr and Mrs Morel because it is the clearest example in the novel of a socially and historically comprehensive problem which is nevertheless interpreted by Lawrence in personal, psychological terms, and because it demonstrates the triumph of Mrs Morel's individualist perspective, which rules the novel as a whole. The class differences between Mr and Mrs Morel are evident. The novel 'follows this idea', Lawrence wrote to his agent in 1912, 'a woman of character and refinement goes into the lower class, and has no satisfaction in her own life'.[3] Lawrence was very much aware of the corresponding class differences between his own parents, and he frequently referred to this social conflict, built into his family, as a means of explaining certain aspects of his own character and thought.

> My mother was a clever, ironical delicately moulded woman of good, old burgher descent. She married below her. My father was dark, ruddy, with a fine laugh. He is a coal miner. He was one of the sanguine temperament, warm and hearty, but unstable: he lacked principle, as my mother would have said. He deceived her and lied to her. She despised him – he drank.[4]

He wrote those words late in 1910, while his mother was dying. In a later poem, much of the sympathy which he had once felt toward his mother's class having vanished, he wrote more bitterly of the social fissure which had divided his childhood:

> My father was a working man
>   and a collier was he,
> at six in the morning they turned him down
>   and they turned him up for tea.
>
> My mother was a superior soul
>   a superior soul was she,
> cut out to play a superior role
>   in the god-damn bourgeoisie.
>
> We children were the in-betweens
>   little non-descripts were we,
> indoors we called each other you,
>   outside, it was *tha* and *thee*.[5]

Aware though he was of this parental class conflict, I do not believe Lawrence fully realised how very near the heart of his work that conflict lay, how fundamentally the contrast between his father's life and his mother's ideas had influenced his own representation of reality....

We have observed that the conflict between Walter and Gertrude Morel is often described in the novel as an opposition between flesh and spirit, an opposition which is reflected by differences in speech: Morel's language is highly sensory and formulaic, presenting a direct account of his emotional responses to immediate experience; Mrs Morel on the other hand demonstrates that, while sharing her husband's capacity for concreteness, she possesses the additional capacity for abstraction, for transcending the present situation towards past and future, for articulating something more than immediate sensations. By the time of writing *Studies in Classic American Literature*, Lawrence had come to view the analogous contrast between his own parents as the paradigm of conflict between body and mind:

> My father hated books, hated the sight of anyone reading or writing. My mother hated the thought that any of her sons should be condemned to manual labour. Her sons must have something higher than that. She won. But she died first. He laughs longest who laughs last. There is a basic hostility in all of us between the physical and the mental, the blood and the spirit. The mind is 'ashamed' of the blood. And the blood is destroyed by the mind, actually.[6]

Here manual labour is explicitly opposed to labour of the mind. Morel's work is almost purely physical; the role of planning, purpose, control – of *consciousness* – is minimal. Only at night or on holiday, when he is mending boots or blacksmithing, does Morel become the conscious, self-directing craftsman idealised by Ruskin and Morris; but these are only sparetime activities, fitfully pursued. He is not a craftsman but an industrial worker. Mental functions in the mines have been transferred to the owners and managers. Like Mrs Morel, they are the educated ones, and they are the ones whose projects and orders are carried out by men such as Morel. There is in the mines a *functional* division between body and mind, which corresponds – as Marx and other nineteenth-century critics of industrial civilisation observed – to the division of labour between workers and managers.

This division was for Lawrence the dominant feature of industrial society: it crops up again and again in his writing. Aside from the account of opposition between workers and owners in *The White Peacock* and *Sons and Lovers*, the manager reappears as a creature of dominating will and mind in such characters as Tom Brangwen, Jr, Gerald Crich, Clifford Chatterley, Fraser (in *The Daughter-in-Law*), and the mine owners of *Aaron's Rod*.[7] ...

Although Lawrence's critique of industrial society has not yet become explicit in *Sons and Lovers*, the raw materials, the condi-

tions which he would later condemn, are all there. During the nineteenth century, as the scale of economic organisation increased, as
automation fragmented the work process, as control over the
process itself receded ever further from the worker and as the relations between workers became increasingly mechanised, the individual human being was reduced to the role of an instrument of
production. We can observe the effects of these economic changes
upon the life of Bestwood. The men become interchangeable tools
in the production process. There is no opportunity for creativity in
their work, nor does their labour seem to produce any durable
results, since the indistinguishable tons of coal are quickly con-
sumed. Slack times in the pit mean hard times in the home, and
there is no redress. The penniless and the powerless in the novel are
intimidated by train stations and restaurants, by waitresses and
paymasters; they queue for Saturday morning charity treatment at
the doctor's surgery; like Mrs Morel they develop 'that peculiar
shut-off look of the poor who have to depend on the favour of
others'. Paul's feeling of terror and humiliation when fetching his
father's pay expresses a child's dread of the 'system', when first
seeking work as a lad fresh out of school, he balks at entry into the
'business world, with its regulated system of values, and its impersonality', because this means becoming a 'prisoner of industrialism'.
In order to work, a man must submit to an alien system, which operates according to its own impersonal laws.

The working people of Bestwood have little sway over those
forces which fundamentally shape their lives – supply and demand
of the market, weather, pay offers, strikes, government decisions,
educational policy, development of industrial uses for coal, accidents in the mine, or the distribution of resources in the earth's
bowels. They are not masters of their condition, either individually
or collectively. As a group they function within an encompassing
political and economic system over which they have practically no
control. For them the larger society has become, to use Marx's
term, *reified*: it seems to be a substantially independent world, in-
habited by irrational, unpredictable and uncontrollable forces
which determine people's lives while remaining oblivious to their
desires.

There are striking similarities between this experience of society
and Lawrence's representation of nature as an autonomous process
over which the individual has no control, but in which he is deeply
enmeshed by virtue of his animality, his existence as a physical

creature. This is the view of nature which is implicit, for example, in the scene in which Paul and Miriam confront a rose tree at evening:

> It was very still. The tree was tall and straggling. It had thrown its briers over a hawthorn-bush, and its long streamers trailed thick right down to the grass, splashing the darkness everywhere with great spilt stars, pure white. In bosses of ivory and in large splashed stars the roses gleamed on the darkness of foliage and stems and grass. Paul and Miriam stood close together, silent, and watched. Point after point the steady roses shone out of them, seeming to kindle something in their souls. The dusk came like smoke around, and still did not put out the roses.

The rose tree is an active subject, the master of transitive verbs, and is not simply alive but *independently* alive, acting on the young lovers who are bound together, as they themselves acknowledge, by something common in nature, something which they recognise to be continuous with their own passions, instincts and desires, something that calls forth a response from their 'souls'. Consistently, Lawrence's human agents for the most part respond passively to impersonal forces which transcend them and which, in sexual relations particularly, are overwhelming.

This subjection of the human to impersonal nature recurs in passages throughout *Sons and Lovers*: the account of Paul and Miriam's first sexual encounter, in which a cherry tree, a sunset and a fir register the harmony between the course of external nature and the course of their young blood; the scene by the flooded Trent, where the surging river functions as objective correlation for the emotions that master Clara and Paul; the scene in which Paul emerges from lovemaking to hear peewits scream:

> It was all so much bigger than themselves that he was hushed. They had met, and included in their meeting the thrust of the manifold grass-stems, the cry of the peewit, the wheel of the stars;

and finally another lovemaking scene in which he merges in consciousness with the encircling natural world:

> Just as he was, so it seemed the vigorous, wintry stars were strong also with life. He and they struck with the same pulse of fire, and the same joy of strength which held the bracken-frond stiff near his eyes held his own body firm. It was as if he, and the stars, and the dark herbage, and Clara were licked up in an immense tongue of flame, which tore upwards and upwards.

After one such encounter Paul reflects that 'It was as if they had been blind agents of a great force': the natural process, like the social, becomes reified, appearing as an autonomous realm of irrational and impersonal forces. Just as unpredictable and uncontrollable social forces rule the lives of common people, so natural forces govern the course of personal relationships. The one realm of impersonal forces is no more hospitable than the other. And just as economic forces reduce human beings to instruments of production, so instinctual forces reduce human beings to instruments of gratification.

Thus Paul justifies his calculated use of Clara by arguing that their intercourse is mutually rewarding – yet she is nonetheless his instrument, serving his needs. To his mother he confesses that, 'Sometimes, when I see her just as *the woman*, I love her, mother; but then, when she talks and criticises, I often don't listen to her.' When Clara charges him with treating her as an object, rather than as a person with her own needs and desires, he excuses himself by appealing to the relentless urge of passion. His relationship with Miriam, though fuller, is corrupted by the same instrumental attitude:

> He had always, almost wilfully, to put her out of count, and act from the brute strength of his own feelings. And he could not do it often, and there remained afterwards always the same sense of failure and of death.

When in a fit of pique he accuses her of trying to 'absorb' him, he is merely echoing his mother's jealous sentiments. Although Lawrence was later to swear by the 'truth' of judgements uttered spontaneously and passionately (basing his faith on the instincts), the judgements which actually appear in his novels, as in the present instance, often merely express unexamined prejudices. When Paul declares an end to his love affair with Miriam – which for his part has been based on intellectual and sexual domination – he is shocked by the girl's bitterness, since he has justified his actions all along by reference to the holy and undeniable passions. In its crudest forms this appeal to the sanctity of instinct becomes in the later Lawrence a variety of sexual determinism, differing little in its ethical implications from the biological determinism of the Social Darwinists. The instrumentalisation of human beings and the mechanisation of personal relationships is equally vicious, whether enforced by an industrial-economic order, or by a natural order....

The sentimental education of a working-class boy, the lives of a mining family, a farming family and a suffragette: these appear to be the chief subjects of *Sons and Lovers*. We are presented with the drama of 'an organic disturbance in the relationships of men and women', to use Dorothy Van Ghent's phrase,[8] and with the Oedipal dilemma of a miner's son. But these materials have an historical content which Lawrence, on account of his psychological focus, did not fully acknowledge. That is to say, the true underlying subject of the novel is a larger historical reality, the movements and qualities of which are concretely focused in the lives of individual characters, who are 'typical' in the sense defined by Lukács.[9] The psychology of these characters can be interpreted as a response to social conditions; their motives and behaviour are comprehensible in terms of their social existence. Whether we examine Mrs Morel's frustrated bourgeois aspirations, Morel's brutalisation, Mrs Leivers' bitterness, Miriam's compensating religiosity, Clara's feminism, Dawes's demoralisation, or the middle-class values and emotional lameness of Paul, we find evidence of crucial trends in contemporary society: the deprivations of working-class life; the increasing mechanisation of society which was to result in the horrors of the 1914–1918 War; the conflict between bourgeois and proletarian ideologies which would lead to revolutions after the war; the proliferating sense of *anomie*; and the movement of women for emancipation. To claim this is not to deny the richness of the novel's world, but on the contrary to indicate the ground of its coherence, to reveal the matrix of social trends which gives it unity. Indeed the novel derives its significance as much from this larger historical reality as from the individual lives through which history is concretely grasped. Although Lawrence focuses on personal relations and subjectivity, it is a subjectivity permeated by social forces, which registers the stress of growing up within a working community that was being transformed by industry, the schools, and the awakening of social consciousness.

Furthermore, Lawrence's own psychology, like that of his characters, is rooted in the social and moral conditions which govern the world of *Sons and Lovers*. Like them, his values and thought developed within the bounds of a specific social existence. His ideas and his art, whatever enduring interest they may possess, represent first and foremost a coherent response to a concrete historical situation. I have suggested certain correspondences between the plane of consciousness and the plane of social existence: the origins of Lawrence's individualistic perspective in bourgeois ideology, with his consequent substitution of psychological for historical explanation; the relation of his mind/body dualism to the dualism of mental and physical functions enforced by the division of labour; the additional parallel between the mind/body dualism and the conflict (practical and ideological) between middle and working classes; the similarity between the representation of nature and of society, each realm being impersonal, autonomous and irrational, and each one reducing the individual to the status of an object in a process which he cannot control. There is at least this much similarity between the structure of his social experience and the structure of ideas which he uses to account for that experience.

From Scott Sanders, *D. H. Lawrence: The World of His Novels* (London, 1973), pp. 21–59.

NOTES

[Scott Sanders's piece is extracted from a longer chapter on 'Society and Ideology in *Sons and Lovers*'. In it he discusses some of the strengths and limitations of Lawrence's portrayal of the working-class community of Bestwood and in particular the characterisation of Walter Morel. He therefore tackles a subject which has not received wide critical comment other than the kind of moral disapproval which Lawrence's novel in some respects encourages. But Sanders broadens the argument to open discussion of more general issues. He is interested in the way Bestwood is described from the point of view of one who has rejected it and he, like Martz (essay 4), Holderness (essay 9) and Pinkney (essay 11), is concerned to elucidate the problem of the novel's realism (see the general Introduction for discussion). Like John Goode (essay 8) and a number of these critics, Sanders also focuses on the theme of isolation in a social world which, he argues, is portrayed as increasingly atomised and alienating. For reasons of space and focus in the argument, this piece has been edited in some places and Scott Sanders' sectional divisions have been removed. No page references are provided. Ed.]

1. I am indebted to Raymond Williams's discussion of the psychology of exile in *Culture and Society, 1780–1950* (Harmondsworth, 1961).

2. D. H. Lawrence, 'The State of Funk', in *Phoenix: The Posthumous Papers of D. H. Lawrence*, ed. Edward M. McDonald (London, 1936), p. 567.

3. Letter to Edward Garnett, 14.xi.12, *Collected Letters of D. H. Lawrence*, ed. Harry T. Moore (London, 1962), p. 160.

4. Letter to Rachel Armand Taylor, 15.xi.10. *Collected Letters*, p. 68.

5. These are the first three stanzas of 'Red-Herring', *Complete Poems of D. H. Lawrence*, ed. Vivian de Sola Pinto and F. Warren Roberts (Harmondsworth, 1977), p. 490. See also the late piece 'Autobiographical Fragment'. On the question generally, see Ada Lawrence, *Young Lorenzo* (Florence, 1932).

6. D. H. Lawrence, *Studies in Classic American Literature* (London, 1924), p. 81.

7. In his *English History 1914–1945* (Oxford, 1965), A. J. P. Taylor observes that the mine-owners in the 1920s, who made a practice of wringing every ounce of coal and every minute of labour from exhausted miners, and who starved out the strikers, 'were about the least worthy element in the British community' (p. 248).

8. Dorothy Van Ghent, *The English Novel: Form and Function* (New York, 1953), p. 247.

9. Georg Lukács, *Studies in European Realism: A Sociological Survey of the Writings of Balzac, Stendhal, Zola, Tolstoy, Gorki and Others*, trans. Edith Bone (London, 1950), 'Preface'.

11

Englishness and Realism in *Sons and Lovers*

TONY PINKNEY

The 'and' of *Sons and Lovers* (1913) announces the book's allegiance to the great achievements of nineteenth-century English realism: *Sense and Sensibility, Pride and Prejudice, North and South* and *Wives and Daughters, Dombey and Son.* Even *Middlemarch*, situating itself in the mid-point between opposites as yet unspecified, is nothing but a single 'and' writ large. The 'and' of these titles registers an initial tension or obstruction – in Mrs Gaskell's classical instance, say, the economic and cultural friction between the split halves of a divided kingdom, North versus South. Yet it also guarantees that tension's overcoming in an act of humane, totalising comprehension which, though it may have its analogues within the book (as when Margaret Hale plights troth with the manufacturer Thornton at the end of *North and South*), is ultimately identical with the act of writing the novel, this kind of novel. No doubt it is never quite unproblematic to be both son and lover, least of all in the very years when Freud was formulating his Oedipus theory; yet the novelistic tradition evoked by that conjunction promises that such limits and resistances will at last be overcome, that the binary opposition is at last subject to a benign sublation, that the novel will – in E. M. Forster's famous phrase – 'only connect'.

This quiet humane confidence might seem peculiarly 'English', but Lawrence was by now setting his English-realist enthusiasms within a wider European perspective. Writing to Blanche Jennings in 1908, he contrasts Balzac favourably to George Eliot's 'padding and moral reflection'.[1] Reading *Eugénie Grandet* a month earlier, he had realised that the French novel might be more English than the English, truer to the native fictional tradition than its own exponents: 'it is rather astonishing that we, the cold English, should have to go to the fleshy French for level-headed, fair unrelenting realism' (*Letters*, 35). If some French authors could be honorary Englishmen, so too could the odd Russian; Dostoyevsky is the author of a mere 'tract, a treatise, a pamphlet compared with Tolstoy's *Anna Karenina* or *War and Peace*'. If the sheer scale of Tolstoy's *magnum opus* dwarfs all its English counterparts, his choice of that most 'English' of conjunctions in his title speaks for a continuity of moral and aesthetic intent. 'And' declares the totalising ambitions of the realist novel, its determination to penetrate beneath the congealed surfaces and apparent oppositions of social relations into their concealed, systemic dynamic. Lawrence's use of the conjunction in titling his first major work might thus be taken to imply a view of realism similar to that espoused by Georg Lukács in the 1930s. For Lukács, the modernist schools from Naturalism on remain 'frozen in their own immediacy'. In contrast:

> Every major realist fashions the material given in his own experience, and in so doing makes use of techniques of abstraction, among others. But his goal is to penetrate the laws governing objective reality and to uncover the deeper, hidden, mediated, not immediately perceptible network of relationships that go to make up society ... in the works of such writers we observe the whole surface of life in all its essential determinants, and not just a subjectively perceived moment isolated from the totality in an abstract and over-intense manner.[2]

Or, in the more homely phrasing of George Eliot in *Felix Holt*, 'there is no private life which has not been determined by a wider public lot.'[3]

There is much in *Sons and Lovers*, clearly, which corresponds to such emphases. In his letters Lawrence habitually refers to his work-in-progress both by its initial title, *Paul Morel*, and as 'my colliery novel', as if he were trying to capture exactly that balanced interaction between the personal and social which Lukács focuses in his notion of 'typicality'. The opening pages of the book evoke a broad historical panorama: the slow, steady, small-scale mining of the countryside by donkey-powered gin-pits ('some of which had been worked in the time of Charles II') suddenly 'elbowed aside' by a brash new phase of capitalist investment and exploitation, the 'large mines of the financiers' and their interlinking railway (p. 35). The house in the Bottoms where the Morel family lives is not just an opaque self-contained object or inert fictional 'setting', but rather the still decipherable trace of a massive historical process in which whole landscapes and populations were entirely remade. And this incisive social perspective, both impressively panoptic and locally impassioned, governs the whole presentation of 'The Early Married Life of the Morels'. The class tensions between father and mother (grounds of their initial sexual attraction but then of the breakdown of the marriage into embittered non-communication), the nagging economic pressures on the family week after week, the harsher physical pressures on Mr Morel at the coal face which he then transmits in rage and violence to his own family, the mutual support mechanisms of the oppressed community (whether institu-tionalised as clubs or Co-op, or in informal habits of neighbourly helpfulness), the complex effects of all this on a younger, better-educated generation – the vivid concrete realisation of all these in-terlocking processes constitutes the undoubted strength of a mode of novelistic analysis in which the political and personal, the sociological and the psychoanalytic, are powerfully fused.

Realism for Georg Lukács is epistemologically 'reflectionist': it is a mirror of a peculiarly active, interventionist kind, reproducing essential deep-structural relations rather than surface details, but a mirror none the less. It is then perhaps no accident that in Lawrence's early novels, English–realist though they generically define themselves to be, mirrors function in a decidedly unsatisfac-tory fashion. In *The White Peacock* Mrs Saxton's mirror 'left gaps and spots and scratches in one's countenance, and even where it was brightest, it gave one's reflection a far-away dim aspect';[4] in *Sons and Lovers*, 'in the little looking-glass nailed against the wall she [Miriam] could see only a fragment of herself at a time' (p. 221). The realist 'and' seems here to be less efficiently totalising than the Lukácsians would claim it to be. North may marry South in Mrs Gaskell's novel, but Paul finds it qualitatively, not quantita-tively, harder to be Son and Lover, discovering at last that he must choose between his mother and his female sexual partners. The title's 'and' is more of a distant utopian aspiration than a secret guarantee that the jigsaw of the dissociated sensibility can in the end be put back together again. Indeed, in moving from the nineteenth to twentieth centuries, the firm starting- and finishing-points of realist totalisation seem to dissolve, leaving only the 'and' itself, moving frenetically from a point it cannot define towards a destination it can never reach, breaking down into that ephemeral 'between-ness' finely evoked by Matthew Arnold in 'Stanzas from the Grande Chartreuse':

> Wandering between two worlds, one dead,
> The other powerless to be born.[5]

'And' then mutates into the modernist 'to'. 'Only connect', wrote Forster; but his finest novel is called *Passage to India*, and Fielding and Aziz do not connect at the end of this; so too does Virginia Woolf's early realist work *Night and Day* give way to her more characteristic *To the Lighthouse*. Yeats wrote the exemplary poem of the modernist 'to' in his 'Sailing to Byzantium' (its successor, 'Byzantium', in which he actually arrives, is much inferior); and Lawrence himself captures something of this destinationless modernist travelling in his 'The Woman Who Rode Away' – not to mention the last twelve years of his life, which were one long pointless 'to'.

Sons and Lovers begins with Lukácsian ambitions, but they soon break down, in two major senses. First, the sociological acumen and impersonality of the book do not after all prevent it from having a self-reflexive 'modernist' dimension. For it is a *Künstlerroman*, a study of the artist's formation comparable to Thomas Mann's *Tonio Kröger* (1903), James Joyce's *A Portrait of the Artist as a Young Man* (1916) or Dorothy Richardson's *Pilgrimage* (1915 onwards). Such works end, at least in principle, at the point where the central character has acquired sufficient maturity and technical expertise to write or 'paint' or 'compose' the text in which he or she appears; there is a self-fulfilling circularity about this sub-genre, with the snake ultimately swallowing its own tail. For Lukács, the great realists achieved a totality of subject and object in the category of action, where history could be seen in its very making by the individuals whom it also determines. The *Künstlerroman* sustains the ambition of totality, but raises it one level, containing it entirely in the aesthetic rather than the phenomenal realm: subject and object now converge when the fledgling artist can write the work which presents him or her to us. Totality in this sense never reaches the community at all, which is felt as threat to it rather than its field of possibility; the novel now evokes that poignant, subject-centred 'transcendental homelessness' that Lukács had analysed in his pre-Marxist *Theory of the Novel* (1916). All readers of *Sons and Lovers* have felt this shift as the book progresses – from the sociological objectivity of the treatment of Paul's parents to a more subjectivistic, almost inchoate intensity as he moves towards manhood. Far from finding succour in the Bestwood community as his family had during his childhood, Paul cuts right away from its sanctions and standards, coming 'more or less to the bedrock of belief that one should feel inside oneself for right and wrong' (p. 314); at the Leivers' home he mocks the Primitive Methodist chapel with a glib arrogance which far exceeds that shown earlier by his brother's London girlfriend. Even his mother, herself antagonistic to the local community in so many ways, sees that his repudiation of it has been carried to a dangerous extreme and seeks to draw him back from the brink, 'to fight for his very life against his own will to die' (p. 316). And if subjectivity takes on a fierce, unmanageable intensity, the social environment fades into mere backcloth for individualist adventures, as when Paul and Clara contemplate the Nottinghamshire landscape from the Castle hill. Whereas Joyce's *Portrait of the Artist* is explicitly and unashamedly a novel of this sort, devoted to aesthetic autonomy not communal solidarity, *Sons and Lovers*, which had sought to be something else and more, also dwindles to these proportions.

But as realism breaks down, more turbulent, primitive literary energies come out of the undergrowth; and these centre on the figure of Miriam, who has been much misunderstood. Misunderstood, however, not just by critics but by the text itself; for they have followed its lead in seeing Miriam Leivers as an excessively intellectualist woman whose rabid virginity creates most of Paul's difficulties – though the more generous of them will then add that he is a fastidiously virginal intellectual of exactly the same kind. And this line of meaning does attach to Miriam: it is one among several threads of her significance; for *Sons and Lovers* is notably unclear about the kind of threat she represents, though that she is a – in fact *the* – threat it has no doubt whatsoever. What I here want to stress is the heavy emotionalism which is assigned to her throughout, felt in the characteristic epithets that attach to her: 'surcharged', 'heavy', 'intense', 'mystical', 'religious', 'romantic', 'ecstatic', 'rhapsodic'. In this respect, she takes further aspects of Emily Saxton, of whom Cyril Beardsall noted 'the extravagance of her emotional nature ... she knows herself powerless in the tumult of her feelings'.[6] But these Miriamesque adjectives do not so much evoke a character as delineate a literary genre. Miriam is not just one woman among others, a possible love-object for the young Paul Morel. She is rather, so to speak, a different kind of *text* which has strayed, as if by mistake, into the precincts of the would-be classic realism of *Sons and Lovers* and must politely but firmly be shown the door. Or perhaps more accurately, as classic realism bit by bit disintegrates, an atavistic fictional mode which it had historically displaced threatens to make an uncanny return – and must then be urgently repressed. For as Paul informs his girlfriend, 'himself, he said, was Norman, Miriam was *Gothic*' (p. 229 – my emphasis).

After visiting London in 1908 Lawrence wrote to Blanche Jennings about this 'Capital of Commercialism':

> a place of stately individualistic ideas, with nothing Gothic or aspiring or spiritual ... It is Lincoln and Ely that are still, and set the soul a-quivering. Silence is strange and mystical and wearying ... it is the noble, the divine, the Gothic that agitates and worries one.
>
> (*Letters*, 29)

A month later he accused her of being 'Brontë-bitten in your taste in heroines' (*Letters*, 34), just as he denounced Jessie Chambers, real-life original of Miriam, for being 'purely emotional': 'He declared I was like Emily Brontë ... "You *are* like her, you are intense and introspective as she was"'.[7] Elsewhere he contrasts Louie Burrows with Jessie (here dubbed Muriel) exactly in terms of the supersession of the Gothic by Victorian realism; Louie's is 'a fine, warm, healthy, natural love – not like Jane Eyre, who is Muriel, but like – say Rhoda Fleming or a commoner Anna Karenina' (*Letters*, 70). For once Miriam enters the book we do indeed seem to be drawn into uncanny Gothic realms; 'if you put red berries in your hair ... why would you look like some witch or priestess?', Paul asks her (p. 240), and together they visit a whole series of historical or ancient monuments, strangely resonant objects or places like Hemlock Stone or Crich Stand or even Wingfield Manor, where Mary Queen of Scots was incarcerated. The Leivers family, most of whom share Miriam's sombre emotionalism, seem to Paul to be a strange race of atavistic throwbacks, '*les derniers fils d'une race epuisée*' (the last sons of an exhausted race). Walking beside the wood with Miriam and Clara, he imagines 'old tribes ... bursting out of their darkness of woods upon all the spaces of light' (p. 296).

Even Mrs Morel, than whom nobody could be more dourly commonsensical, inclines to see Miriam as vampire, as 'one of those who will want to suck a man's soul out' (the fact that vampires do not have reflections may account for Miriam's difficulties with mirrors). We can once more formulate all this in terms of the 'and' of *Sons and Lovers*. Nineteenth-century realism overcomes its initial opposition, but in doing so does not wholly cancel out the identities of the competing terms; North and South are reconciled in Mrs Gaskell's text, yet the piquancy of their surface differences remains. But if in one sense there is too little realist *rapprochement* between Sons and Lovers, since for Paul maternal and adult-sexual relationships prove incompatible, in another sense there is too much – so much so indeed that the *rapprochement* ceases to be 'realist' at all. The 'and' now proves so powerful that it breaks down the dualism altogether: Paul's mother *is* his lover, as a host of details and similes stresses throughout the book. But this means that the incest-taboo, keystone of the whole order of culture and of its classicist and realist literary modes, has broken down. And as culture travels back, Tardis-like, to and beyond its primordial origins in this prohibition, so do more archaic forms – Miriam's Gothic – which are not bound by its edict begin to emerge.

Miriam represents a formidable principle of anti-realism. 'She was prepared for the big things and the deep things, like tragedy. It was the sufficiency of the small-day life she could not trust' (p. 271). Every term thrown at her accusingly by Paul glances laterally at the literary mode to which *Sons and Lovers* is seeking (but by now failing) to align itself: ordinary, human, unexaggerated, common, normal, restraint, reserve. At the very moment when Paul is relentlessly cutting himself away from his community, he is ruthlessly prepared to invoke its norms against Miriam – as she realises, wondering 'why he always claimed to be normal when he was disagreeable' (p. 276). She is both external threat to the novel's realist ambitions and internal scapegoat for its own failure to achieve them. If it could project its own failure onto Miriam, blaming an inner fissuring of the English-realist form into *Künstlerroman* on to its traditional rival the Gothic, then it might salve its own uneasy conscience; to this extent, the novel's dealings with Miriam repeat those of its hero, always eager to read his own sexual inadequacies into her behaviour.

But then there is in these matters a close bond between genre and gender. The Gothic is a rich notion, encompassing medieval

cathedrals (Lincoln, Ely) at one end, and a specifically female subversive literary form at the other (the Brontës). All we need to note
here is that what the novel identifies as the Gothic 'absorptiveness'
of Miriam is simply the fact of female sexuality itself. 'She wanted
to draw all of him into her', we learn; 'her lips were parted, and her
dark eyes lay open to him. His look seemed to travel down into
her' (p. 210). Earlier, as they play on the swing, she experiences
'the exactly proportionate strength of his thrust, and she was afraid.
Down to her bowels went the hot wave of fear' (p. 200). Much of
what the book hates in Miriam is simply femaleness as such, or its
social consequences. The intellectual 'intensity', of which we hear
so much, is in fact a function of her educational deprivation in a
boorish, male-dominated household; she can never be quite easy
among books and ideas after having been starved of them for so
long – something one would have expected the 'sociological' side of
Sons and Lovers to appreciate keenly. But as often as not what the
novel and hero diagnose as a white heat of abstract intellectualism
is simply female sexual desire, as Clara Dawes at least perceives:
'she doesn't want any of your soul communion. That's your own
imagination. She wants you' (p. 338). The 'violence' of the relationship is thus not Miriam's possessiveness but Paul's brittle, 'phallic'
unyieldingness; 'his body seemed one weapon, firm and hard
against her' (p. 274). When Paul does finally, briefly, achieve a
'Miriamseque' Gothic intensity in his sexual relations with Clara,
the novel's realist protest against this is displaced on to his partner.
'Is it me you want, or is it *It*?', she asks (p. 431), seeking to reduce
her own sexuality to the manageable, individuated proportions of
the realist text. Paul's attempt to hold out for a 'mythic' interpretation necessarily breaks down, given that his own allegiances for the
greater part of the novel have been on the other side of the argument. Classicist realism seeks to expel a menace that is always both
sexual and generic.

That process of expulsion is at least as importantly a matter of
style as of plot and theme; but to understand the very texture of the
language of *Sons and Lovers* as realist stratagem, we need to set it
in the context of contemporary stylistic options, which are best
focused in the poetic debates of the first two decades of this
century. In 1912 one of Lawrence's poems appeared in *Georgian
Poetry 1911–1912*, an anthology edited by Edward Marsh to introduce what he saw as a new trend in English poetry; Lawrence
thereafter appeared in four out of the five Georgian collections that

Marsh put together between 1912 and 1922. Yet in both 1915 and 1916 he also contributed poems to Amy Lowell's annual anthology *Some Imagist Poets*, a movement founded on militantly anti-Georgian lines. Was this schizophrenia, or unscrupulousness (he certainly needed the money), or a case of a unique poetic talent which cannot be pigeonholed in any of the glib, doctrinaire '-isms' of the modernist movement? All these answers have been suggested; but I want to explore a different logic for Lawrence's participation in both Georgianism and Imagism – a logic which has important bearings on the style of *Sons and Lovers*, which was published one year after the first Georgian and one year before the first Imagist anthology, and whose pressures Lawrence eventually found himself victim rather than master of.

Georgianism has on the whole sunk below the contemporary critical horizon, yet in reviewing Marsh's 1912 anthology Lawrence took a passionate stand on the movement's behalf:

> What are the Georgian poets, nearly all, but just bursting into a thick blaze of being? ... It is the return of the blood, that has been held back, as when the heart's action is arrested by fear. Now the warmth of the blood is in everything.[8]

His enthusiasm springs from the closeness of the Georgian project to the aesthetic of 'Englishness' which underpins his own first novel: the *Quarterly Review's* notice of Marsh's first volume described its content as 'realism running riot'.[9] But given the new movement's devotion to the concrete, we ought to have an instance of it in front of us before seeking to elicit its aesthetic credo. Edward Thomas's 'Tall Nettles' can serve as representative:

> Tall nettles cover up, as they have done
> These many springs, the rusty harrow, the plough
> Long worn out, and the roller made of stone:
> Only the elm butt tops the nettles now.
>
> This corner of the farmyard I like most:
> As well as any bloom upon a flower
> I like the dust on nettles, never lost
> Except to prove the sweetness of a shower.

Modesty is the term that springs to mind here: formally, in the brevity of the poem; lyrically, in its calm, poised, judicious emotions ('like', not 'love'); thematically, in the humble, neglected nature of the objects it fastens upon – not even nettles as such but the dust upon them. Clearly, this is a poetry of fugitive, transient impressions, catching those aspects of the rural scene which a busily utilitarian or 'officially' poetic imagination ('bloom upon a flower') overlooks. Avoiding the grand gesture, the poem's understatement conveys a peculiar lyrical authenticity – one which gains in authority by the tenacious, quietly precise grip of the language upon the objects it conveys. 'Liking' here is a matter of 'showing' rather than 'telling', residing more in photographic fidelity to the details of the local scene than in overt statement. Place – 'this corner' – is evidently important to the Georgian poet. Poetic virtue resides, precisely, in the depth and honesty of one's inherence in it: if the particular impression is a fleeting one, the scene itself is regularly visited ('these many springs'). And we are perhaps not generalising too far beyond this particular text if we claim that this place, this scene, and the quietly faithful tones of the poem that renders it, are somehow distinctively 'English'.

T. S. Eliot finely captured the essence of Georgian poetic 'modesty' in remarking 'how often the word "little" occurs; and how this word is used, not merely as a piece of information, but with a caress, a conscious delight'.[10] Such modesty was in its context a cultural–political stance, the disownment by a generation of liberal intellectuals of the strident imperialist rhetoric of their poetic elders (Kipling, Newbolt). As in *The White Peacock*, a 'sober' local Englishness repudiates the grand sonorities of official Britishness. As James Reeves argues:

> The celebration of Englishness, whether at peace or at war, became a principal aim of Georgian poetry. The English countryside, English crafts, and English sports offered suitable subject-matter. Poems about country cottages, old furniture, moss-covered barns, rose-scented lanes, apple and cherry orchards, village inns and village cricket.[11]

To such English themes there corresponded an 'English' diction and imagery; 'you English words', enthused Edward Thomas with appropriate sobriety in his poem 'Words'. Mistrusting rhetoric, the Georgian poem remains close to the rhythms of common speech, sparing and precise in its adjectives, homely and concrete in its metaphors. It tended – to employ a term more theoretical than its own genial amateurism could allow – towards an aesthetic minimalism, of both situation and poetic means.

And it is precisely here that this shy English modernism comes to look uncannily like its brash, cosmopolitan challenger Imagism, which, with Ezra Pound at its helm, was never short on theories and manifestos. Of the founding triumvirate of Imagism (Pound, Aldington, H. D.), two were American, and the transatlantic connection was strengthened when Amy Lowell arrived in London from Boston in 1914 to throw her weight behind the fledgling movement. Moreover, the Imagists owed an avowed debt to French symbolism, initially using the French form *Imagistes* to testify to their exoticism in the torpid London intellectual atmosphere. None the less, for all these internationalist affiliations, Imagist aesthetics are to a point clearly consistent with the major emphases of Georgianism. When F. S. Flint propounded the first two 'rules for Imagistes' in 1913 he was adding little to Georgian principles of linguistic economy:

1. Direct treatment of the 'thing', whether subjective or objective.
2. To use absolutely no word that did not contribute to the presentation.

And when Pound added, 'Go in fear of abstraction ... Use either no ornament or good ornament', most Georgian poets would have concurred; these were the very values of their own 'English' poetic realism, not its overthrow.[12] Thematically too, there are strong parallels in the attention paid to fugitive impressions and marginalised objects. The distance is not after all very great from Thomas's dusty nettles to Pound's 'In a Station of the Metro':

> The apparition of these faces in the crowd;
> Petals on a wet, black bough.

Donald Davie has suggested that the clipped, no-nonsense laconicism of Imagist utterances may have owed much to upper-class English speech-forms,[13] and Amy Lowell certainly detected continuity of a sort between English poetic localism and its internationalist successor when she abruptly informed the young Georgian D. H. Lawrence that he was an Imagist without knowing it.

But if there are grounds of thinking of Imagism as an intensification rather than a repudiation of the Georgian programme, there is at least one major Imagist tenet that cannot be so easily reconciled with Englishness. Images are, ideally, 'definite', toughly objective: aggressive and iconoclastic, they violently disrupt our complacent everyday habits of perception and reading. 'Hard light, clear edges', fulminated Pound as he saw Amy Lowell diluting the original project towards a hazy Impressionism. Georgianism, by contrast, is decidedly 'soft', mild in tone, mellow in its landscapes, gentle in its Englishness. Or, more precisely, it is all this in its middle-class adherents. But to a working-class Georgian like Lawrence, English realism would have to encompass the pits of Bestwood as well as the valley of Nethermere, the industrial as well as the rural, mutating in the process into something grittier than his genteel fellow anthologists could tolerate, and closer to the 'harshness' that Pound and T. E. Hulme were espousing. And *Sons and Lovers* may accordingly be a good candidate for the title of the first Imagist novel.

Jessie Chambers applied a key Imagist epithet to the novel in speaking of the 'hard brilliance of its narration',[14] and Lawrence himself referred to its 'hard violent style full of sensation and presentation' (*Letters*, 259). Stylistically speaking, the novel begins with a simple, sparing prose very close to the linguistic Englishness of Georgian poetry – as becomes evident if we set a few lines beside a verse of Edward Thomas:

> Morel took off his coat. Jerry held the hat containing the money. The men at the tables watched. Some stood with their mugs in their hands. (p. 56)

> The steam hissed. Someone cleared his throat.
> No one left and no one came
> On the bare platform. What I saw
> Was Adlestrop – only the name.
>
> ('Adlestrop')

Thomas's adjective 'bare' adequately characterises both passages; Lawrence's novel too is packed with epithets which serve both as objective description and as oblique announcement of the text's own stylistic desiderata. Only, given that the Midlands coalfields are a harsher human environment than Thomas's beloved Wiltshire, Georgian simplicity gravitates towards Imagistic hardness. That such aesthetic toughness was also, for Lawrence, a distinctively English mode is implied by a remark he made about the Midlands in 1926: 'it's real England – the hard pith of England' (*Letters*, 953). A negative equation of *Sons and Lovers* and Englishness is made in a letter of July 1912, where in the course of a single paragraph Lawrence announces, 'I loathe the idea of England ... I *loathe Paul Morel*' (*Letters*, 135).

If the Midlands are hard, so must be the novel's style; it is this faithfulness of language to the experience of the narrated community which earns Raymond Williams's praise in his *The English Novel*. He finds in early Lawrence 'a sort of miracle of language', a powerful attempt to break beyond the classicist transcendentalism of the George Eliot narrator. 'The language of the writer is at one with the language of his characters, in a way that hadn't happened'; Lawrence alters 'the novelist's language of description and analysis to the colloquial and informal from the abstract and polite'. Yet when Williams goes on to term this linguistic quality 'flow' – 'a particular flow – what he once called sympathy but it isn't that formal' – one's reservations begin.[15] For that noun, imported back from Lawrence's later social and sexual thinking, does not register the clipped, staccato hardness of the novel's language. Community here is more endured than enjoyed, and up to a point this is, as Williams insists, to keep faith with it. The novel's prose is as grimly tight-lipped, as rigidly tensed against almost intolerable pressures, as the lives of the working people themselves. 'Hardness' is thematically reflected upon as well as stylistically enacted, as industrial capitalism takes its blighting toll of human life. '"It seems hard"', reflects Mrs Morel after her husband's pit accident; in the mine he works in shaft 'Number 42. Hard'; his pit trousers are 'too dirty, and the stuff too hard, for his wife to mend' (p. 103). The harshness of this working environment deforms the human bodies that labour within it, which themselves acquire the stylistic qualities of the novel, as with the 'small work-hardened fingers' of Mrs Morel, or the tough but scarred and twisted physique of her husband. Even the more liberal regime of Thomas Jordan's Surgical Appliances Factory involves such dehumanising; Clara longs to 'smash the trivial coating of business which covered him [Paul] with hardness' (p. 419).

To this extent, language keeps faith with labour, admiringly enacting its tenacious, exact attention to its object but also registering the humanly diminishing effects of this process under capitalist social relations. But then in a more fundamental sense this is a language that refuses community – not just tensing itself against this (capitalist) community but against the very value of communality in general. Loyal to the exhausting grind of mining in one sense, the novel's lean linguistic exactitude in another sense repudiates the positive values incarnated in its central mining figure. For whereas *it* is dry, hard and cold, Paul's father is 'warm' and 'soft'. Unlike the book in which he features, Mr Morel has 'a warm way of telling a story', and in a passage compulsorily cited by every critic, *Sons and Lovers* speaks of 'the dusky golden softness of this man's sensuous flame of life ... soft, non-intellectual, warm' (p. 45). As far as Morel is concerned, the novel's language is an *anti*-style, contracting itself against all he represents. It is – *pace* Williams – more a style of and for the mother than the local community, enacting in its very texture the gestures of fierce repudiation which are her psychic response to Morel; if the mother 'clipped her language very clear and precise' (p. 386), so too does her son's novel. After she learns that Morel does not own the house they live in, 'something in her proud, honourable soul crystallised out as hard as rock' (p. 48); and thereafter, in a mounting chorus, the novel's key stylistic epithet is applied to her over and over. Paul 'marvelled at his mother's hardness'; Miriam feels upon him 'the hardness, the foreignness' of her influence; Clara too senses 'something so hard and certain in his mother'.

The book's scrupulous economy of linguistic means might initially seem to guarantee its stern impartiality between the various conflicting voices it sets in motion. But Miriam has already noted Paul's habit of claiming to be normal precisely when he is most disagreeable – though Jessie Chambers herself failed to draw the connection between the 'hard brilliance' of *Sons and Lovers* and what she regarded as its outrageous weighting in favour of the mother. This style could never be a successful tool of analysis of the class and Oedipal problems at the novel's heart because it is more their symptom than solution. Far from being enlightenedly neutral, it is haplessly in the grip of past traumas. The 'peculiar slight knitting of the brows' that marks Paul almost from birth exactly captures the taut, strained quality of the prose itself; if Paul 'walked with something screwed up tight inside him', so too does every sentence in this book. As the generous Victorian realism which the novel harks back to in its title breaks down in its second half, so the text's claim to realist achievement becomes a purely negative one: if it can say often enough, in relation to Miriam, I am not Gothic, then it sustains at least some faint formal continuity with the great realisms of the past. So too does the typical sentence of *Sons and Lovers* become a purely negative gesture, repeating in this Paul's relations with Miriam where 'it seemed as if virginity were a positive force' (p. 339). In this tight, constrained prose, George Eliot's broad-minded clarity becomes dry disillusion, precision turns to watchful repudiation, a warding off of alternative human possibilities. A 500-page novel ends up doing little more than eternally repeating one of the mother's tiny characteristic gestures, as 'the mouth closed tight from suffering and disillusion and self-denial' (p. 105).

That the stylistic hardness of the book aligns itself with the mother is clear even in those episodes which have often been taken to show a positive reponse to the father's sensuous gaiety. A much cited instance is that in which the children help him make fuses for the mine:

> Morel fetched a sheaf of long sound wheat-straws from the attic. These he cleaned with his hand till each one gleamed like a stalk of gold, after which he cut the straws into lengths of about six inches ... He always had a beautifully sharp knife that could cut a straw clean without hurting it. Then he set in the middle of the table a heap of gunpowder, a little pile of black grains upon the white-scrubbed board. He made and trimmed the straws while Paul and Annie filled and plugged them.   (p. 103)

Here at least, it would seem, the virtues of clarity and precision are attached firmly to the father – the visual sharpness of the prose rendering the scene as dexterously as Mr Morel cuts a straw. This is certainly an Image in Ezra Pound's sense, a hard, definite concretion vividly realising an intellectual and emotional complex in an instant – the 'complex' in this case being that tangle of distance and desire for the father which *Sons and Lovers* finds so hard to translate into overt analysis (at that level, all it can say is that Morel has 'denied the God in himself'). And the whole book is composed of crisply visualised episodes of this kind: Mrs Morel locked out in her garden at night, Paul and Clara clambering up and down the banks of the Trent, and so on. Hence it is that the label 'Imagist novel' seems apt.

Yet even a scene which registers the merits of the father may be cast in a mode which ultimately disowns him; and this, surely, is the case with the gunpowder fuses. As Lawrence began work on what would become *The Rainbow* and *Women in Love*, he remarked that the new novel 'is quite different in many ways from my other stuff – far less visualised ... all analytical – quite unlike *Sons and Lovers*, not a bit visualised' (*Letters*, 183, 193). If the style of *Sons and Lovers* is hard where Morel is soft, its narrative mode, analogously, is visual where he is blind. As a miner, he is a creature of the underground, darkness, night; and he becomes increasingly ineffectual and ill at ease in the daylight world as the novel progresses. 'It makes me feel blind', his wife-to-be exclaims when he first describes his work to her, and he agrees:

> 'Like a moudiwarp!' he laughed. 'Yi, an' there's some chaps as does go round like moudiwarps.' He thrust his face forward in the blind, snout-like way of a mole, seeming to sniff and peer for direction.
>
> (p. 45)

Mrs Morel, by contrast, is a creature of pure visuality, and as she wastes away later in the novel becomes almost nothing but vision: 'her blue unfailing eyes... . . He felt if only they had been of a different colour he could have borne it better' (p. 441). The contrast is then repeated, as we should expect, in terms of Miriam and Paul, Gothic and Norman; she is hopelessly short-sighted, and 'resented his seeing everything ... that he saw too much' (p. 194). Clara too finds that when she is with Paul 'it seemed to her that she had never *seen* anything before' (p. 384). The dry visualism of the book, as anti-impressionistic as Paul's own paintings with their 'rather definite figures', is thus ultimately aligned with Mrs Morel, whatever local concessions it may make to the father and working-class community.

Not that the novel is wholly unable to launch a critique of its own linguistic hardness and Imagistic visualism. Intermittently throughout *Sons and Lovers* a sense of the cost of this fictional mode breaks through. When Paul has his first interview at Jordan's 'he was so much stunned that he noticed only the outside things' (p. 136); the book's own externalist aesthetic is here recognised as psychic trauma. Later, during Mrs Morel's final illness, the relation between this aesthetic and an unmastered inner pain and scarring is more explicitly fomulated. Paul's 'mind was clear and hard, but his body was crying' (p. 438); and this insight finds passionate expression as his mother fights death, in a passage which virtually counsels us to re-read the entire preceding novel against the grain:

> She was holding herself rigid, so that she might die without ever uttering the great cry that was tearing from her. He never forgot that hard, utterly lonely and stubborn clenching of the mouth.
>
> (p. 455)

But once this has been said, *Sons and Lovers* is no longer *Sons and Lovers*; the book has repudiated itself. Accordingly, it ends with one of the great (and literal) 'turns' in British literature, erasing its entire former self in the process. Paul has repudiated community throughout the book, but now, 'no, he would not give in. Turning sharply, he walked towards the city's gold phosphorescence' (p. 492).

From Tony Pinkney, *D. H. Lawrence* (Hemel Hempstead, 1990), pp. 27–49.

NOTES

[Though in some respects compatible in terms of both political outlook and emphasis on themes of isolation and rootlessness, the argument Tony Pinkney here presents on the social bearing of *Sons and Lovers* is somewhat different from that offered by John Goode, Graham Holderness and Scott Sanders in essays 8, 9 and 10. Pinkney works, for example, from very different assumptions about literary realism (these are explored in the general Introduction), and he presents *Sons and Lovers* as a radically splintered and divided text. His startlingly original account of the novel provokes new ways of thinking about several areas of it, including the description of Miriam. Unlike other critics in this collection, Pinkney is not primarily interested in Miriam as a human character about whom various claims can be made as to the justice or otherwise of her treatment by Lawrence or Paul. Instead, he depicts her as a kind of embodiment of a different, more disruptive kind of *writing* – the Gothic – which destabilises the balanced conventions of the realist novel. This focus on the writerly, as distinct from the human or sympathetic, dimensions of literary texts follows the spirit of much recent criticism, and Pinkney's piece is comparable to those of Diane Bonds (essay 6) and Terry Eagleton (essay 3) in that it sees the literary text as a volatile and often contradictory assembly of forces rather than a finished, rounded product. In portraying Miriam's Gothic qualities as 'an atavisitic fictional mode', Pinkney, like Eagleton, represents the novel in terms of psychoanalytic mechanisms. Lurking below the accommodating ambitions of its realistic surface, he argues, there are disturbing, unconscious textual forces and Pinkney illuminatingly relates these to issues concerned with English national identity. These disquieting elements in the novel, he suggests, parallel the forces working below the apparently unruffled surface of Edwardian life in the period just before the First World War. This essay is extracted from a longer chapter on Lawrence's early work and has been lightly edited to sustain focus. Page references to *Sons and Lovers* are incorporated into the text and are to the Penguin edition edited by Keith Sagar (1981), Ed.]

1. *Collected Letters of D. H. Lawrence*, ed. Harry T. Moore (London, 1962), p. 39. Hereafter abbreviated in the text to *Letters* followed by page number.

2. Georg Lukács, 'Realism in the Balance' in Ernst Bloch *et al., Aesthetics and Politics* (London, 1977), pp. 38–9.

3. George Eliot, *Felix Holt, The Radical* (1866), ch. 2.

4. D. H. Lawrence, *The White Peacock*, ed. Alan Newton (Harmondsworth, 1982), p. 268.

5. Matthew Arnold, 'Stanzas from the Grande Chartreuse', in *The Poems of Matthew Arnold*, ed. Miriam Allot (London, 1979), p. 305.

6. *The White Peacock*, p. 156.

7. Jessie Chambers, *D. H. Lawrence: A Personal Record* (London, 1935), p. 130.

8. D. H. Lawrence, 'Georgian Poetry: 1911–1912' in *Selected Literary Criticism*, ed. Anthony Beal (London, 1967), p. 74.

9. Cited in C. K. Stead, *The New Poetic: Yeats to Eliot* (London, 1964), p. 92.

10. T. S. Eliot, 'Reflections on Contemporary Poetry', *The Egoist*, September 1917.

11. James Reeves (ed.), *Georgian Poetry* (Harmondsworth, 1962), p. xv.

12. F. S. Flint, 'Imagisme', and Ezra Pound, 'A Few Don'ts by an Imagist', in *Imagist Poetry*, ed. Peter Jones (Harmondsworth, 1972), pp. 129–31.

13. See Donald Davie, *Ezra Pound: Poet as Sculptor* (London, 1965).

14. Chambers, *Lawrence: A Personal Record*, p. 202.

15. Raymond Williams, *The English Novel: Dickens to Lawrence* (London, 1971), pp. 172–3.

12

Lawrence and the Decline of the Industrial Spirit

PAUL DELANY

In Galsworthy's *The Silver Spoon* the aristocratic beauty Marjorie Ferrar begins an expensive lawsuit against Fleur Mont, then finds herself five thousand pounds in debt. The only escape from her difficulties, she decides, is to get married. When her grandfather, the Marquess of Shropshire, learns of her engagement he invites her to breakfast. His hobbyhorse is electrification, so he is delighted to hear that Marjorie's fiancé, an industrialist MP, is 'dead keen on electricity'.[1] The conversation then comes around to wedding presents, and Shropshire asks Marjorie if she would like some of his antique lace:

> 'Oh! no, please, dear. Nobody's wearing lace.'
> With his head on one side, the marquess looked at her. 'I can't get that lace off,' he seemed to say.
> 'Perhaps you'd like a Colliery. Electrified, it would pay in no time.'
> Marjorie Ferrar laughed. 'I know you're hard up, grandfather; but I'd rather not have a Colliery, thanks. They're so expensive. Just give me your blessing.'[2]

The breakfast takes place in January 1925, fifteen months before the General Strike; but Marjorie looks her gift colliery in the mouth because she knows that the industry is already in a bad way. The Germans must sell coal abroad in order to make their reparation payments, and British mine owners want to cut wages to remain competitive. Marjorie's joke shows that the aristocracy has lost faith in coal and would rather put its capital somewhere else. She is in fact a shrewd prophet, for what lies ahead is sixty years of decline for British mining. Whether it is lace or mines, she has no wish to be stuck with something that is out of fashion.

It is far cry from Marjorie Ferrar's offhand joke to D. H. Lawrence's deep involvement with mining and miners; but careless and thoughtless people may sometimes be closer to the truth than experts. I want to argue that Lawrence's personal experience caused him to assume that mining was as central to British culture generally as it was to him individually, and to overestimate the political and industrial power of the mine-owning classes. It is true that mining has long held a special place in the British cultural imagination; but that is because mining, more than any other industry, is 'known' in terms of myth (which exists, in part, because practically no one except the miners themselves has ever been down a mine). Myth and economic necessity have always been opposed; at certain crucial moments they have been brought into bitter confrontation – notably in the great strikes of 1926 and 1984, and in the nationalisation of 1945.

By the myth of mining I mean a cluster of popular responses: about the danger of mining, the solidarity of the workers, the insularity of their communities, their fondness for singing, and the like. Part of the myth, indeed, is the miner's sensitive son who becomes a teacher or writer. And most of the myth is grounded on social fact. It is mythical not because it is untrue, but because it is incomplete: it obscures the profound changes in the industry over the past century, and it makes mining into an archetype that is not necessarily relevant to British industry as a whole. Furthermore, the industrial myth does not live independently, but as the counterpart to something older and more powerful: the myth of Britain as it was before industry came to change it.

Let us call this rival idea the 'rural myth'. It has recently been the subject of a seminal book by Martin Wiener, *English Culture and the Decline of the Industrial Spirit, 1850–1980*. 'The leading problem of modern British history', Wiener begins, 'is the explanation of economic decline'.[3] In Britain, he argues, the industrial revolution was crippled just when it was being wholeheartedly exploited by Germany, the United States, and Japan. During the first half of the nineteenth century there was national enthusiasm for the British industrialist and engineer, culminating in the Great Exhibition of 1851 at the Crystal Palace. But the advance of industry also provoked strong opposition from traditionalist interest groups. This opposition prevailed, and it bears the final responsibility for Britain's long and notorious economic crisis. The present condition of Britain has not been determined by the loss of empire or the strains of the two world wars. It has older and deeper roots, visible in the dominance of landed and financial interests over industrial ones, of the rentier over the manager, of the South over the North.[4] Nominally Britain is ruled by either the Conservative or the Labour Party; effectively, it is ruled by the Garden Party.

From Cobbett and Blake onward, those sages who pronounced on the 'condition of England' spoke with one voice on the issue of industry, regardless of whether they were right or left politically. Their common ideal was the 'organic' rural community, devoted to spiritual rather than material values. They established the Rural Myth as the country's most important received idea, the uncontested premise of most cultural production. 'England's green and pleasant land' must be saved, over and over again, from 'those dark satanic mills'. The 'red rust' of semi-detached housing – and all that goes with it – creeps from *Howards End* to Eliot's Waste Land to Orwell's 'Lower Binfield' in *Coming Up for Air*. Liberal, reactionary, or socialist, all unite in a mystified love of Olde Englande and in contempt for whatever is new.

It is assumed by the Rural Myth that industry and urbanisation have no moral basis; they express only a materialism without aim or limit. 'High wages are not an end in themselves,' said Arnold Toynbee, a leading disciple of Ruskin. 'No one wants high wages in order that working men may indulge in mere sensual gratification' (qtd in Wiener p. 82). Sixty years later, G. M. Trevelyan lamented the decline of rural England in his lifetime. 'Agriculture is not merely one industry among many', he wrote, 'but is a way of life, unique and irreplaceable in its human and spiritual values' (Wiener p. 87). Toynbee and his followers (such as the Hammonds) established certain axioms in cultural history: that traditional rural societies were better than their successors, that modernity represented the triumph of 'gross materialism' over spiritual ideals, and that the industrial revolution was 'a period as disastrous and as terrible as any through which a nation ever passed' (Wiener p. 82).

The demonology of the Rural Myth lumps together the factory and the town. 'I am always haunted by the awfulness of London', went one lament in 1891, 'by the great appalling fact of these millions cast down, as it would appear by hazard, on the banks of this noble stream.... [London is a] tumour, an elephantiasis sucking into its gorged system half the life and the blood and the bone of the rural districts' (Wiener p. 106). This was not some rustic sage speaking, but Lord Rosebery, who had just completed his term as the first chairman of the London County Council. Leonard Bast's trajectory in *Howards End* – from rural Wiltshire origins to a job as an insurance clerk to parasitic unemployment – made the point, for E. M. Forster, that the English race has degenerated in moving from the open field to the factory or office.

If we accept Wiener's definition of what is particularly English about English culture, it follows that D. H. Lawrence is not such an outsider and iconoclast as he has commonly been painted. Rather, he has his place in the great stream of anti-industrial sentiment that runs continuously from Blake to Orwell. F. W. Bateson described English Romanticism as 'the shortest way out of Manchester'; for Lawrence, the shortest way out of Eastwood was the road to Felley Mill farm. His family, after all, had its roots and its fortunes in industry. His maternal grandfather was an engineer in the naval dockyard at Sheerness, his father a miner and skilful amateur mechanic, and his elder brother George a manager of an engineering company in Nottingham. Yet Lawrence, as an adult, made virtue of his incompetence to deal with a car or a typewriter. His youthful letters say almost nothing about technology, and his first major literary project was pastoral idyll, *The White Peacock*. His cultural formation alienated him from the industrial society of the Midlands long before he physically left it, on his long pilgrimage in search of an ideal South.

In his youth Lawrence could afford to take industry for granted because it was in a phase of relatively untroubled expansion. Between 1885 and 1913 production of coal in Britain rose by about 60 per cent. Almost all coal was still cut by hand and seams were getting more inaccessible; as a result, employment in mining more than doubled, from half a million to over a million men.[5] The Nottinghamshire coalfield was more modern and productive than most, and its workers less militant than those farther north or in Wales.[6] They were influenced by being closer to London and living more intermingled with the middle classes (exemplified, of course, in Lawrence's own divided family). *Sons and Lovers* leaves us with the impression that Morel has been steadily degenerating both personally and socially. But a walk around Eastwood shows that the

Lawrence family had a better house each time they moved, as Arthur Lawrence shared in the general prosperity of the mining industry.

Lawrence himself wanted to move much farther than just up the hill from 'The Breach'. But he also had a lifelong need to return and re-create the world of his youth, beginning with *Sons and Lovers*. The depiction of industry there is primal – what would be taken in by the eyes of a mother-fixated child who himself never went 'down pit'. In contrast with agricultural or artisan societies, industry brought about a complete separation of work between the sexes. Before, they worked at different tasks in the same place; now one sex worked at home, the other in the factory or mine. So Morel is not shown in his work, but only as a brutal domestic intruder. Each sex makes the rules for its own territory and resists intrusion by the other: men have the pit and the pub, women the house and the chapel. The fundamental opposition is one sex against the other, rather than people against machinery. In this novel, then, Lawrence has not yet established a polarity between the sensual and the mechanical. By sharing a physical task, the miners can affirm their sensuality together; but they are sensually alienated from their spiritual and moralistic womenfolk.[7]

When Paul Morel writes his first letter of application, the narrator calls him 'already ... a prisoner of industrialism' (p. 89). But the novel as a whole does not show industry as closing off the development of those who take part in it. It is surely significant that Lawrence extended his three months at Haywood's in 1901 into a fictional stay at 'Jordan's' that covers ten years of his life, up to his mother's death in 1911. His emotional development as student and teacher during this period is mapped onto the life of a factory clerk, with no obvious difficulty of fit. Despite his occupation, Paul Morel preserves his dignity and sensitivity, and is the credible hero of one of the major *Bildungsromane* in English.[8] As with Lawrence himself, Paul's hostility to industry derives from cultural tradition rather than from direct perception of its malignancy.

In his early work, then, Lawrence followed the middle road of the anti-industrial tradition; he showed preference for rural settings, a measured distaste for factories and towns, and an escapist or romantic attitude toward sex. His inclusion in the earlier volumes of *Georgian Poetry* marked his acceptance as a relatively orthodox Edwardian writer. Between 1912 and 1916, however, he shifted to a much more radical view of the industrial question. This shift was motivated by upheavals in his personal life rather than by working through the traditional debate over the 'condition of England'. Lawrence's anti-industrial vision was the product of his lived experience of sexual liberation, economic independence, exile and war. This was its strength; but this strength came at the cost of dissociation from the everyday concerns and perspectives of most of his countrymen.

By eloping with Frieda, Lawrence chose also to be a writer rather than a teacher, and to live among peasants rather than on the fringes of London. The sexual fulfilment that he enjoyed in Germany and Italy led him to situate his phallic and sensual ideals within the peasant way of life instead of within the masculine comradeship of the mines. Having abandoned or even annihilated his personal past, he liked to imagine how the society he had left behind might literally be destroyed; and the outbreak of war promised to turn his projective fantasy into sober truth. This vision – we might call it Lawrence's industrial apocalypse – is expressed in one of his most powerful poems, 'The North Country':

> In another country, black poplars shake themselves over a pond,
> And rooks and the rising smoke-waves scatter and wheel from the
> works beyond:
> The air is dark with north and with sulphur, the grass is a darker
> green,
> And people darkly invested with purple move palpable through the
> scene.
>
> Soundlessly down across the counties, out of the resonant gloom
> That wraps the north in stupor and purple travels the deep, slow
> boom
> Of the man-life north imprisoned, shut in the hum of the purpled
> steel
> As it spins to sleep on its motion, drugged dense in the sleep of the
> wheel.
>
> Out of the sleep, from the gloom of motion, soundlessly, somnam-
> bule
> Moans and booms the soul of a people imprisoned, asleep in the rule
> Of the strong machine that runs mesmeric, booming the spell of its
> word
> Upon them and moving them helpless, mechanic, their will to its will
> deferred.
>
> Yet all the while comes the droning inaudible, out of the violet air,
> The moaning of sleep-bound beings in travail that toil and are will-
> less there

> In the spellbound north, convulsive now with a dream near morning, strong
> With violent achings heaving to burst the sleep that is now not long.[9]

Lawrence's anti-industrialism was born in exile; it was a set of emotions and fantasies that never amounted to a serious programme, except during his association with Bertrand Russell in 1915.[10] Contemporaries like Ford, Belloc, Forster, or Galsworthy made a careful study of how English rural life could be revived, though each looked to different groups to take the lead: 'small producers', the Catholic church, liberal intellectuals, or the country gentry. *Sons and Lovers*, however, shows no real concern for the economics or social viability of Felley Mill farm. The Leivers are ineffectual dreamers, and it is taken for granted that they will in due course go bankrupt. For Lawrence, what matters about the country is its spiritual opposition to industry and the city. Indeed, this opposition can only be spiritual because the rural way of life cannot and will not defend itself against the profound wish of modern man 'to create the great unliving creators, the machines, out of the active forces of nature that existed before flesh'.[11] When Lawrence awoke to the power of industry, he tended to see it as the only real force in civil society – something demonic and overwhelming that would expand, without effective resistance, until it reached a destructive consummation. 'Anything that *triumphs*, perishes', he wrote in 'The Crown'; but the industrial juggernaut must drive on until it *has* triumphed.[12]

Lawrence's impassioned elegy for Garsington, in 1915, assumes that everything the house stands for is obsolete and therefore doomed:

> this house of the Ottolines – It is England – my God, it breaks my soul – this England, these shafted windows, the elm-trees, the blue distance – the past, the great past, crumbling down, breaking down.... So vivid a vision, everything so visually poignant, it is like that concentrated moment when a drowning man sees all his past crystallised into one jewel of recollection.[13]

The actual instrument of this doom is left vague; but in *John Thomas and Lady Jane* Lawrence makes the conflict between old and new England into a moralised tableau:

> The great houses, 'stately homes of England', still loom and make good photographs. But they are dead.... The mines were blotting out

the halls. It was inevitable. When the great landowners started the mines, and made new fortunes, they started also their own obliteration.... The old England was doomed to be blotted out, with a terrifying absoluteness, by a new and gruesome England.[14]

'Stateliness is on its last legs', observes Gerald Barlow in *Touch and Go*, explaining how his colliery has taken an abandoned eighteenth-century hall and made it into offices.[15] His former mistress Anabel Wrath and his sister Winifred are both appalled by Gerald's boundless ambitions:

> **Winifred**   ... if Gerald was a bit different, he'd be really nice. Now he's so *managing*. It's sickening. Do you dislike managing people, Anabel?
> **Anabel**   I dislike them extremely, Winifred.
> **Winifred**   They're such a bore.
> **Anabel**   What does Gerald manage?
> **Winifred**   Everything. You know he's revolutionised the collieries and the whole Company. He's made a whole new thing out of it, so *modern*.... [He] adores electricity.[16]

The argument of these passages is that when the landed gentry collaborated with the rise of industry, they signed their own death warrant as a class. Modern historians would see this as a simplistic view of English culture. In fact, the landed interests shifted much of their wealth into British (and later foreign) industry, but without radically changing their way of life or losing their cultural hegemony. Within Lawrence's own circle, Lady Ottoline Morrell was a good example of how wealth derived from coal could be devoted to artistic enterprises and ambitions. The Bell family history shows the actual shift away from industry toward a more prestigious style of life. William Heward Bell made his fortune as a colliery owner and mining engineer in Wales. He then established his family in mock-Jacobean splendour in Wiltshire, went by the name of 'Squire Bell' among the local rustics, and made sure that his tenants joined him at Anglican services though he was privately an atheist.[17] His son Clive made the final step into the bohemian intelligentsia. In this family the hall blotted out the mines, rather than the other way around!

Lawrence fails to appreciate the flexibility of the landed gentry and to understand how they are more visible as a caste than as a class. Their traditional manners are preserved, while the actual management of their wealth is carried on first by the financial interests of the City of London, then, at second hand, by the industrial managers and technicians who have never, in Britain, achieved parity of status and power with the traditional owning (and ruling) classes. One of the chief concerns of this system is to make its own workings invisible. So Lawrence responded to the dynamism of Midlands industry as he had observed it in his youth, but failed to see how, in the long run, Britain was not imbued with the 'industrial spirit'.[18] On Lawrence's own ground, the last two mines in Eastwood closed down in the year of his centennial.

Lawrence felt keenly, of course, the general crisis of British industry in the twenties. But he still took the primacy of industry for granted and focused on the internal struggle between management and labour rather than on the place of industry in British society as a whole. Gerald Barlow in *Touch and Go*, Gerald Crich in *Women in Love*, and Clifford Chatterley are demonic magnates, examples of 'the human soul worshipping at the mystery of Matter'.[19] Their interest in machinery is shown as a compensation for some essential flaw, such as a death wish in Crich or paralysis in Chatterley. At the managerial level, Ursula's uncle Thomas Brangwen in *The Rainbow* reveals his unhealthiness by his affinity with the lesbian Miss Inger. Those who have lost contact with the 'Body Electric' become obsessed with the electrified colliery and must follow out that obsession to its limit – which is some form of psychic death. Industrial modernisation and expansion are thus reduced to modes of sexual pathology, and Lawrence ceases to be a social novelist, that is, one who works within Britain's complex dialectic of class and regional interests.[20]

How might my argument affect Lawrence's status as writer or thinker? Wiener's study puts forward two propositions: that the central fact of modern British history is the country's decline relative to other developed nations; and that the cause of this decline is not narrowly economic but rather a pervasive *cultural* hostility to the 'industrial spirit'.[21] Literature, Wiener argues, has helped disseminate this hostility, and insofar as economic performance is the measure of a country's success, literature bears a large share of the responsibility for Britain's failure. British intellectuals, said C. P. Snow in 1959, are 'natural Luddites'.[22]

A number of polls taken in the seventies found that *The Rainbow* was the novel most widely read and admired by British students. Can it be that Lawrence had ceased to be a heretical author; or was his message, as I have tried to show, never too far removed from the crucial pieties of his culture? How much of *The Rainbow's* popularity, we may ask, derived from its nostalgic view of social evolution; from its pastoral bias, its hostility to large-scale organisation; or from the vision of deindustrialisation with which it ends? Did these features appeal especially to that generation of youth, or do they permeate all levels of British culture? How far does Lawrence's popularity depend on the anti-industrial sentiments of teachers as a class? What are the social responsibilities of novelists and poets, and are they the same for each kind of writer?

One might begin to answer these questions by recognising that there are two traditions of anti-industrial literature in modern Britain: the 'soft' and the 'hard'. The soft version centres on Bloomsbury but also includes novelists like Ford, Galsworthy, and Evelyn Waugh. Its worldview is that of the southern rentier class, oriented toward some version of the country house (or country cottage) ideal.[23] The hard version alternates between nostalgia for antique or primitive societies and dystopian visions of modernity. Its leaders include Lawrence, Eliot, Pound, Yeats, Orwell. In their works, a debased contemporary world is often starkly opposed to an innocent nature: Birkin's fantasy of a world swept clean of people, Winston and Julia escaping from the London of Big Brother into a sexualised landscape.

Writers who choose the 'soft' option tend to have substantial or sentimental ties with the dominant financial and landed classes; they retain these ties even as they deplore what Britain is coming to. They are the insiders of the anti-industrial tradition. The outsiders, less compromising and compromised, either never belonged to the English upper classes or, like Orwell, resigned from them. The former group tend to be 'little Englanders' by politics and temperament; the latter see England from a European, or even a global, perspective. The insiders work over the classic 'middle ground' of the English novel; the outsiders are mythmakers, religious revivalists, or primitivists.

I would argue that Lawrence began as traditional 'soft' pastoralist, became a 'hard' primitivist in his middle period, and tried to reconcile the two modes in *Lady Chatterley's Lover*. *The White Peacock* and *Sons and Lovers* are faithful to the Edwardian 'country cottage' ideal, which also contributes to Will and Anna's life at Cossethay in *The Rainbow*. These earlier novels incorporate the standard dialectic of the Rural Myth: traditional values are pitted against the encroachments of modernity, but the struggle is conducted within gradualist and indigenously English terms. In early 1915, when Lawrence debated postwar reconstruction with Bertrand Russell, he proclaimed a far more radical opposition to the modern industrial system. 'But we shall smash the frame', he told Russell. 'The land, the industries, the means of communication and the public amusements shall all be nationalised.... Then, and then only, shall we be able to *begin* living. Then we shall be able to *begin* to work.... Till then, we are fast within the hard, unliving, impervious shell.'[24] From these new convictions Lawrence made a new, apocalyptic conclusion to *The Rainbow*, showing industry and urbanisation as 'a dry, brittle, terrible corruption spreading over the face of the land'.[25]

The traditionalists viewed the Great War as a defence of the English 'unofficial rose' against Prussian mechanised destruction. Lawrence did not believe in such limited rules of engagement. Either the war would bring about the end of the machine age in Europe, or else Moloch would reign and Lawrence himself would have to flee into a primitive exile. Whatever the outcome, his novels from 1915 on would assume the 'smashing of the frame': he would abandon the classic middle ground of the English novel and embrace the Savage God. The Second World War inspired a corresponding move in Orwell's fiction from mimesis to fable in *Animal Farm* and *Nineteen Eighty-Four*.

Lawrence and Orwell courted similar dangers in making this shift. Assuming a radical opposition between the 'human' (pastoral) and industrial worlds, they ruled out any evolving mediation between the realms of nature and technique. But in Britain, I have argued, the industrial revolution was hedged around by powerful countervailing social interests. The northern manufacturing classes never achieved a cultural hegemony over the existing landed, commercial, or financial elites; rather, they tried to acquire the social prestige of these older classes by aping their style of life. When Lawrence returned to the 'condition of England' novel in *Lady Chatterley's Lover*, he was still strongly committed to the apocalyptic and symbolic modes that he had deployed in the fiction of his middle period. Clifford Chatterley thus becomes an overdetermined embodiment of war, industry, and sexual inadequacy, complete with mechanical wheelchair. If Clifford Chatterley is postwar England personified, then Connie and Mellors have no viable social agenda; they can only plot their escape to the virgin forests of British Columbia. In *Sons and Lovers* the Leivers farm represents a complete and credible alternative to the industrialism of Bestwood;

but in *Lady Chatterley* the alternative has shrunk to the cramped and vulnerable space of the gamekeeper's hut. Somewhere along the way, Lawrence has charged sex with the exclusive responsibility for confronting the modernist juggernaut. John Thomas and Lady Jane, fragile redeemers of an age of iron, are the sole positive terms in Lawrence's final politics of cultural despair.

From *The Challenge of D. H. Lawrence*, ed. Michael Squires and Keith Cushman (Madison, 1990), pp. 77–88.

NOTES

[Paul Delany's is the most wide-ranging essay in this collection and examines an issue which has been widely debated over recent years. It concerns issues of British – or, more strictly, English – cultural and national identity and thus continues discussion of a topic raised by Tony Pinkney in essay 11. Lawrence's iconoclastic, anti-industrial views defined his radicalism for many influential early commentators, including those associated with Leavisite criticism. But Delany places these views in the context of other writers holding similar opinions in the period. What emerges is that, though Lawrence's views on industrial culture sharpened abruptly during the First World War, in some respects the account of Bestwood in *Sons and Lovers* is moderate in attitude and falls more into line with mainstream Edwardian literary opinion than is usually supposed. The novel's vision of English life is, Delany argues, in important respects essentially pastoral in manner, and, despite the coalfield setting, industrial culture is kept largely out of sight. These kinds of issues have been of interest over recent years partly because of the debate in Britain about the 'enterprise culture' in which it is argued that a 'Rural Myth' (as Delany puts it) about British culture impedes wealth creation. Whether this is true or not, Delany identifies an important feature of literary debate, at both ends of the twentieth century, in which Lawrence participated thoroughly. Page references to *Sons and Lovers* are incorporated into the text and are to the Penguin edition edited by Keith Sagar (1981). Ed.]

1. John Galsworthy, *The Silver Spoon* (New York, 1926), p. 242.

2. Ibid., p. 245.

3. Martin J. Wiener, *English Culture and the Decline of the Industrial Spirit, 1850–1980* (Cambridge, 1981), p. 3.

4. Wiener focuses on the complex, two-sided opposition between these forces; however, a comprehensive treatment of the issue would include the three elements of South, North, and the 'Celtic fringe' (Scotland, Wales, and Ulster).

5. See M. W. Kirby, *The British Coalmining Industry 1870–1946* (London, 1977), pp. 6–7. Employment peaked at one and a quarter million in 1920; currently (1988) it is about one-tenth of that.

6. In 1984–5 the Nottinghamshire miners generally refused to join the national strike (as they had also refused in 1926); a majority voted in October 1985 to secede from the National Union of Mineworkers.

7. At Jordan's warehouse, the sexes have correspondingly different attitudes to factory work: 'The man was the work and the work was the man, one thing, for the time being. It was different with the girls. The real woman never seemed to be there at the task, but as if left out, waiting' (p. 155). See also Marko Modiano, *Domestic Disharmony and Industrialisation in D. H. Lawrence's Early Fiction* (Uppsala, 1987).

8. However, there is the sense in which Jordan's has only one foot in the camp of industry – because, for Paul at least, it is still part of the woman's realm and his important relations there are with women. An exclusively male work environment would be much more threatening to him, as is indicated in the scene where he goes to pick up his father's pay.

9. *The Complete Poems of D. H. Lawrence*, ed. Vivian de Sola Pinto and F. Warren Roberts (Harmondsworth, 1977), pp. 148–9. The poem was probably drafted at Croydon, then put into its published form at Porthcothan in early 1916, when two other poems – 'In Church' and 'At the Front' – were split off from it. See Carol Ferrier, 'D. H. Lawrence's Pre-1920 Poetry: A Descriptive Bibliography of Manuscripts, Typescripts and Proofs', *D. H. Lawrence Review*, 6 (1973), 333–59.

10. For the failure of Lawrence's political collaboration with Russell, see my *D. H. Lawrence's Nightmare: The Writer and His Circle in the Years of the Great War* (New York, 1978), chs 3 and 4.

11. D. H. Lawrence, *Twilight in Italy* (Harmondsworth, 1960), p. 60.

12. D. H. Lawrence, *Phoenix II: Uncollected, Unpublished and Other Prose Works by D. H. Lawrence*, ed. Warren Roberts and Harry T. Moore (New York, 1968), p. 373.

13. *The Letters of D. H. Lawrence, Vol. 2. June 1913–October 1916*, ed. George J. Zytaruk and James T. Boulton (Cambridge, 1981), pp. 431, 459.

14. D. H. Lawrence, *John Thomas and Lady Jane* (London, 1972), pp. 153–4.

15. See Wiener, *English Culture* (p. 143) for an instructive account of the fate of Winnington Hall. When a giant chemical complex grew up around this Tudor manor house, it was preserved by ICI as an exclusive club for its executives.

16. D. H. Lawrence, *The Complete Plays of D. H. Lawrence* (New York, 1966), pp. 365, 334.

17. Frances Spalding, *Vanessa Bell* (London, 1983), pp. 67–71.

18. It would perhaps be more accurate to say that Britain preserved the industrial spirit – so long as the industry was overseas. The City of London gathered together the country's capital and invested it largely in the expanding economies of Britain's colonies, or rivals. The distaste for 'trade' and the cult of the 'private income' were sustained by massive foreign investments. The moral complications of this system are examined in Forster's *Howards End*; see my '"Islands of Money": Rentier Culture in E. M. Forster's *Howards End*', *English Literature in Transition: 1880–1920*, 31 (1988), 285–96. It is a weakness of Wiener's book that he neglects the complicity between the Rural Myth and the export of capital from Britain.

19. Lawrence, *John Thomas and Lady Jane*, p. 335.

20. For example, Lawrence makes a passion for the machine, or for making money, equivalent expressions of the sterile, materialist character. However, the crucial opposition in the British economy is between industry and finance; the latter is less 'materialistic' but more 'sterile'. It is also the economic base of the southern rentier class, whose mentality is brilliantly allegorised in 'The Rocking-Horse Winner'.

21. The impressive performance of the British economy over the past four years (1984–8) may, if continued, lead to a revision of the Wiener thesis. However, British industrial production is still lower than in 1979, the year Thatcher was elected; and industrial employment is substantially lower. On the subordination of industry to finance, see Perry Anderson, 'The Figures of Descent', *New Left Review* (Jan./Feb. 1987), 20–77, and Geoffrey Ingham, *Capitalism Divided? The City and Industry in British Social Development* (London, 1984).

22. In *The Two Cultures and the Scientific Revolution* (Cambridge, 1959). Snow's main adversary in the ensuing debate was Britain's leading Lawrence critic, F. R. Leavis.

23. Lawrence entertained both ideals at times: one was represented by Garsington, the other by his occasional fantasies of living obscurely in a cottage with his mother, Louie Burrows, or even Frieda. He recognised, however, that the latter style of life could never accommodate artistic ambitions on the level that he set himself. (During the war he was obliged to live in country cottages, but he resisted the traditional ideals of village life – what Orwell called the cult of 'beer and cricket'.)

24. *Letters*, II, 286.

25. D. H. Lawrence, *The Rainbow*, ed. Mark Kinkead-Weekes (Cambridge, 1989), p. 458.

Further Reading

EDITIONS AND TEXTUAL ISSUES

Three very good editions of *Sons and Lovers* are available. All provide help for the reader in terms of introduction, notes and other information.

Helen Baron and Carl Baron (eds), *Sons and Lovers*. The Cambridge Edition of the Letters and Works of D. H. Lawrence (Cambridge: Cambridge University Press, 1992). This prints the 'revised' text of the novel based on Lawrence's manuscripts. The expensive hardback edition contains excellent notes on all points of information and textual detail.

Macdonald Daly (ed.), *Sons and Lovers* (London: Everyman, 1994). A recent paperback edition based upon the 1913 first edition with helpful notes and other critical apparatus and a good introduction.

Keith Sagar (ed.), *Sons and Lovers* (Harmondsworth: Penguin, 1981). A reliable text with helpful notes based on the 1913 first edition. Probably the most widely used modern edition, it provides the point of reference for this New Casebook and page references have been standardised to it throughout.

Note

The textual situation of *Sons and Lovers* has become much more complicated since the publication of the recent Cambridge edition. For the reasons explained in 'Note on the Text of *Sons and Lovers*' on pp. 19–20, this New Casebook continues to use the Penguin edition of the novel, edited by Keith Sagar, as its point of reference. But it is important to note that the complexity of the textual issues introduced by the Cambridge edition mirrors in some respects a more general problem. As will be clear from many of the essays collected here, recent critical thinking stresses the instability of literary meaning and the variety of approaches critics can make to it.

The existence of different versions of even the very words on the page of *Sons and Lovers* only serves to underline the point, and this has been a matter for some critical comment:

Paul Eggert, 'Opening-Up the Text: The Case of *Sons and Lovers*', in *Rethinking Lawrence*, ed. Keith Brown (Milton Keynes: Open University Press, 1990), pp. 38–52.

Mark Spilka, 'For Mark Schorer with Combative Love: The *Sons and Lovers* Manuscript', in *D. H. Lawrence: A Centenary Consideration*, ed.

Peter Balbert and Philip L. Marcus (Ithaca, NY: Cornell University Press, 1985), pp. 29–44.

BIOGRAPHICAL

[Jessie Chambers], *D. H. Lawrence: A Personal Record by 'E.T.'* (1935: Cambridge: Cambridge University Press, 1980). An important memoir by the original of Miriam.

D. H. Lawrence, *The Letters of D. H. Lawrence: Vol. 1: September 1901–May 1913*, ed. James T. Boulton (Cambridge: Cambridge University Press, 1979).

Edward Nehls (ed.), *D. H. Lawrence: A Composite Biography*, 3 vols (Madison: University of Wisconsin Press, 1957). A fascinating compilation of recollections and opinions about Lawrence from those who knew him. Volume 1 deals with the years 1885–1919.

Keith Sagar, *D. H. Lawrence: Life into Art* (Harmondsworth: Penguin, 1985).

John Worthen, *D. H. Lawrence: The Early Years, 1885–1912* (Cambridge: Cambridge University Press, 1991). An outstanding account of Lawrence's life up to and including the writing of *Sons and Lovers*.

GENERAL CRITICAL STUDIES OF LAWRENCE

All of these offer helpful accounts of aspects of Lawrence's work, including *Sons and Lovers*. For discussion of Lawrence's career beyond *Sons and Lovers*, the reader should, of course, also consult the books by Bonds, Holderness, Kermode, Millett, Pinkney, Sanders and Simpson, and the essay by Goode, from which extracts are included in this volume.

Michael Bell, *D. H. Lawrence: Language into Being* (Cambridge: Cambridge University Press, 1991).

Keith Brown (ed.), *Rethinking Lawrence* (Milton Keynes: Open University Press, 1990).

Aiden Burns, *Nature and Culture in D. H. Lawrence* (London: Macmillan, 1980).

Emile Delavenay, *D. H. Lawrence: The Man and His Work: The Formative Years, 1885–1919*, trans. Katherine M. Delavenay (London: Heinemann, 1972).

R. P. Draper (ed.), *D. H. Lawrence: The Critical Heritage* (London: Routledge, 1970).

G. M. Hyde, *D. H. Lawrence* (London: Macmillan, 1990).

Allan Ingram, *The Language of D. H. Lawrence* (London: Macmillan, 1990).

F. R. Leavis, *D. H. Lawrence/Novelist* (1955: Harmondsworth: Penguin, 1964).

Peter Widdowson (ed.), *D. H. Lawrence: A Critical Reader* (London: Longman, 1992).

John Worthen, *D. H. Lawrence and the Idea of the Novel* (London: Macmillan, 1979).

STUDIES OF *SONS AND LOVERS*
General
Michael Black, *D. H. Lawrence: Sons and Lovers*, Landmarks of World Literature (Cambridge: Cambridge University Press, 1992).

Harold Bloom (ed.), *D. H. Lawrence's Sons and Lovers: Modern Critical Interpretations* (New York: Chelsea House Publishers, 1988).

Brian Finney, *Sons and Lovers*, Penguin Critical Studies (Harmondsworth: Penguin 1990).

Geoffrey Harvey, *Sons and Lovers: The Critics Debate* (London: Macmillan, 1987).

Ross C. Murfin, *Sons and Lovers: A Novel of Division and Desire* (Boston: Twayne, 1987).

Gāmini Salgādo (ed.), *D. H. Lawrence: Sons and Lovers: A Casebook* (London: Macmillan, 1969). The first Casebook volume: it contains a good range of traditional approaches to the novel and some useful contextual and biographical material.

Psychoanalytic
These items include psychoanalytic readings of the novel or discussion of the connection between Freud's work and that of Lawrence.

Calvin Bedient, *Architects of the Self: George Eliot, D. H. Lawrence and E. M. Forster* (London: University of California Press, 1972).

Ann Fernihough, *D. H. Lawrence: Aesthetics and Ideology* (Oxford: Clarendon Press, 1993), ch. 3.

Evelyn J. Hinz, '*Sons and Lovers*: The Archetypal Dimensions to Lawrence's Oedipal Tragedy', *D. H. Lawrence Review*, 5 (1972), 26–53.

A. B. Kuttner, 'A Freudian Appreciation', in *D. H. Lawrence: Sons and Lovers: A Casebook*, ed. Gāmini Salgādo (London: Macmillan, 1969), pp. 69–94. This is an early – 1916 – but influential and detailed psychoanalytic account of the novel.

Giles Mitchell, '*Sons and Lovers* and the Oedipal Project', *D. H. Lawrence Review*, 13 (1980), 209–19.

Shirley Panken, 'Some Psychodynamics in *Sons and Lovers*: A New Look at the Oedipal Theme', *Psychoanalytic Review*, 61 (1974–5), 571–89.

Daniel J. Schneider, *D. H. Lawrence: The Artist as Psychologist* (Lawrence, KS: University Press of Kansas, 1984).

John E. Stoll, *The Novels of D. H. Lawrence: A Search for Integration* (Columbia: University of Missouri Press, 1971).

E. W. Tedlock, Jr (ed.), *D. H. Lawrence's Sons and Lovers: Sources and Criticism* (New York: New York University Press, 1965). Usefully collects a range of psychoanalytic materials.

Philippa Tristram, 'Eros and Death (Lawrence, Freud and Women)', in *Lawrence and Women*, ed. Ann Smith (London: Vision Press, 1978), pp. 136–55.

Daniel A. Weiss, *Oedipus in Nottingham: D. H. Lawrence* (Seattle: University of Washington Press, 1962).

Gender and Sexual Analysis

These items include specific discussion of *Sons and Lovers* from this point of view, or discussion of general issues in relation to Lawrence arising from essays 5, 6 and 7 in this volume.

Peter Balbert, *D. H. Lawrence and the Phallic Imagination: Essays on Sexual Identity and Feminist Misreading* (London: Macmillan, 1989).

Janet Barron, 'Equality Puzzle: Lawrence and Feminism', in *Rethinking Lawrence*, ed. Keith Brown (Milton Keynes: Open University Press, 1990), pp. 12–22.

Gavriel Ben-Ephraim, *The Moon's Dominion: Narrative Dichotomy and Female Dominance in Lawrence's Early Novels* (London: Associated University Presses, 1981).

Simone de Beauvoir, *The Second Sex*, ed. and trans. H. M. Parshley (Harmondsworth: Penguin, 1953).

Lydia Blanchard, '"Love and Power": A Reconsideration of Sexual Politics in D. H. Lawrence', *Modern Fiction Studies*, 21 (1975), 431–43.

Carol Dix, *D. H. Lawrence and Women* (London: Macmillan, 1980).

Adrienne E. Gavin, 'Miriam's Mirror: Reflections on the Labelling of Miriam Leivers', *D. H. Lawrence Review*, 24 (1992), 27–42.

Janice H. Harris, 'Lawrence and the Edwardian Feminists', in *The Challenge of D. H. Lawrence*, ed. Michael Squires and Keith Cushman (London: University of Wisconsin Press, 1990), pp. 62–76.

Nigel Kelsey, *D. H. Lawrence: Sexual Crisis* (London: Macmillan, 1991), ch. 3.

Mark Kinkead-Weekes, 'Eros and Metaphor: Sexual Relationships in the Fiction of Lawrence', in *Lawrence and Women*, ed. Ann Smith (London: Vision Press, 1978), pp. 101–21.

Sheila MacLeod, *Lawrence's Men and Women* (London: Heinemann, 1985).

Cornelia Nixon, *Lawrence's Leadership Politics and the Turn Against Women* (Berkeley: University of California Press, 1986).

Faith Pullin, 'Lawrence's Treatment of Women in *Sons and Lovers*', in *Lawrence and Women*, ed. Ann Smith (London: Vision Press, 1978), pp. 49–74.

Judith Ruderman, *D. H. Lawrence and the Devouring Mother: The Search for a Patriarchal Ideal of Leadership* (Durham, NC: Duke University Press, 1984).

Marion Shaw, 'Lawrence and Feminism', *Critical Quarterly*, 25 (1983), 23–7.

Ann Smith (ed.), *Lawrence and Women* (London: Vision Press, 1978).

Margaret Storch, *Sons and Adversaries: Women in William Blake and D. H. Lawrence* (Knoxville: University of Tennessee Press, 1990), ch. 5.

Sons and Lovers *in Social Context*

Patricia Alden, *Social Mobility in the English Bildungsroman: Gissing, Hardy, Bennett and Lawrence* (Ann Arbour: UMI Research Press, 1986), ch. 4.

Terry Eagleton, *Exiles and Emigrés: Studies in Modern Literature* (London: Chatto and Windus, 1970).

Terry Eagleton, *Criticism and Ideology: A Study In Marxist Literary Theory* (London: New Left Books, 1976), ch. 4.

Kim A. Herzinger, *D. H. Lawrence in his Time: 1908–15* (Lewisburg: Buckness University Press, 1982).

Malcolm Pittock, '*Sons and Lovers*: The Price of Betrayal', in *Rethinking Lawrence*, ed. Keith Brown (Milton Keynes: Open University Press, 1990), pp. 120–32.

Peter Scheckner, *Class, Politics and the Individual: A Study of the Major Works of D. H. Lawrence* (London: Associated University Presses, 1985).

E. P. Shrubb, 'Reading *Sons and Lovers*', in *D. H. Lawrence's Sons and Lovers: Modern Critical Interpretations*, ed. Harold Bloom (New York: Chelsea House Publishers, 1988), pp. 109–29.

David Trotter, *The English Novel in History 1895–1920* (London: Routledge, 1993).

Raymond Williams, *The English Novel From Dickens to Lawrence* (London: Chatto and Windus, 1970).

Other

Elizabeth A. Campbell, 'Metonymy and Character: *Sons and Lovers* and the Metaphysics of Self', *D. H. Lawrence Review*, 20 (1988), 21–32.

Paul Delany, '*Sons and Lovers*: The Morel Marriage as a War of Position', *D. H. Lawrence Review*, 21 (1989), 153–65.

Daniel R. Schwarz, 'Speaking of Paul Morel: Voice, Unity and Meaning in *Sons and Lovers*', *Studies in the Novel*, 8 (1976), 255–77.

Wayne Templeton, 'The Drift Towards Life: Paul Morel's Search for a Place', *D. H. Lawrence Review*, 15 (1982), 177–94.

INTRODUCTIONS TO CONTEMPORARY CRITICAL THEORY

The following are helpful guides to aspects of the modern critical theory drawn upon by critics collected in this volume.

General

M. H. Abrams, *A Glossary of Literary Terms*, 5th edn (New York: Holt, Rinehart & Winston, 1988).

Terry Eagleton, *Literary Theory: An Introduction* (Oxford: Blackwell, 1983).

Jeremy Hawthorn, *A Concise Glossary of Contemporary Literary Theory* (London: Edward Arnold, 1992).

Anne Jefferson and David Robey (eds), *Modern Literary Theory: A Comparative Introduction*, 2nd edn (London: Batsford, 1986).

Rick Rylance (ed.), *Debating Texts: A Reader in Twentieth-Century Literary Theory and Method* (Milton Keynes: Open University Press, 1987).

Raman Selden, *A Reader's Guide to Contemporary Literary Theory* (Brighton: Harvester, 1985).

Psychoanalytic Criticism

Malcolm Bowie, *Jacques Lacan* (London: Fontana, 1991).
Juliet Mitchell, *Psychoanalysis and Feminism* (Harmondsworth: Penguin, 1974).
Elizabeth Wright, *Psychoanalytic Criticism: Theory in Practice* (London: Routledge, 1984).

Feminist Criticism

Catherine Belsey and Jane Moore (eds), *The Feminist Reader: Essays in Gender and the Politics of Literary Criticism* (London: Macmillan, 1989).
Toril Moi, *Sexual/Textual Politics* (London: Routledge, 1985).
K. K. Ruthven, *Feminist Literary Studies* (Cambridge: Cambridge University Press, 1984).
Elaine Showalter (ed.), *The New Feminist Criticism: Essays on Women, Literature and Theory* (London: Virago, 1986).

Poststructuralism and Deconstruction

Catherine Belsey, *Critical Practice* (London: Methuen, 1980).
Christopher Butler, *Interpretation, Deconstruction and Ideology* (Oxford: Clarendon Press, 1984).
Gerard Doherty, 'White Mythologies: D. H. Lawrence and the Deconstructive Turn', *Criticism*, 29 (1987), 477–96.
Christopher Norris, *Deconstruction: Theory and Practice* (London: Methuen, 1982).
William Ray, *Literary Meaning: From Phenomenology to Deconstruction* (Oxford: Blackwell, 1984).

Marxist Criticism

Tony Bennett, *Formalism and Marxism* (London: Methuen, 1979).
Terry Eagleton, *Marxism and Literary Criticism* (London: Methuen, 1976).
Terry Eagleton, *Ideology: An Introduction* (London: Verso, 1991).
Raymond Williams, *Marxism and Literature* (Oxford: OUP, 1977).
Raymond Williams, *Problems in Materialism and Culture* (London: Verso, 1980).

Debates about Realism

Ernst Bloch *et al.*, *Aesthetics and Politics* (London: Verso, 1977).
Catherine Belsey, *Critical Practice* (London: Methuen, 1980).
Georg Lukács, *Studies in European Realism*, trans. Edith Bone (London: Hillway Publishing, 1950).
Colin MacCabe, *James Joyce and the Revolution of the Word* (London: Macmillan, 1978).
Raymond Williams, 'Realism and the Contemporary Novel' in *The Long Revolution* (Harmondsworth: Penguin, 1965).

Notes On Contributors

Diane S. Bonds holds an administrative post in the theology school of Emory University in Atlanta, Georgia, where she also teaches writing and literature. Her publications include *Language and the Self in D. H. Lawrence*, scholarly articles on modernist and contemporary writers, and poetry appearing in a number of American literary periodicals.

Paul Delany is a Professor of English at Simon Fraser University, Canada. His books include *D. H. Lawrence's Nightmare: The Writer and His Circle in the Years of the Great War* (1978) and *The Neo-Pagans: Friendship and Love in the Rupert Brooke Circle* (1987).

Terry Eagleton is Thomas Warton Professor of English Literature, University of Oxford, and Fellow of St Catherine's College, Oxford. He is author of numerous books of literary criticism and theory, as well as a novel and two plays.

John Goode taught English at Reading and Warwick before becoming Professor of English at Keele University in 1989. He wrote *Tradition and Tolerance in Nineteenth Century Fiction* (1966) with David Howard and John Lucas, edited a collection of essays on Henry James, *The Air of Reality* (1972), and was author of *George Gissing: Ideology and Fiction* (1978) and *Thomas Hardy: The Offensive Truth* (1988). He also wrote numerous articles on George Eliot, William Morris and other nineteenth-century topics. John Goode died in January 1994.

Graham Holderness is Professor and Dean of the School of Humanities at the University of Hertfordshire. His numerous publications include *D. H. Lawrence: History, Ideology and Fiction* (1982), *Wuthering Heights* (1985) and *Women in Love* (1986). He has edited general books on Shakespeare and is co-author of *Shakespeare: The Play of History* (1988) and *Shakespeare: Out of Court* (1990).

Sir Frank Kermode describes himself as a long-retired professor of English who has written a number of books, the best of which he takes to be *The Genesis of Secrecy: On the Interpretation of Narrative* (1979) and *Forms of Attention* (1985).

Louis Martz is Sterling Professor of English, Emeritus, at Yale University. His essay 'The Second Lady Chatterley' appeared in *The Spirit of D. H. Lawrence*, ed. Gāmini Salgādo and G. K. Das (Macmillan 1988). He has published numerous articles and books on authors of the Renaissance, the latest of which is *From Renaissance to Baroque* (1991). He has also edited both the *Collected* and *Selected Poems* of H.D.

Kate Millett is a writer, sculptor, film-maker and pioneer of contemporary Anglo-American feminism. She has written numerous books including, most recently, *The Politics of Cruelty* (1994).

Tony Pinkney is Lecturer in English at the University of Lancaster. He is the author of *Woman in the Poetry of T. S. Eliot: A Psychoanalytic Approach* (1984), *Raymond Williams: Post-modern Novelist* (1991) and many articles on literature and literary and cultural theory. He is editor of the journal *News From Nowhere*.

Scott Sanders earned a PhD at Cambridge University, before going on to teach at Indiana University, where he is Professor of English. His books include novels, such as *Bad Man Ballad* and *The Invisible Company*, collections of stories such as *Wilderness Plots* and *Fetching the Dead*, and works of non-fiction such as *The Paradise of Bombs* and *Secrets of the Universe*.

Hilary Simpson studied at the University of York and subsequently at Reading during the 1970s. For the last fourteen years she has worked in local government, where she has pioneered a number of initiatives to improve the position of women in employment. She continues to study and teach literature, and has recently contributed to the Open University course on 'Literature in the Modern World' and to the Longman Critical Reader on Lawrence edited by Peter Widdowson (1992).

Index